✦✦✦ THE ✦✦✦
ORTHODOX REALITY

··· THE ···
ORTHODOX REALITY

CULTURE, THEOLOGY, AND ETHICS
IN THE MODERN WORLD

VIGEN GUROIAN

Baker Academic
a division of Baker Publishing Group
Grand Rapids, Michigan

Published by Baker Academic
a division of Baker Publishing Group
PO Box 6287, Grand Rapids, MI 49516-6287
www.bakeracademic.com

Printed in the United States of America

Library of Congress Cataloging-in-Publication Data
Names: Guroian, Vigen, author.
Title: The Orthodox reality : culture, theology, and ethics in the modern world / Vigen Guroian.
Description: Grand Rapids : Baker Publishing Group, 2018. | Includes bibliographical references.
Identifiers: LCCN 2018001813 | ISBN 9780801099342 (cloth)
Subjects: LCSH: Orthodox Eastern Church—Doctrines. | Orthodox Eastern Church—History.
Classification: LCC BX260 .G876 2018 | DDC 230/.19—dc23
LC record available at https://lccn.loc.gov/2018001813

18   19   20   21   22   23   24   7   6   5   4   3   2   1

For
Will Herberg (1901–1977)
teacher, mentor, and friend

Contents

Part 4 Theological Ethics: *On Marriage and Family*

Acknowledgments

This book is dedicated to the late Will Herberg, Jewish philosopher and theologian, who was my teacher and mentor during my doctoral study at Drew University from 1972 to 1977. In the fall of 1971, I visited Drew having spent a disappointing semester in a PhD program at the University of Pennsylvania. I walked from the parking lot to nearby Bowne Hall where the Caspersen School of Graduate Studies was housed. I climbed the narrow flight of back stairs to Will's office in a dormer room and was met by a squat, broad-waisted, partially balding, gray-bearded man who instantly reminded me of Socrates.

Will immediately stood up from behind his desk, greeted me, and then just as swiftly seated himself. I grabbed a wooden chair and pulled it up nearer to Will's desk. Brusquely, as was his manner, Will asked, or more rightly stated, "You have an Armenian name. *Parev, inch'pes yes?*" (This is the Armenian greeting: *Welcome. How are you?*) I answered, "*Lav yem*" (I am well.) "Did your grandparents emigrate from Armenia about the time of the First World War?" I answered, "Yes, they did." Will then inquired, "What did your grandfathers do for a living?" I responded that my paternal grandfather worked in a shoe factory. "Then he must have lived near Brocton, Massachusetts." I answered that my father grew up in Bridgewater where my grandfather worked. (Bridgewater is fewer than ten miles from Brocton.) Later I surmised that during the research for his classic sociological study of religion in America, *Protestant, Catholic, Jew*, Will must have come across this detail in American ethnography and remembered it!

"You want to study at Drew?" I answered that I did, but that more especially I wished to study under him. Will smiled. It was a bright smile in an otherwise dim room. He then looked directly into my eyes and stated, "You may study under me with one condition. I expect that you will attend the Armenian Church regularly. I know that there are several parishes in this area."

And that is how it began. Some might think this a most unorthodox beginning. Who today would ask such a thing of a prospective graduate student? But I understood what Will was telling me. Theology must begin with prayer and in one's own tradition.

At this time in my life, a list of persons to whom I owe thanks and special mention would be far too long. I do want to remember, however, Thomas C. Oden, who was also at Drew in the formative years of my graduate study and who passed on in December 2016. I took just one course with Tom, his seminar on Reinhold Niebuhr. It, however, launched me into the study that would be the backbone of my dissertation on the politics of Reinhold Niebuhr and Edmund Burke. Will became incapacitated with a cancerous brain tumor that finally took his life in 1977, and Tom participated in my doctoral defense in Will's stead. But my relationship with Tom Oden continued until his death. As he began to look to the writings of the great patristic authors and then launched the monumental series Ancient Christian Commentary on Scripture, for which he served as the general editor, our ongoing conversation turned to my work in Orthodox theology and ethics. For years Tom was a source of wise counsel and comfort to me as I struggled to carve a niche in the religious academy. We even shared together, as members of a religious delegation, an extraordinary adventure to Russia in September 1991, just a month after the failed coup that brought about the end of the Soviet Union.

Last, Tom Oden introduced me to Howard and Roberta Ahmanson. Eventually, through their foundation, Fieldstead and Company, they supported a leave from teaching at Loyola College and seven years' presence at the University of Virginia from 2008 to 2015. During those years, I composed important articles that have become chapters in this book. I will be forever grateful for the Ahmansons' faith in my efforts to integrate Orthodox Christianity into the study of religion in the academy.

ABBREVIATIONS

General

chap(s).	chapter(s)	SJ	Society of Jesus
ed.	edition, edited by, editor	Sr.	Sister
e.g.	*exempli gratia*, for example	trans.	translated by, translation,
Fr.	Father		translator
i.e.	*id est*, that is	v(v).	verse(s)
para.	paragraph	vol(s).	volume(s)
rev. ed.	revised edition	WCC	World Council of Churches

Modern Versions

NKJV	New King James Version	SAAS	St. Athanasius Academy
REB	Revised English Bible		Septuagint
RSV	Revised Standard Version		

Old Testament

Gen.	Genesis	1 Sam.	1 Samuel
Exod.	Exodus		

New Testament

Matt.	Matthew	Phil.	Philippians
Mark	Mark	Col.	Colossians
Luke	Luke	1–2 Tim.	1–2 Timothy
John	John	Titus	Titus
Acts	Acts	Heb.	Hebrews
Rom.	Romans	2 Pet.	2 Peter
1–2 Cor.	1–2 Corinthians	1 John	1 John
Gal.	Galatians	Rev.	Revelation
Eph.	Ephesians		

Introduction

In this introduction, I will do the obligatory and try to prepare readers for what to expect in the pages that follow. Yet I also want to take this opportunity to reflect on my past work as an Orthodox theologian in order to put into perspective the essays that belong to this book. This seems appropriate as I enter my seventieth year and commence a fourth decade since my first book, *Incarnate Love: Essays in Orthodox Ethics*,[1] was published. At that time, Orthodox theologians in America had written very little in ethics. In the introduction to *Incarnate Love*, I could name but one book on Orthodox ethics written by an American, Fr. Stanley S. Harakas's *Toward Transfigured: The Theoria of Eastern Orthodox Ethics*.[2] Much more was available in historical, dogmatic, and liturgical theology. Fr. Georges Florovsky, Fr. John Meyendorff, and Fr. Alexander Schmemann, all stationed in America, were early inspirations to me.

Nonetheless, it is significant that these three, and others that were doing theology in America at the time, were of an immigrant generation that had come to the United States via Russia, Greece, and Western Europe, or were children of immigrants. As I started to write in the late 1970s, I was acutely aware that my identity as a third-generation Orthodox American was a critical factor for what I was setting out to do. When all is said and done, it is the

---

1. Vigen Guroian, *Incarnate Love: Essays in Orthodox Ethics*, 2nd ed. (Notre Dame, IN: University of Notre Dame Press, 2002).

2. Stanley Harakas, *Toward Transfigured: The Theoria of Eastern Orthodox Ethics* (Minneapolis: Light and Life, 1983). Thirty-five years later there are more names and a growing body of literature. Among those to be consulted are John Breck, David Bentley Hart, Alexander F. C. Webster, John Chryssavgis, Gayle Woloschak, Perry Hamalis, Philip LeMasters, and Aristotle Papanikolaou.

background of the American experience of Orthodoxy, seen through the eyes of a third-generation Orthodox, that shaped my theological thinking.

The same holds true for this book. Whether the subject is Constantine and Christendom, the challenge of secularism for the Orthodox churches, or an Orthodox understanding of marriage and family, I write as one located in North America. With *Incarnate Love*, I intentionally set a course for an "American" Orthodox theology. On several occasions early in our friendship and collaboration, Fr. Harakas applauded the "pan-Orthodoxy" of my writing and its idiomatic attunement to American ears. At the outset, I also entertained the wild imagining that the many Orthodox churches, once separated by mountain ranges and oceans, languages and customs, had been gathered together to be reunited in a great American Pentecost. I continue to hold on to that vision.

As my teacher and mentor the late Will Herberg explains in his classic study on American religious identity, *Protestant, Catholic, Jew*, the first-generation immigrant is ambivalent and divided in mind about his or her American belonging, whereas members of the third generation feel fully American, all but for the important qualification that they sense that the process of acculturation also jeopardizes the unique value of the faith. Although they may cherish the ethnic or national identity that the immigrants brought with them, they do not choose ethnic separateness. They may well seek, however, to hold on to the truth in the religion of their heritage and further investigate it. In other words, the religion of their parents and grandparents may yet play a powerful role in their American identity.[3] My writing has in large measure been an endeavor to reclaim and apply to American life the enduring truth of my Orthodox inheritance.

When I penned *Incarnate Love*, I felt very much alone in this endeavor, especially within the rarefied and antiseptic environs of the American religious academy. When I became a member of the Society of Christian Ethics in the early 1980s, Fr. Stanley Harakas was its sole Orthodox member. When Paul Ramsey and Franz J. van Beeck, SJ, nominated me for the American Theological Society in 1988, I became just the third Orthodox member to belong since the Society's founding in 1912.[4] John Meyendorff and Alexander Schmemann preceded me.

Almost always, I was the only Orthodox theologian present at professional meetings or conferences. And it sometimes gave me pause when a female or an African American colleague expressed a similar sentiment about being a

3. See Will Herberg, *Protestant, Catholic, Jew: An Essay in American Religious Society* (Garden City, NY: Anchor Books, 1960), 22–23, 30–31.
4. Fr. Stanley Harakas was also admitted in this year, so I share this distinction with him.

minority. They had every right to express that sentiment, but few of them had even the vaguest notion of what it might mean to be the only Orthodox in the hall, leave aside the sole person of Armenian ancestry whose grandparents also survived the first genocide of the twentieth century.

Very often, these colleagues were trying to distinguish themselves and their work from what they regarded as an oppressive hegemony of North American theology. I too felt the pressure of that hegemony, but in a different way that called for a different kind of response. For the most part, feminist and African American liberationist theologians took for granted their American belonging as they endeavored to step back from and even rebel against it in order to strike an independent path free of sexist or racist shibboleths. But I felt the need to embrace an American identity in order to speak intelligibly and forcefully about Orthodox Christianity. There was no easy alliance to be forged with others. I was, indeed, very much alone.

In 1983 at the annual meeting of the Society of Christian Ethics, I delivered my first academic paper. It was titled "Love in Orthodox Ethics: Trinitarian and Christological Reflections." Gene Outka of Yale University, whose *Agape: An Ethical Analysis* has achieved status as a classic in its field, convened the session. At the close of the session, Outka drew me aside and quietly remarked, "Vigen, you shouldn't feel as if you must explain all of Orthodoxy in one paper. It is simply not possible." This counsel was sensible, but not so easily followed when I could expect that my audience would have little or no knowledge of the tradition from which I spoke.

My second book, *Ethics after Christendom: Toward an Ecclesial Christian Ethic*, was published in 1994.[5] In it I continued my practice of drawing from Orthodox liturgies and rites. I addressed the use of the Bible and the role of tradition in Orthodox ethics, deepened my analysis of the Orthodox encounter with American culture, and included chapters on marriage, ecology, and care for the dying. Between *Incarnate Love* and the publication of *Ethics after Christendom*, many colleagues had thanked or congratulated me for making Orthodox Christianity accessible to those who knew little about it. I successfully introduced and mined Orthodox sources, ancient and modern, while also referencing and engaging in a critical manner the growing canon of North American theology and ethics. I hope that the essays in this book are of the same quality.

All of the chapters herein were published earlier in books and journals. All have also been revised. In several of the essays, I draw from Orthodox liturgy

5. Vigen Guroian, *Ethics after Christendom: Toward an Ecclesial Christian Ethic* (Grand Rapids: Eerdmans, 1994).

as was my practice in *Incarnate Love* and *Ethics after Christendom* or in my later books *Life's Living Toward Dying: A Theological and Medical-Ethical Study* (1996) and *The Melody of Faith: Theology in an Orthodox Key* (2010).

As I look over the corpus of my writings on Orthodox theology and ethics, it strikes me that this book most resembles my first two books in its broad perspective on American culture. I think in particular of my critiques of secularism and individualism and ruminations over how the Orthodox churches might retain their theological and religious integrity in North America. I return also to the subjects of Christian love and marriage. The difference is that here I am developing a theology of culture, whether I address myself to the nature of culture, and Christian culture in particular, or reflect on the meanings of family, parenthood, and childhood.

Religion and Culture

In chapter 1, I discuss what culture is and how it and religion relate to one another. I argue that culture and religion are companionate. Both—not God—are human creations. Both issue from our human nature and are specifically connected to our creation in the image of God, the *imago Dei*. We are endowed by God with a capacity to create, though we do not create as God does, bringing other beings and things into existence out of nothing—creation *ex nihilo*. The things we "create" furnish culture, which in the deepest sense issues from a nature that is theonomous. There is no such thing as religion in the abstract, a religion sans culture. Likewise, there is no such thing as a culture without its source in religion. These claims are arguable, I understand. But over a forty-year career and seventy years on this earth, I have pondered the alternatives and have settled on these conclusions.

In his writing, Reinhold Niebuhr states that the community is as primordial as the individual. We can add to this that religion is as primordial as both. I entirely agree with the seasoned judgment Robert Louis Wilken (my former colleague at the University of Virginia) makes in his immensely erudite and readable book *The First Thousand Years: A Global History of Christianity* that "Christianity is a culture-forming religion." Throughout, Wilken demonstrates how, in its first millennium, Christianity planted and grew new "Christian communities" that remade "the cultures of the ancient world" and brought into existence "a new civilization, or more accurately, several new civilizations."[6] Another way of speaking about this historical reality is that conversion to the

6. Robert Wilken, *The First Thousand Years: A Global History of Christianity* (New Haven: Yale University Press, 2012), 2.

faith is not simply about conversion of the "naked" individual, for no such individual exists. When conversions happen, they happen within communities and cultures and are mediated by these communities and cultures.

It is unfortunate that today Niebuhr's wisdom about the individual and the community scarcely obtains in American Christianity, much of which has become wedded to a radical individualism that regards culture and society, implicitly if not explicitly, as artificial constructs that individuals build. As to how Christianity takes form as a social reality, the many Orthodox sagas and hagiographic accounts of the conversion of the "ethnos" or "nation" more accurately grasp what constitutes a living faith than the notion that faith spreads and takes hold when individuals are "born again" and multiply in the same manner. I believe that, on the whole, North American culture is awash in a feckless brew of expressive individualism, moral relativism, and godless utilitarianism that does grave damage to the human spirit and most certainly challenges the church to reassert its mission to claim this world for God.

Exaggerated Influences of Yoder and Hauerwas

In my early writing, I wanted to present a distinctly Orthodox critique of contemporary American society. I was profoundly influenced by Fr. Alexander Schmemann. I read deeply into the mystical and neopatristic theology of Vladimir Lossky. I was inspired by Russian religious philosopher Nicholas Berdyaev's prophetic critique of modernity and approach to ethics in such books as *The Destiny of Man* and *Slavery and Freedom*. And I took instruction from Greek philosopher-theologian Christos Yannaras's exploration of Orthodox liturgy's ethical meaning in his book *Freedom and Morality*. Throughout this study, I was more than aware that the theological and philosophical writings of these four, and others I have not named, were not wholly compatible. I experienced the dissimilarities as stimulus to my own thought.

Looking to other places, I found that John Howard Yoder's and Stanley Hauerwas's acute and penetrating critical stances toward modernity helped me to think and speak in terms oriented to North American theology and ethics. At the time, both were riding a wave of influence throughout American religious thought. In *Incarnate Love* and *Ethics after Christendom*, I cited Yoder and Hauerwas and frequently grappled with what they were saying.

It should not have surprised me that in his comments for the back cover of *Ethics after Christendom*, the late Max Stackhouse judged: "Here, his [Guroian's] Eastern Orthodox sensibilities meet Western Anabaptist suspicions of modern secularism in a quest for a renewed spirituality."[7] Nonetheless I initially winced at what Stackhouse wrote, knowing, however, that I had left myself open to such a characterization and that Stackhouse's description was not entirely inaccurate. Stackhouse had limited familiarity with the deeper soundings of the Orthodox social vision that I was attempting to propound in a new idiom and, quite understandably, could find no other way to describe the otherwise odd juxtaposition of sources in my writing.

In my first two books, I used Yoder's moniker "Constantinianism" in my own analysis of the church's surrender to the secularism and liberalism of North American society and its political systems. This was how Hauerwas was employing the term as well. Yet Yoder made historical claims for this term with which I was never comfortable. He traced the culturally and politically compromised position of contemporary Christianity—its apostasy from the teachings of Jesus, as he would have it—back to the Roman emperor Constantine himself who, at the beginning of the fourth century, granted Christianity legal status. I was uneasy with this claim from the start, and now regret having taken up the term in my own writing.

During the mid-1990s, at meetings of the Society of Christian Ethics, Yoder and I had several conversations in empty hallways while others were attending meetings. We discussed Orthodox history and the Orthodox religious ethos. Yoder was very curious about the latter as he saw parallels with the Mennonite ethos. I realized as we spoke, however, that he had only superficial knowledge of Byzantium. Yet I did not ask him, in view of this lacuna in his otherwise considerable historical learning, just how he was sure that his moniker, "Constantinianism," accurately represented the real legacy of Emperor Constantine. I suspect Adolf von Harnack and Ernst Troeltsch, whose views on the history of the church in the East are laden with misleading prejudices, were not far in the background. It also goes without saying that the Anabaptist narrative of the church's early deviation from Jesus's ministry and teachings was well and alive in Yoder's imagination.

Although I was drawn to Yoder's and Hauerwas's critiques of modernity, I was not at all taken with the ecclesiology they were expounding at that time within their early and highly influential books: Yoder's *The Politics of Jesus* (1972) and *The Priestly Kingdom* (1984) and Hauerwas's *A Community of Character* (1981) and *The Peaceable Kingdom* (1983). I concluded that their Anabaptist ecclesiology lacked a vital sense of the church as the sacrament of the world and as a *communio sanctorum* that is not just synchronic but also

---

7. This is an excerpt from Stackhouse's lengthier comments on the back cover of *Ethics after Christendom*.

diachronic throughout all ages.[8] In my own writing, I was striving to demonstrate how Orthodox ethics are grounded in liturgy and how the liturgy lends a powerful, transformative, and eschatological vision to Orthodox ethics.[9]

Thus, while Hauerwas and Yoder did deeply inform *Incarnate Love* and *Ethics after Christendom*, I followed them only so far. Hauerwas recognized this almost from the start. He, as well as Paul Ramsey, strongly encouraged me to continue to work out of Orthodox liturgy. When I asked Hauerwas to write a preface for *Incarnate Love*, he responded that this would not be a service to me, as it would give others the opportunity to pigeonhole me unfairly as a disciple of his. Yet even without a "Hauerwas preface," some concluded that Hauerwas was the muse of *Incarnate Love* and that I was committing the same sins of "sectarianism" as he. This was confounding precisely because the ecclesiology I expounded was at the farthest remove from being sectarian.[10] In the preface to the second edition of *Incarnate Love* in 2002, I answered this misperception. If I had a muse, it was Alexander Schmemann.[11]

Schmemann's influence is no less pronounced in this book. Nowhere is this more evident than in chapters 2 through 5. These explore the meaning of Orthodoxy's presence in the West, especially its struggle to make sense of its American presence within a culture that it has had no direct role in shaping. This inquiry into religious truth and identity necessarily addresses pluralism and secularism, on the one hand, and the nature of ecclesial unity on the other.

Schmemann's influence on these topics may seem strange at first. After all, the consensus is that Schmemann's liturgical theology is his great achievement. But scattered throughout his writing, often in incidental papers delivered to non-Orthodox audiences, Schmemann unleashed a cutting critique of modernity and the Orthodox encounter with it. In fact, his liturgical theology is that much more compelling precisely because in it he frequently contrasts

8. In following decades, Hauerwas's ecclesiology becomes more "catholic." See, for example, *In Good Company: The Church as Polis* (Notre Dame, IN: University of Notre Dame Press, 1994).

9. See for example, chap. 5, "Seeing Worship as Ethics," in *Incarnate Love*, 75–101; chap. 2, "Tradition and Ethics," in *Ethics after Christendom*, 29–52; and chap. 2, "The Luminous Moment of the Apocalypse," in *The Melody of Faith: Theology in an Orthodox Key*, 25–41 (Grand Rapids: Eerdmans, 2010). In *Ethics after Christendom* I express my appreciation for Yoder's eschatological perspective but also note that it is not embedded in a sacramental understanding of the church. Thus, in this chapter I move from some of Yoder's good thoughts on tradition as "vine" and "stream" to Orthodox theologians John Zizioulas's and Alexander Schmemann's discussions of eucharistic epiclesis and anamnesis.

10. I was aware, however, that an Orthodox ethic, drawn from a baptismal and eucharistic ecclesiology, might well appear countercultural within a secular society long distanced from anything that looks like Christendom. In this case there are bound to be those who regard that ethic (or stance toward the world) as "sectarian."

11. Guroian, *Incarnate Love*, x–xi.

"this world" with the eschatological kingdom of God. Schmemann's deeply intuitive perceptions about the church and modernity follow from a profound prophetic vision, not sociological learning.

Constantine and Beyond

Long ago I ought to have conducted my own quiet inquiry into Constantine and his world. In 2011, I was invited to participate in a symposium on Peter J. Leithart's *Defending Constantine: The Twilight of an Empire and the Dawn of Christendom*. This afforded me the opportunity to make that inquiry. Four years hence, I developed my thoughts further in a lecture titled "Did It Make a Difference that Constantine Ended Sacrifice and Was Baptized?" This was given at an annual conference of the Center for Catholic and Evangelical Theology. Chapter 2 is a revision of that lecture. There I assess Yoder's thesis about Constantine and Constantinianism, but, more important, I propose an alternative interpretation of Constantine's legacy and its significance for Christian social ethics.

I suspect that after reading chapter 2, there will remain readers who want yet more from it, who are not satisfied with where I leave matters. For in it I stop short of discussing how an Orthodox public or political theology for today might look. The Byzantines certainly did have a political theology, as the chapter demonstrates. It was an almost logical outcome of the Byzantine church's theology, especially its Christology, and privileged status as the religion of the empire. But do I wish for the same in America? Do I think this would be a profitable project for Orthodoxy in America? My answer to both hypotheticals is no.

Byzantium was a sacral social order. America today is in no real sense a sacral society. Regarding Christianity's historical relationship to the political order, America is a special case, vastly different, even today, from the European nations or England. Uniquely, almost all of global Christianity has found its way to America or originated from it. Yet American Christianity has never enjoyed state establishment or a form of cultural establishment over which one single church has presided. Disestablishment and religious pluralism have been the rule and a good thing for America.

Yet since the founding, the establishment and free exercise clauses of the First Amendment, which James Madison conceived as protective of the *freedom* of the church, have been hammered and molded by court decisions and legal precedent into a doctrine of the separation of church and state that treats religious faith as if it resides solely in the *individual* and assumes that the church is nothing more than a voluntary association comprised of otherwise disconnected individuals. In point of fact, this late doctrine is antichurch, in the only way Orthodoxy can conceive of the church, as the veritable body and polity of Christ in the world.

Proposals for a public theology, even those that issue from Orthodox theologians, generally uphold this reductive doctrine of church and state separation. For instance, Aristotle Papanikolaou has tried his hand at this in his book *The Mystical as Political: Democracy and Non-Radical Orthodoxy* (2012).[12] Papanikolaou urges Orthodoxy to embrace the church and state doctrine in its own public theology.[13] He also verges on subordinating the church to the authority of liberal culture when he maintains that "the logic of [Orthodoxy's] eucharistic ecclesiology demands the existence of a liberal democracy,"[14] as if the liberal democracies of our time are superior to all other forms of political regime that have preceded them, as if, to use Francis Fukuyama's turn of phrase, they are "the end of history."[15] Eusebius erred similarly in the fourth century when he thought the monarchic Roman Empire had become the very image of the kingdom of God on earth.

My criticism of the late American doctrine of church and state does not presuppose that Orthodoxy is wedded to an establishmentarian view on the relationship of church and state, as obtained in Byzantium or as exists today in Russia and other Eastern European nations. Establishment belongs to the history of these countries. A working establishmentarian arrangement is feasible, but the risk of an unhealthy alliance of church and state, especially one in which the truth of the church is distorted by nationalism or subordinated to the *raison d'être* of the state, is also very real. In the last analysis, our juridically expounded doctrine of separation of church and state is a specific manifestation of the broad secularist heresy I discuss in chapters 3 and 4.

12. See my "Godless Theosis," *First Things* (April 2014): 53–55, a review of Aristotle Papanikolaou's *The Mystical as Political: Democracy and Non-Radical Orthodoxy* (Notre Dame, IN: University of Notre Dame Press, 2012). As another example of an "Orthodox" interpretation of church and state, see Nathaniel Wood, "'I Have Overcome the World': The Church, the Liberal State, and Christ's Two Natures in the Russian Politics of *Theosis*," in *Christianity, Democracy, and the Shadow of Constantine*, ed. George E. Decacopoulos and Aristotle Papanikolaou (New York: Fordham University Press, 2017). There are in this volume several other essays that explore possibilities for an Orthodox political theology in liberal democratic societies. In *Incarnate Love* and other locations, I have argued, as other Orthodox have also, that it is not the "business" of the church to confirm the superiority of any one form of government over another. See Guroian, *Incarnate Love*, 159.

13. See my analysis of the separation of church and state in chaps. 7 and 8 of *Incarnate Love*, 141–88.

14. Papanikolaou, *Mystical as Political*, 77.

15. Francis Fukuyama, "The End of History?," *The National Interest* 16 (1989): 3–18.

Orthodox Christology, with its strong emphasis on the hypostatic union
of the two natures (divine and human, without confusion) in one Lord Jesus
Christ, weighs heavily against a strict separation of church and state, as has
evolved in America.[16] The Byzantine *symphonia*, or harmony of church and
state, presumed that the empire would interpret its existence under the lordship of Christ.[17] I am not opposed in principle to an Orthodox political or
public theology. But I am convinced that it is much too early in the Orthodox
Church's American experience to embrace a political theology without grave
risk of undercutting its fundamental ecclesiology. I explore that ecclesiology
in chapters 5 and 6.

Chapter 5, "Orthodoxy and American Religion," demonstrates that the
Orthodox Church's first priority in America must be to straighten out its
ecclesiology, not just on the theoretical plane but, more important, in the
daily existence of the church.[18] This process would also allow Orthodoxy to
develop a "secondary" speech about its relationship to the American order
that would support a political theology firmly grounded in experience and
history.

In an essay titled "How (Not) to Be a Political Theologian," Stanley Hauerwas writes that "the Church is God's politics for the world," and that if
"Christians are well-formed by this politics, they . . . [can] serve the world
well by developing an 'ecclesial squint.'"[19] This is an intriguing locution; yet
it needs amendment. The "ecclesial squint" should also be an "eschatological
squint" (or vision) learned especially within the church's eucharistic worship.[20]

In chapter 2, I cite Paul's charge to the Philippian Christians that by their
eucharistic existence in Christ they become God's eschatological polity in
the world. "But our commonwealth [our *politeuma*] is in heaven," he states,
"and from it we await a Savior, the Lord Jesus Christ, who will change our
lowly body to be like his glorious body, by the power which enables him even

16. The same can be said my own Armenian Church's non-Chalcedonian miaphysite Christology that insists even more emphatically than Chalcedonian Christology on the unity of
divine and human in Christ.

17. More than three decades ago, Stanley Harakas attempted to reconcile the Byzantine
theory of *symphonia* with American democracy and the Constitution. To his credit, Harakas
carefully considered James Madison's theologically informed justification of the separation of
church and state and strong regard for the freedom of the church. However, Harakas's endeavor
is strained and, in the end, is not persuasive. See Harakas's article, "Orthodox Church-State
Theory and American Democracy," *The Greek Orthodox Review* 21, no. 4 (1976): 285–307.

18. I say something about this in the preface to the second edition of *Incarnate Love*, x.

19. Stanley Hauerwas, "How (Not) to Be a Political Theologian," in Decacopoulos and
Papanikolaou, eds., *Christianity, Democracy, and the Shadow of Constantine*, 269.

20. I suspect that Hauerwas would accept this amendment, based especially on the ecclesiology he develops in his later writings.

to subject all things to himself" (Phil. 3:20–21 RSV). Thus, according to Paul, God's "politics," and *only* God's "politics," is genuinely transformative.

I do not know whether Hauerwas intends his "ecclesial squint" as a metaphor in the full sense that I hear it. It reminds me of the manner in which a painter squints at a composition to block out distracting details so that the eye captures the composition's essence, the full spectrum of color within it, or the shapes and forms, absent their rough edges, that compose it. In like manner, might not the Christian "squint" enable us, or better still the church's squint enables it, to detect the ominous shadow of despotism and totalitarianism that hangs over every species of ideology and politics, progressivist or populist, that promises to transform the world? Here is a calling and witness that Orthodoxy can perform within the American milieu.

The Ecumenical Horizon

Chapter 6, the first chapter of part 3, is titled "The Agony of Orthodox Ecclesiology." This chapter was originally composed as a supporting document for The Princeton Proposal for Church Unity issued in 2003.[21] The Princeton Proposal was the work of sixteen theologians and ecumenists, of which I was one, who met together over three years. "The Agony of Orthodox Ecclesiology"[22] expands my analysis in chapter 5 of the contradiction between Orthodoxy's high churchly theology of unity and the actual organization and conduct of Orthodox churches here in America and in other places. In both chapters I try to imagine a way forward by which Orthodox churches come to terms with the challenges to their ecclesiology and can be of more service to other Christian churches.

Although fragmentation and division of Christianity into new sects and denominations has continued in late modernity, at the same time ancient divisive wounds and grievances have also been healed. The news media has been virtually blind to these developments and their tremendous significance. Barely has the media taken notice of a rapprochement that has mounted over the past fifty years between the two largest bodies of Christians in the world, the Roman Catholic Church and the Orthodox Church—a rapprochement that by any historical measure is near to astonishing.

21. The formal title of the Princeton Proposal is *In One Body Through the Cross: The Princeton Proposal for Church Unity*, ed. Carl E. Braaten and Robert W. Jenson (Grand Rapids: Eerdmans, 2003).

22. This chapter appeared in an earlier form as "The Crisis of Orthodox Ecclesiology," *The Ecumenical Future*, ed. Carl E. Braaten and Robert W. Jenson (Grand Rapids: Eerdmans, 2004), 162–75.

In 1964 Pope Paul VI and Greek Ecumenical Patriarch Athenagoras met in Jerusalem. Not since 1438 had a bishop of Rome met with a bishop of Constantinople. From the start of his papacy, John Paul II strove to reconcile ancient grievances and heal old wounds that hindered the ultimate goal of unity between the Roman Catholic Church and the Orthodox Church. I report a piece of that history in chapter 7 of this book, "The Problem of Papal Primacy." In 1979, Pope Paul VI and Ecumenical Patriarch Demetrios I established the Joint International Commission for Theological Dialogue between the Catholic Church and the Orthodox Church. The commission has continued to the present and addresses a variety of subjects, including sacraments and sacramental communion, the theology of ordained ministry, the historical role of the bishop of Rome, and primacy and synodality in the church.

To mark the fiftieth anniversary of the meeting of Pope Paul VI and Ecumenical Patriarch Demetrios I, in May 2014 Pope Francis and Ecumenical Patriarch Bartholomew joined in a pilgrimage to the Holy Land for a symbolic meeting at the Church of the Holy Sepulchre in Jerusalem. And in February 2016 Pope Francis met with Patriarch Kirill of Moscow, the head of the Russian Orthodox Church. Not for a millennium had such a thing happened. Both of Pope Francis's predecessors, John Paul II and Benedict XVI, had already reached out to the Byzantine Eastern Orthodox churches and the Oriental Orthodox churches (churches of the East that did not accept the fifth-century Council of Chalcedon's christological formula) and met with many of their leaders. Furthermore, there were and continue to be numerous bilateral consultations between the various Orthodox churches and the Roman Catholic Church on sacramental and ecclesiological matters that, historically, have divided them.

In chapter 7 I weave together two stories. The first is from the nineteenth century. It illustrates the historically strained relations that over the centuries have prevailed between the Armenian Church and the Roman Catholic Church. The second story concerns a meeting in 1996 at the Vatican of Pope John Paul II and Karekin I, Supreme Patriarch and Catholicos of All Armenians, which gave hope for unity. Through juxtaposing these two stories, I explore not only how the Armenian and Roman Catholic churches have differed on and disagreed over the meaning of papal primacy but also how, in their meeting, John Paul II and Karekin I opened up new possibilities for full communion between their churches.

Chapter 7 was initially prepared for a 2005 conference at the University of Aberdeen. A gathering of theologians from the United States and Great Britain engaged in a dialogue on John Paul II's encyclical *Ut Unum Sint* (That They May Be One). In his encyclical, John Paul II invokes Ignatius of Antioch's second-century expression that the bishop of Rome "presides in love."

For this reason I titled my conference paper, "A Communion of Love and the Primacy of Peter." In that paper (now chap. 7 in this volume) I explore, especially through Armenian hymns that celebrate Peter's ministry, how the bishop of Rome's "priority" among peers in a context of a "communion of love" might replace an ideology of papal power and jurisdictional supremacy.

Chapter 8, "Love That Is Divine and Human," is not in itself an essay on or about ecumenism. Nonetheless, this chapter examines the meaning of that love through which the priority or primacy of the papacy may be interpreted. I believe that this exploration of the Orthodox theological understanding of love, grounded in and growing out of its trinitarian and christological teachings, reveals a deep conviction about the essential unity of the church. This love that is both divine and human is a power that enjoins communion and demands of Christians full unity as the one church of Jesus Christ. It is this conviction about love and unity that moved the Orthodox Church to join the modern ecumenical movement at its inception and keeps the Orthodox in it despite so many obstacles thrown up along the way. As it is the last of the three essays in this section, I am confident also that readers will find it to be an appropriate and helpful bridge to the final section on marriage and family.

Marriage and Family

This subject matter has concerned me since the beginning of my theological career. The lengthiest chapter of *Incarnate Love* is on marriage and is arguably the chapter that has been most cited. Marriage and family are also very much at the center of contemporary discussions about the state of our society. Opinions conflict about the health or lack thereof of marriage and the family today. The final three chapters of this book reveal where I stand on these matters. Nonetheless, the chapters are not opinion pieces. Rather, in them I am seeking to clarify through theological and ecclesial lenses the meanings that marriage, parenthood, and childhood obtain within the Christian life.

Chapter 9 was written and revised several times "on the fly" as opportunities arose, before and after the 2015 Supreme Court decision *Obergefell v. Hodges*, to address the controversy over same-sex marriage. The Orthodox understanding of marriage differs in important ways from Protestant and Roman Catholic teachings. The Orthodox understanding is deeply sacramental. Unlike other churches, the Orthodox Church does not regard marriage's essence to be contract, covenant, or divine ordinance. Rather, as with the other sacraments, marriage is a blessing that heals. It restores to health the broken body of Adam-Eve humanity that the fall brought about, which set male and female at enmity with each other. Also, like all the other sacraments, marriage entails the use and transfiguration of specific nonsubstitutable elements, in this case, male and female human beings. The sacrament, thus understood, exposes as a falsehood the notion that same-sex partnerships can be a marriage.

Last, I believe that churches opposing same-sex marriage must use the controversy as an occasion to instruct their people about what marriage truly is. This truth, ironically, has been obscured by centuries-long arrangements with the state to marry men and women under the certification of civil law.

Chapter 10 has a different shape and tenor. It examines the exceptionally rich writings of the fourth- and fifth-century Christian bishop John Chrysostom on the responsibilities of parenthood. Chrysostom discussed marriage and family more than any other patristic writer. Although his thought belongs to antiquity, his wisdom about the role of parents in their children's lives is surprisingly relevant for today. For example, when he chastises parents for their obsession with the worldly success of their children at the price of neglecting the moral formation of their character, Chrysostom speaks to us. His description of the Christian family as an "ecclesial" entity, a small church, also directs our attention to the solemn responsibility of parents for the souls of their children. God holds parents accountable for the kinds of persons their children become. Salvation lies in the balance. This responsibility means seeing properly to their religious education. Chrysostom was a pioneer of Christian pedagogy, often speaking and writing about how to instruct children in the Christian faith.

The final chapter was originally written for inclusion in a volume on children and their Christian calling as sons and daughters of God. The assignment turned me toward a topic that I had flirted with for some time in essays like those just discussed. It also gave me the opportunity to think through why I recoiled from contemporary views of the child, whether represented by developmental (or stage) theories of maturation and growth or postmodernist notions of childhood as a social construct. The stage theorists are committed to an "essentialist" concept of the child, while postmodernist theories deny that there is anything distinct about the child qua human being that sets him or her apart from older human beings.

The distinctively Christian way of thinking about the child is grounded in the Christian truth that God became incarnate as a helpless babe and grew to be a child under the care of his mother, Mary, and his stepfather, Joseph. Christianity, but for a few exceptions such as John Chrysostom, comes late to a "theology of the child." Two great Victorian Christian writers, John Henry Newman and George MacDonald, broke new and incredibly rich ground for a theological understanding of the child, and both figure prominently in chapter 11.

The "Conclusion"

My editor at Baker Academic, Dave Nelson, asked that I write a conclusion for this book. We tossed some ideas back and forth, and I settled on something more like an "invitation" to read further. For the final seven years of my teaching career, a generous private grant gave me the opportunity to develop and teach courses specifically on Orthodox Christianity at the University of Virginia. These courses invited students, undergraduate and graduate alike, to inquire into what I have come to call the "lost tribe of Christianity" in religious studies and theology departments across North America. It is a very big tribe at that, that is, if one takes in view global Christianity. Why "lost tribe"? Because in North America, Orthodox Christianity is virtually absent from the academic study of religion and Christianity.

This is nothing less than a scandal. It is fraudulent to teach about Christianity as if everything that happened in the East ended with the Cappadocian fathers of the fourth century, if they are even spoken of. Standard textbooks on the history of Christianity do no better than summing up in but one or two chapters what happened in the East, in the Levant, in Africa, in Asia, in Byzantium, and with the conversion of the Slavs. And what makes the thing even more peculiar is that my own church, the Armenian Church, is one of the smallest of the Orthodox churches. Yet I have been busy trying to remedy the absence of greater Orthodoxy in the academy for most of my professional career and representing this "lost tribe" in so many places.

There seems no reason to stop trying. So, I have written a conclusion, which by way of discussing two syllabi of courses I taught at the University of Virginia, invites interested lay readers and academics alike to study further. In the first instance, I hope I will open a way for readers to broaden and deepen their personal knowledge and, perhaps, prompt conversations in other churches about Orthodox Christianity. In the second instance, I hope to encourage those who teach religion in higher education to expand the scope of their courses to include the study of Orthodoxy in its various aspects of ecclesial life and ethics as well as theology, and not limited to the ancient world but present, dynamic, and thriving in our day.

PART 1

Culture

1

The Meaning of Culture

T. S. Eliot once said that Matthew Arnold "set up Culture in the place of Religion, and . . . [left] Religion to be laid waste by the anarchy of feeling."[1] Eliot's comment prompts one to consider whether Arnold, the quintessential Victorian, was also the prototypical modern who, unable to muster belief in the God of Christian orthodoxy, embraced culture as a substitute for religion. And this question can certainly prompt further reflection on the meaning of culture and how Christians, especially, ought to be disposed toward it.

We are here concerned with the latter question, that of the meaning of culture and how Christians ought to comport themselves toward it. Nonetheless, it is helpful to start with the special case of Matthew Arnold. Even if Eliot was right to suggest that Arnold substituted culture and duty to it in place of religion, the great Victorian remained sufficiently sympathetic to the spirit of historic Christianity that his vision of culture was neither atheistic nor thoroughly secularist. And if this is so—and I believe it is—then Arnold may also be viewed as a transitional figure from whom we can learn a lot about the late modern context of our topic.

In his day, Arnold was eminent among a company of critics who believed high culture cannot be accounted for apart from a stable historical religion and a shared religious piety. Indeed, he worried that a contemporary spirit of thoughtless experimentation and frivolous innovation was shifting into a

---

An earlier version of this chapter originally appeared as "Christians and Culture," in *Oxford Handbook of Theological Ethics*, ed. Gilbert C. Meilaender and William Werpehowski, 381–97 (Oxford: Oxford University Press, 2005). Used by permission of Oxford University Press.

1. T. S. Eliot, *Selected Essays* (New York: Harcourt, Brace, 1950), 387.

crass new barbarism. He writes, "The danger now is, not that people should obstinately refuse to allow anything but their old routine to pass for reason and the will of God, but either that they should allow some novelty or other to pass for these too easily, or else that they should underrate the importance of them altogether, and think it enough to follow action for its own sake, without troubling themselves to make reason and the will of God prevail therein."[2]

Arnold had caught the scent of a rising new secularism and a practical atheism, both driven by a utilitarian spirit that the people's passions fueled. In this respect, Eliot may have unfairly accused Arnold of opening the gates to "an anarchy of feeling."

I believe that Arnold does not so much "set up Culture in the place of Religion" as overstate the case for it. This is because he collapses religion into culture. He is a fish who swims and breathes in the brackish waters of late Christendom. He values biblical religion in anthropological terms as educative, inspirational, and supportive of culture. "Religion [is] the greatest and most important of the efforts by which the human race has manifested its impulse to perfect itself," he opines. "Religion comes to a conclusion identical with that which culture, culture seeking the determination of this question [of the nature of perfection and how to achieve it] . . . reaches." Culture, in its pursuit of this perfection, includes pursuits of "art, science, poetry, philosophy, history, as well of religion [itself]."[3] Arnold concludes that the present time "is the moment for culture to be of service, culture which believes in making reason and the will of God prevail, believes in perfection, [and] is the study and pursuit of perfection."[4]

Eliot vigorously objects to such formulations. Art, literature, and poetry may well convey religious ideas and sentiments. They, however, are not a substitute for, or the equivalent of, faith and dogma, ecclesiastical authority, and corporate worship of God. Religion is concerned with a transcendent and supernatural reality and is not a subset of culture. It is, rather, the source of culture. "Man is man because he can recognize supernatural realities, not because he can invent them," Eliot argues in his criticism of the New Humanism, represented by Irving Babbitt, his former teacher at Harvard, that had gained attention and stirred controversy in the 1920s and 1930s. "Either everything in man can be traced as a development from below, or something must come from above," Eliot insists. "There is no avoiding that dilemma: you must either be a naturalist or a supernaturalist."[5] Not by its own power

2. Matthew Arnold, *Culture and Anarchy* (Cambridge: Cambridge University Press, 1961), 46.
3. Arnold, *Culture and Anarchy*, 47.
4. Arnold, *Culture and Anarchy*, 46.
5. Eliot, *Selected Essays*, 433.

or on the basis of naturalism or mere humanism can culture rescue or repair a fraying and disintegrating civilization, or hold at bay an emerging, dehumanized mass society, the "Wasteland" of Eliot's poetry.

The Arnoldian claim that culture is our guide to perfection is a dangerous pursuit. Seeking perfection by and through culture is at minimum a path to grave disappointment, Eliot warns. It may even bring down the gloomy curtain of nihilism, when disappointment sours into disillusionment or despair. Nevertheless, the inverse of Arnold's proposal that religion, rather than culture, is a means to perfection in this world is just as false. In "The Idea of a Christian Society," Eliot outright rejects the use of the Christian faith as an instrument of social progress. "And what is worst of all is to advocate Christianity, not because it is true, but because it might be beneficial. . . . To justify Christianity because it provides a foundation of morality, instead of showing the necessity of Christian morality from the truth of Christianity, is a very dangerous inversion."[6]

Many in Arnold's generation who no longer believed in the biblical God nonetheless continued to be sympathetic to Christianity's cultural legacy. They welcomed and found comfort in Arnold's analysis. His vision supported the easy Victorian and the increasingly less confident Edwardian assumption that Western culture could carry all the valuable Christian truths about human nature and human possibilities without faith in the biblical God or subscription to formal religion.

Important late nineteenth- and early twentieth-century theologians and religious philosophers sought to correct this assumption. They maintained that culture grows from the religious cult. "Culture is the development of the religious cult, of its differentiation and the unfolding of its content,"[7] argues Russian religious philosopher Nicholas Berdyaev. When the cult's vitality diminishes, the culture becomes exhausted, turns brittle, and hollows out; although after the well of faith has dried up, there still might persist for a time a pragmatic and instrumental use of religion.

Defining Culture

Lay and learned people alike often make pronouncements about culture with wild inexactitude as to its meaning. So permit me to clarify my use of the word. In point of fact, the meaning of culture that I favor is near to Arnold's understanding. I part company with Arnold in his belief that culture is well-nigh

6. T. S. Eliot, "The Idea of a Christian Society," in *Christianity and Culture* (New York: Harcourt, Brace, 1949), 46.
7. Nicholas Berdyaev, *The Meaning of History* (New York: Scribner's Sons, 1936), 212.

redemptive. Rather, culture, even as it may issue from a religion, is always religiously and morally ambiguous.

That having been said, I define culture as follows:

> Culture is the cultivation, development, and exercise of certain distinctively human capacities of freedom, reason, conscience, and imagination. Culture is embodied in manners and mores and is promoted by education: producing art, craft, music, poetry and literature, science and the like.

This definition differs from the anthropological and sociological definition of culture that started to take hold in the social sciences during the latter half of the nineteenth century and that today dominates higher learning. It states that

> culture is a distinctive way of belonging to a particular group or a historically formed people. This way of belonging is grounded in social tradition and values, expressed through a variety of symbolic forms, rituals, and activities, and embodied in institutions, art, literature, religion, and the like.

According to this definition, culture is in essence equivalent to the entire human social world. It is next to interchangeable with society and civilization. H. Richard Niebuhr adopts this definition for his classic study *Christ and Culture*. In that book, he describes culture as "the 'artificial, secondary environment' which man superimposes on the natural. It comprises language, habits, ideas, beliefs, customs, social organization, inherited artifacts, technical processes, and values." Niebuhr adds that "this 'social heritage' [is what] New Testament writers frequently had in mind when they spoke of the 'world,' which is represented in many forms but to which Christians like other men are inevitably subject."[8]

Yet in order to support his thesis about Christianity and culture, Niebuhr misrepresents what New Testament authors like John and Paul meant when they spoke of the "world." When Niebuhr gathers, classifies, and interprets a host of important historical thinkers' views on Christianity and culture in similar terms, he compounds the confusion. Whether one speaks of Clement of Alexandria or Tertullian, John Chrysostom or Augustine, Dante or Thomas More, Kant or Kierkegaard, Tolstoy or F. D. Maurice, not one understood culture as Niebuhr defines it.

The Greek words that John and Paul use for world are *kosmos* and *aeon*. John does not have culture in mind but rather the whole created order that is in need of redemption, when, for example, he announces, "It was not to judge

8. H. Richard Niebuhr, *Christ and Culture* (New York: Harper and Row, 1975), 32.

the world [*kosmos*] that God sent his Son into the world [*kosmos*], but that through him the world [*kosmos*] might be saved" (John 3:17 REB). Here the evangelist is contemplating much more than mere human existence and its artifacts. Instead, he has in mind the whole creation that in its fallen condition is in need of salvation. Neither the authors of the New Testament nor their ancient audience conceived of culture in the manner of our modern social sciences.

Nonetheless, the early Christian apologists and Greek fathers did adopt a word that over time came to mean *culture* as I am employing it in this chapter. That word is *paideia*. Werner Jaeger, in his monumental study *Paideia: The Ideals of Greek Culture*, explains that the original meaning of *paideia* was education or the whole process of educating. Like the Latin *cultura* and the English *culture*, however, *paideia* eventually referred to not only the process of educating but also its content, issuance, and endurance as intellectual, moral, and artistic inheritance. Jaeger explains that after the fourth century, Greeks (and Greek speakers) regularly invoked *paideia* "to describe all the artistic forms and the intellectual and aesthetic achievements of their race, in fact the whole content of their tradition."[9]

For example, in *Panegyric on St Basil*, Gregory of Nazianzus (ca. 330–390) employs *paideia* both as education in the strict sense and more generally as culture. He states,

> I take it to be admitted by men of sense, that the first of our advantages is education; and not only this our more noble form of it, which disregards rhetorical ornaments and glory, and holds to salvation and beauty in the objects of contemplation; but even that external culture which many Christians ill-judgingly abhor, as treacherous and dangerous, and keeping us afar from God. . . . [So], from secular literature we have received principles of inquiry and speculation, while we have rejected their idolatry. . . . Nay, even these have aided us in our religion, by our perception of the contrast between what is worse and what is better, and by gaining strength of our doctrine from the weakness of theirs. We must not then dishonor education, because some men are pleased to do so, but rather suppose such men to be boorish and uneducated, desiring all men to be as they themselves are, in order to hide themselves in the general, and escape the detection of the want of culture.[10]

The etymology of the English word *culture* take us back to the Latin *colere*, which means "to till." The verb meaning "to cultivate" is derived from the

9. Werner Jaeger, *Paideia: The Ideals of Greek Culture*, vol. 1, Archaic Greece: The Mind of Athens (New York: Oxford University Press, 1939), 303.

10. "The Panegyric on S Basil," Oration 43, in *A Select Library of Nicene and Post-Nicene Fathers of the Christian Church* (Grand Rapids: Eerdmans, 1978), 7:398–99.

past participle *cultus*, as is our English word *cult*. The Roman Stoic Seneca taps into this etymological background when he states, "As the soil, however rich it may be, cannot be productive without culture, so the mind, without cultivation, can never produce good fruit."[11] Culture, thus conceived, means much the same thing as *paideia*.

The Difference between Culture and Society

Classical liberal political philosophy sharply distinguishes between the state and civil society. In a similar manner, we may make a distinction between culture and society. Culture grows in society, where it may or may not flourish, just as the political state functions within society, where it may or may not prosper. Culture, like the state, is more discrete and limited than society. This analogy between state and civil society and culture and society, of course, is not precise and can only be taken so far. Culture and society overlap and interpenetrate in ways that, according to classical liberal theory, state and society do not, or at least ought not to do.

Society exists in animal nature as well as in human history. In the natural world, society is determinate. It is the product of what, for lack of greater precision, we sometimes call instinct or laws of nature. Natural society is repeated without significant innovation. For example, the beehive is essentially the same in form and function time and again, according to the life cycle of that insect. There is in the beehive not a trace of freedom, personality, or self-transcendence. By contrast, human society entails reason, imagination, memory, and, most significant for our purposes, freedom and creativity. Thus, human society varies considerably, although it does not transcend natural determinacy entirely. As a person is comprised of both nature and spirit, so also is human society.

Society may be historical, as in human history, or natural, as in the recurrence of beehives, but culture is distinctively historical and exclusively human. Human art is qualitatively different from even the intricately woven and otherwise remarkable spider's web. Human art does not necessarily serve a "useful" purpose. It may simply express form and beauty. Human music is qualitatively different from the purely imitative, but otherwise impressive, repertoire of the mockingbird. Human music expresses sadness or joy, conscious memory or sentiment, emotions and capacities that we do not ascribe to the mockingbird's song. There may be similarities of movement between the mating gesticulations of the bird of paradise and a human dancer. Yet

---

11. Tryon Edwards, compiler, *The New Dictionary of Thoughts*, ed. C. N. Catrevas and Jonathan Edwards (New York: Standard Book Company, 1954), 111.

human dance, even when man and woman perform it romantically, is much more than an instinctive mating ritual. It expresses rhythm and story. A human home may include a complex of "rooms," as in a rabbit warren, and provide shelter from the elements, as does the warren. But a human home may also include architecture, decorative art, and furnishings that express the personal tastes, histories, hopes, and expectations of the family members.

In addition to having historicity, culture is personal; this, inasmuch as culture expresses freedom and does not conform to determinate laws of nature. Culture manifests the human spirit, freedom, and self-transcendence more freshly and with greater immediacy than society does. It is nearer than social order and organization to the wellspring of creative inspiration. Culture helps to form and shape human society, but it is not reducible to society; just as human personality, which expresses itself through culture, is not reducible to mere individuality as member and number of the species *Homo sapiens*. Individuality belongs solely to material, spatial, and temporal existence, while personality pertains to spirit. Personality is the human being created in the image and likeness of God. Spirit may exist without individuality; thus, the Godhead is triune personality but is not individuated.

Toward a Christian Theological Vision of Culture

During the period in which *paideia* began to take on the meaning of culture, Christian attitudes toward classical culture ran the full spectrum from highly positive to strongly negative. Yet this spectrum reflects opinions about pagan culture and not necessarily culture per se. Tertullian, who speaks harshly of contemporary culture, agrees no less than Clement of Alexandria, who is more sympathetic to it, that Christians should create their own culture. Yet this is not the impression H. Richard Niebuhr leaves with the reader in *Christ and Culture*. Rather, he gives the impression that Christianity has been divided against itself on whether faith is compatible with culture, and this in fact may well have to do with the definition of culture that he adopts.

Niebuhr's *Christ and Culture* is famous for its fivefold typology that ranges from "Christ against Culture" to "Christ of Culture." Whatever one's judgment about that typology, it is indisputable that Christians differ, sometimes dramatically, in their estimates of the value of the culture in which they live and whether it is compatible with the Christian faith. In the fourth century, both in the Latin West and Greek East, we discover Christian writers wrestling with how to define culture within the framework of the entire Christian theological vision of creation and salvation.

In his Gifford Lectures of 1992–93, "Christianity and Classical Culture: The Metamorphosis of Natural Theology in the Christian Encounter with Hellenism," Jaroslav Pelikan brilliantly analyzed the fourth- and fifth-century synthesis of faith and culture that expresses this vision. The subject of Pelikan's study are the three Cappadocian churchmen and theologians Basil of Caesarea, Gregory of Nyssa, and Gregory of Nazianzus, as well as Macrina, the sister of Basil and Gregory of Nyssa. They lived roughly during the same time as Augustine of Hippo, who was developing his own account of culture, history, and the Christian faith, most notably in his monumental tome *The City of God*.

Pelikan argues that the Cappadocians negotiated and defined the terms on which Byzantine Christianity continued to engage the classical cultural heritage.[12] Their influence on Orthodox theology is considerable even today. They "stood squarely in the tradition of Classical Greek culture," Pelikan writes. Yet "each was at the same time intensely critical of that tradition."[13] Each of the Cappadocians, however, carried on his or her criticism of classical culture in a somewhat different key from the others. Collectively, they represent a broad view of Christianity and culture that allows for a range of defensible assessments of and engagements with culture.

Of the four, Gregory of Nazianzus is the most positively disposed toward classical culture and learning. He finds very little inconsistency or conflict between its best wisdom and the Christian gospel. Gregory of Nyssa has the broadest and most penetrating insight into Greek *paideia*. Yet he is also attuned to "the cultural differences between more cultivated and 'more barbarian people.'" In his profound work of spirituality *The Life of Moses*, Gregory maintains that the great Hebrew patriarch was the best example of "how to properly benefit from pagan learning. . . . [He] had, according to the Book of Acts 'received a *paideia* in all the *sophia* [wisdom] of the Egyptians' [Acts 7:22]." More so than Gregory, Basil emphasizes the desultory effects of sin on human learning and conduct. He refuses to elevate Moses as high as does his brother, recalling that Moses, too, was a member of fallen humanity. "Macrina . . . drew on the ideas of the pagan philosophers,"[14] according to Pelikan. She regarded the ancient philosophers as wise men, but we know less about her thought and its nuances. It is significant, however, that both she and her brother Basil founded monastic communities, suggesting that, like Basil, she too held to a strong sense of human sin and the need for reforming human nature and society.

12. Jaroslav Pelikan, *Christianity and Classical Culture* (New Haven: Yale University Press, 1993), 6.
13. Pelikan, *Christianity and Classical Culture*, 9.
14. Pelikan, *Christianity and Classical Culture*, 10.

The Cappadocians grounded their synthesis of Christianity and culture not just in a doctrine of universal sinfulness but also in the doctrine of the image of God (the *imago Dei*) that their great predecessors Irenaeus, Origen, and Athanasius propounded and developed. This belief in the human person as *eikōn* of God is at the center of Cappadocian anthropology. It is an important reason why none of them rejected classical culture outright. For however "disfigured" by the ancestral (original) sin, the image of God has not been erased in human beings. What is more, because Christ restored the *imago Dei* in his own person for the whole of humanity, culture itself may be positively understood as sacramental, soteriological, and eschatological image (*eikōn*) of the kingdom of heaven. The twentieth-century Russian Orthodox theologian Paul Evdokimov carries this tradition into the present when he states, "If every human being in the image of God is His living icon, culture is the icon of the Kingdom of God."[15]

Orthodoxy credits culture, in its highest expression, with the capacity to elevate society above and beyond its natural form to a truly human status of personality and communion. "Culture indicates the fashioning of material by the action of spirit, the victory of form over matter. It is . . . closely connected with the creative act of man,"[16] Berdyaev explains. This "creative act of man expresses the *imago Dei*," he adds, and brings it forth into the world through culture. "The Creator gives to man, to his own image and likeness, free creative power. Man's creativity is like that of God—not equal and identical, but resembling it."[17] Evdokimov echoes Berdyaev's sentiments when he declares that "God is the creator, poet or maker of the universe and man, who resembles him is also creator and poet in his own way.[18] If "art is the signature of man," as G. K. Chesterton once said,[19] then culture is humanity's letter to God.

The Ambiguity of Culture

In its best moments, humanity reaches toward divine similitude. In its worst moments, it demonically parodies God. The initial chapters of Genesis introduce and explore these polar possibilities. God created human beings in his own image so that they could grow into his likeness, becoming more like

15. Paul Evdokimov, *In the World, of the Church: A Paul Evdokimov Reader*, ed. Michael Plekon and Alexis Vinogradov (Crestwood, NY: St. Vladimir's Seminary Press, 2001), 132.

16. Nicholas Berdyaev, *Slavery and Freedom* (New York: Scribner's Sons, 1944), 122–23.

17. Nicholas Berdyaev, *The Meaning of the Creative Act* (New York: Harper and Brothers, 1954), 136.

18. Evdokimov, *In the World, of the Church*, 196.

19. G. K. Chesterton, *The Everlasting Man* (San Francisco: Ignatius, 1993), 34.

God (Gen. 1:26). The descendants of Adam and Eve, whom God intended to live in community, created culture and technology. They practiced agriculture, invented music, made tools, and fashioned artistic artifacts (Gen. 4:17–22). These things, when exercised and used properly to glorify God, increase the stature and well-being of humankind, which is God's intension. The builders of the Tower of Babel (Gen. 11:1–9), however, abused their freedom and creativity. With Promethean pride and ambition, they perversely endeavored to fashion their city so that it would be equal to heaven. They would have stolen God's glory to increase their own power and reputation among the rest of humankind.

The Orthodox Christian tradition builds on all these biblical insights for its understanding of culture. But it categorically rejects the gnostic or Manichaean outlook that denies the goodness of the material creation and culture itself. Orthodoxy embraces the profound wisdom of the prologue to John's Gospel that recapitulates the Genesis account of creation in the new key of the Word made flesh (John 1:14). The divine Word is cocreator with God the Father (John 1:3). In having become a human being, the only begotten Son (John 1:18) reaffirmed the Father's original blessing that declared the creation to be good and beautiful (Gen. 1:31). (The Greek of the Septuagint Old Testament, the Bible of the early church, translates the Hebrew *tob* with not the expected *agathos* [good], but instead *kalos*, which means beautiful. This is possible because *tob* may be rendered as not only "good" but also as "truly fitting" or "perfect.")

Thus, by his divine power and in and through his perfect humanity, Jesus Christ translates fallen human life and culture into a new creation that is beautiful and good. This passage of the old *aeon* into "a new heavens and a new earth" (2 Pet. 3:13) is symbolically expressed in the New Testament account of Jesus's transformation of the poorest water into the finest wine at the marriage celebration in Cana of Galilee (John 2:1–11). Temporal marriage is revealed by Jesus as an eschatological symbol of the great "marriage supper of the Lamb" (Rev. 19:9) that will come about at the dawn of the new creation.

Berdyaev explains that "the appearance in the world of the God-man marks a new moment in the creativity of the world, a moment of cosmic significance."[20] The Holy Spirit's descent upon the apostles and disciples at Pentecost, and every person whom the Church baptizes, breathes new life into man and reignites the ecstatic flame of creativeness in the human spirit. Inside the Church, the Spirit proleptically perfects the *imago Dei*, so that it may be magnified in the world.

20. Berdyaev, *Meaning of the Creative Act*, 137.

In his Letter to the Colossians, Paul writes that Christ "is the image of the invisible God" (Col. 1:15). This means that the visible humanity of the Son is itself the image or symbol of God's invisible divinity. We see in the Incarnate Son's human face the face of God that was hidden even from Moses (Exod. 33:20). We also see the face of sanctified humanity because in Christ these two are the same.

Traditional Christian iconography expresses this belief about the divine image in people and the humanity of God through its depictions of Christ and the saints. It does not strive for naturalism; rather, it portrays divinized humanity both as archetype in Christ and perfection in the saints. This informs and inspires the Orthodox ideal of culture. Just as Christ and the saints embody and confirm the biblical truth about human beings as having been created in the image of God, so human culture may be an expression of that divine image extended into the world. God intends the humanization of the world but also its divinization. God would have humanity imprint the *imago Dei* on the world through the culture it creates: in other words, enstamp Christ on the world, the same who is "the brightness of [God's] glory and the express image of His [the Father's] person" (Heb. 1:3).

Viewed in this light, culture is humanity's artistic response to God's act in Jesus Christ to renew the world. Paul informs believers that they "are God's fellow workers; you are God's field, you are God's building" (1 Cor. 3:9). This is the high calling of culture: to become an icon of the kingdom of God. "At the great moment when the world passes from time into eternity," Evdokimov writes, "the Holy Spirit will touch this icon lightly with His fingers, and something of the Spirit will remain in it forever. In the 'eternal Liturgy' of the age to come, it is by means of all such elements of culture as have passed through the fire of purification that human beings will sing the praises of the Lord."[21] All the externalities of civilization and the political state may pass away with the old *aeon*, but the human spirit embodied in culture, "this treasure in earthen vessels" (2 Cor. 4:7), shall not pass away but shall be "transformed . . . from glory to glory" (2 Cor. 3:18).

Liturgy and Culture

Thus even in a fallen world, culture is not discontinuous with the new creation. To begin to explain the meaning in this, however, we must look at the relationship between worship and culture. Since time immemorial, human

21. Paul Evdokimov, *Women and the Salvation of the World* (Crestwood, NY: St. Vladimir's Seminary Press, 1994), 132–33.

beings have recognized and affirmed the positive value of culture and its relationship to a transcendent order in their worship of divinity and celebration of creation as gift of that divinity.

In *Leisure: The Basis of Culture*, the Roman Catholic philosopher Josef Pieper carries out a stunning phenomenological analysis of the connection between the worship of divinity and the rise of culture. He extends his analysis to make some very particular claims about Christian worship. This analysis functions as the bridge to my closing comments. I am not so concerned, however, with Pieper's powerful and persuasive claim that leisure, defined as "everything that lies beyond the utilitarian world," is the basis of culture, the precondition for its birth, as with his correlative proposal that "culture lives on religion through divine worship."[22]

In other words, Pieper maintains that worship is the basis of leisure, which, in turn, is the fountainhead of true culture. Berdyaev argues similarly when he states that "philosophy, science, architecture, painting, sculpture, music, poetry and morality are integrally comprised in the ecclesiastical cult in undifferentiated form."[23] Pieper insists that genuine leisure is not "killing time." It is not "idle" time. It is not "wasted time." It is none of these because it is not a state of existence, the value of which can be measured over and against time spent in economic labor or work whose purpose is to produce goods external to the actual performance. Religious worship—not limited to the Christian Eucharist—is the quintessential home of leisure because religious worship is nothing less than a freely performed celebration of the divine presence and thanksgiving for the goodness, beauty, and truth that the divinity brings into the lives of those who worship it. Within liturgical time there are no "in order tos," "wherefores," or "whyfores." Neither time nor work tyrannize human existence any longer.

Worshipful liturgical time liberates its participants from time as necessity, imperative "to do," or inevitability. It is, rather, proleptic participation in the freedom and creativeness of the divine nature (2 Pet. 1:4). Worship, says Pieper, marks off the *artes liberales* from the *artes serviles*. From worship's sacred ground and hallowed time, we are able to see and experience a play of Shakespeare as a work of the *artes liberales*. Its value and purpose lie within the creative act itself. This is culture, as contrasted with business marketing for example. Business marketing, whether taught as a subject in the university or practiced in the marketplace, belongs to the realm of *artes serviles*. It is not culture, although culture can potentially elevate and humanize it. Its purpose,

22. Josef Pieper, *Leisure: The Basis of Culture*, trans. Alexander Dru (New York: Random House, 1963), 61.
23. Nicholas Berdyaev, *Meaning of History*, 212.

to sell products, is external to the activity itself. The value of the activity is fundamentally instrumental.

Much as it can hardly fathom C. S. Lewis's observation that joy is a "surprise" that cannot be conjured by well-planned recreational events, the pragmatic or utilitarian mind has difficulty grasping how the *artes liberales* differ from other "necessary" kinds of human activity and productivity. "Celebration of God in worship cannot be done unless it is done for its own sake,"[24] Pieper states. Yet, if this is so, then culture itself is at least as much a gift from divinity as a human achievement, more a surprise than something securable by government grants to the humanities.

Culture, as I have been defining it, is among humanity's highest expressions of freedom, for genuine worship is not compelled; it is "done" voluntarily. The human person, made in the image of God, "creates" culture in a manner analogous to, although by no means in the same way as, how God brings all things into being not from necessity but with perfect freedom. "The object of God's creativity, the world, is not only a universe," writes the twentieth-century Russian Orthodox theologian Sergius Bulgakov, "but an artistic work, the *kosmos* in which the artist rejoices."[25] Human beings dwell in a "divine culture," a divine milieu, even "before" (I mean this in an ontological sense, as state of being, not temporally) they make human culture. Indeed, divine culture is the precondition of human culture. Divine culture is paradise before the fall; it is forgotten and lost through the ancestral sin; it is remembered and regained through prayer and sacrament.

Pieper writes that the notion of "the origin of arts in worship, and of leisure derived from its celebration is given [to us by Plato] in the form of a magnificent mythical image: man attains his true form and his upright attitude 'in festive companionship with the Gods.'"[26] In our epoch, however, the world of the market and economically driven labor claims to be the entire field of valuable human activity.

This state of mind (or habit of being) is secularism, as I discuss it in chapters 3 and 4. Says Pieper, "What in our days is called 'secularism' represents perhaps, not so much the loss of a Christian outlook, as rather the loss of some more fundamental insights that have traditionally constituted humanity's patrimony of natural wisdom."[27] If the Cappadocians were alive today, they no doubt would agree with him.

24. Pieper, *Leisure*, 62.
25. Sergius Bulgakov, *Sergius Bulgakov: Toward a Russian Political Theology*, ed. Rowan Williams (Edinburgh: T&T Clark, 1999), 195.
26. Pieper, *Leisure*, 61.
27. Josef Pieper, *Josef Pieper: An Anthology* (San Francisco: Ignatius, 1989), 142.

Shifting from the general to the specific, something more needs to be said about the singularity—even the uniqueness—of Christian worship and, therefore, Christian culture. Bulgakov states the crux of the matter when he writes, "Man is the son of eternity plunged in the stream of time, the son of freedom" caught in a fallen world. The church in its liturgy calls on human beings to "lift up your hearts," whereas the modern spirit beckons ordinary humanity to think that the answer to the mystery of its origin, nature, and destiny is no mystery at all but a fact found beneath human existence in animal and inanimate nature. Bulgakov continues, "It cannot with impunity be dinned into a man's ear that he is a two-legged brute, that his nature is purely animal, and that therefore the only thing left him is to recognize this and to worship his own brutishness. . . . One cannot deprive man of the ideal of personality and hide Christ's image from him without devastating his soul."[28]

Bulgakov maintains that this existential and cultural crisis of human meaning is the essence of modernity and postmodernity. He judges that the current condition of Western culture is inextricably and unavoidably intertwined with the decline of Christian orthodoxy, and the future of Western culture with the future of the Christian faith. This is, of course, contrary to contemporary conventional wisdom wedded as it is to one or another ideology of progress.

For two millennia, through sacraments and liturgy, Christians have remembered the divine image. Out of this worship they have drawn the hope and inspiration to build up culture in a world that modern science tells them is doomed to end in ice and fire. Christians have understood the Eucharist as God's gift of health and renewal to humanity and to the whole world. God calls on human beings to act as priests of his creation, to recollect and return the entirety of it with whole heart and mind to God as matter and subject (Rev. 5:13) of the "eternal liturgy" (Heb. 8:1–2) in which the old creation is translated into a new one. "Now I saw a new heaven and new earth, for the first heaven and the first earth had passed away" (Rev. 21:1), reports the seer of the book of Revelation.

The sacred and hallowed death that the Eucharist commemorates is not only the last and final bloody sacrifice acceptable to God; it is the ultimate sacrifice that sanctifies and renews the entire creation. For Christ gave not only himself as a sacrifice, but rendered to God, through his body and blood, all of creation as one holy oblation transformed into his resurrected body.

In light of this sacramental character of the world, revealed in and fulfilled by the Christian liturgy, the true value of culture comes to light.

---

28. Sergius Bulgakov, *A Bulgakov Anthology: Sergius Bulgakov, 1871–1944*, ed. James Pain and Nicholas Zernov (Philadelphia: Westminster, 1976), 63.

Indeed, it needs to be said that the Eucharist renders human beings fit to make culture itself sign and image of the kingdom of heaven. This culture may be a great cathedral, the work of many, or the simple prayer of one small child.

"Three exclamations of the celebrant and three short replies from the gathering comprise an introductory dialogue by which the sacrament of the [Byzantine] anaphora begins,"[29] writes Alexander Schmemann in *The Eucharist*. The three exclamations are: "The grace of our Lord . . . be with you all," "Let us lift up our hearts," and "Let us give thanks to the Lord." The three responses assent to and affirm these declarations to be fitting and right. Thus, in eucharistic worship, through the offering of the holy oblation, Christians realize that their words, actions, and achievements participate in the goodness, truth, and beauty of the life of God. They remember that all their words, deeds, and creations attain value only insofar as they themselves dispose their whole self to that which is "high" and "heavenly." And they express gratitude to God that in and through this holy sacrifice their lives and the life of the world are redeemed, renewed, and sanctified. These are the three liturgical movements of the soul that mystically (hidden from unbelieving eyes) have given birth to the culture we call "Western."

Conclusion

In his criticism, Matthew Arnold proved himself a true late child of nineteenth-century liberal Christianity and of modernity. He could leave creed and dogma and prayer and worship behind yet remain paradoxically (perhaps contradictorily) attached to Christendom and convinced that culture would continue to be perfected. Today we are living at the end of that self-contradictory and self-delusory modern legacy. Against this backdrop, postmodernity rises up to reject Christendom and, with no qualms, to leave it behind completely.

A path, which there is not room here to follow in detail, may be traced from the Arnoldian belief in culture to the aggressive, monolithic secularism of today. This secularism asserts the absolute autonomy of human beings and experiments with a new Prometheanism. The twentieth-century Roman Catholic theologian Romano Guardini once described modernity "as a movement that in its beginning denied the Christian doctrine and a Christian order of life even as it usurped its human and cultural effects." In the midst of this,

---

29. Alexander Schmemann, *The Eucharist* (Crestwood, NY: St. Vladimir's Seminary Press, 1988), 166.

Christian men and women "found ideas and values, whose Christian origin
was clear, but which were declared the property of all." Guardini predicts that
the new coming age "will do away with [even] these ambivalences . . . [and]
declare that the secularized facets of Christianity are sentimentalities. This
declaration will be clear." He continues, "The world to come will be filled
with animosity and danger but it will be a world open and clean."[30] No one
will be able to doubt any longer what is at stake.

Guardini tendered these penetrating observations almost three quarters of
a century ago. The term *culture wars*, which has become stock parlance in
our day, can mislead and obscure the real drama unfolding. *Culture wars* is a
hopelessly inadequate description of the choices that contemporary society
is making for the future of humankind. It does register, however, a widening
gap of disagreement between secularists and the religiously orthodox about
the meaning and value of culture. Secularists are believers in progress through
education, economics, social science, diversity,[31] multiculturalism, feminism,
and deconstructionism. They often reject transcendental reality, or at least
regard the possibility that it exists as irrelevant to human endeavor. They are
persuaded that the perfect or best of all possible worlds is a strictly human
and historical project. Whatever the secularists' precise definition of culture,
culture is the "end game" without closure or fulfillment in final meaning.
"Culture is opposed to eschatology, to the apocalyptic. . . . [It] is opposed to
an ending; its secret hope is to remain in history."[32]

Christianity defines culture not merely in anthropological and sociological
terms but, more important, soteriologically, sacramentally, and eschatologi-
cally. For two millennia, this religious vision provided Western civilization
with a unifying image of human excellence. Culture was understood as the
expression and concretization of the spiritual element of human nature writ
large, the *imago Dei* growing out into the world and transforming it into
the eschatological kingdom of God. Because this is a fallen world, deeply,
ontologically rooted in the habit of sin, culture was also understood as profoundly ambiguous. On the one hand, it is the manifestation of the godlike
creative capacities of human beings, owing to the fact that they are endowed
with the divine image. On the other hand, owing to the fall, culture can express the most destructive proclivities of human beings. Culture is neither
humanity's perfection nor our salvation. Culture is historical and finite,
and not an end in itself. "Culture, in its essence . . . is the search in history

30. Romano Guardini, *The End of the Modern World* (Wilmington, DE: ISI Books, 1998), 105.
31. Diversity and multiculturalism have become ideologies. One can reject both and still
embrace genuine plurality.
32. Evdokimov, *Women and Salvation*, 127.

for what is not found in history, for what is greater than history and leads outside its boundaries,"[33] states Evdokimov. No culture, however "Christian," is able to convert the sinful human being and render the human condition blessed. The perfection of culture, like that of humankind, is completely dependent on God's initiative in and through the incarnation by the power of the Holy Spirit.

Postmodernity rejects this vision. I do *not* mean to suggest, however, that the vision has completely vanished. For it continues to reside in the "cult" that gave birth to it and infused it into the decadent, hollowed-out culture of late antiquity, and transmuted that dying world into what we call Christendom.

"Every culture has its spiritual origin in a cult, from which little by little it becomes detached, until it is entirely cut off and self-contained, even perhaps the reserve of an elite," observes the contemporary Orthodox theologian Olivier Clément. Ironically, as it enters its decadent phase, a culture may achieve "high refinement, subtlety and consciousness," Clément adds; but there is a loss of focus, wholeness, and spontaneity. With higher consciousness comes objectification, "skepticism, tolerance of diversity, a dislike of sharp distinctions, a readiness to see shades of grey, rather than black and white."[34]

Because of Western civilization's Christian past, growing indifference to the incarnation and rejection of it can only mean decadence and demise of the culture. "In its decadent phase (using the phrase with no pejorative intent) a culture becomes accessible and in a way that simultaneously enfeebles and enriches it, when it spreads beyond its traditional organic community," Clément writes. It is like a dying sun, growing weaker and more diffuse until it implodes. "This accessibility and openness are accompanied by a certain predilection for the unknown, what Spengler called 'secondary religiosity,'"[35] after which complete secularity follows.

An agnostic or atheistic culture, however, "can only be a parasite plant on an alien stock, and one which kills the tree upon which it is feeding," Bulgakov warns. "Self-deification [through culture] is not life-giving but . . . death-bringing."[36] Some will claim similarities between contemporary Western civilization and the late Roman Empire into which Christianity entered. Social scientists and historians can accept or reject these comparisons on so-called "objective" grounds. But in all this, a fundamental claim of the Christian faith

33. Evdokimov, *Women and Salvation*, 132.
34. Olivier Clément, *On Human Being* (New York: New City, 2000), 132.
35. Quoted in Clément, *On Human Being*, 132.
36. Bulgakov, *Bulgakov Anthology*, 62.

does not figure. It is that the course of human history, and so this culture too, has been altered fundamentally and irreversibly by the incarnation.

Post-Christian society cannot be like pre-Christian society; it cannot return to its pagan past because God has unveiled his face as the face of humanity in Christ. The One (God) who was hidden behind ancient mythologies has become flesh. It cannot remain agnostic indefinitely either. New gods may be invented, but that is just it: they would be inventions. Pieper argues that after Christ "there is only *one* true and finally valid form of cultic worship, which is the sacramental Sacrifice of the Christian Church." On the cross, Jesus Christ ended ritual sacrifice and the pre-Christian cult forever. "For the student, Christian or non-Christian, of the 'history of religions,'" Pieper continues, "it really is not possible to meet with any actually established cult other than the Christian, in the world-wide European culture."[37]

Our "post-Christendom civilization" might turn aggressively atheistic, but this atheism can only be with reference to biblical faith. Thus, postmodernity is not a new culture. It is the rotting corpse of a thoroughly desacralized Christendom or, alternatively, the empty shell of the Christian cult inhabited by alien ideologies. An institutionalized postmodernity inside the old Christendom, lately called modernity, would be the "incarnation" of the antichrist. It would be culture that is anticulture.

Guardini says that such a future would entail two phenomena: "the non-human man and the not-natural nature." In such a "new" heathen or atheistic future, humans would exercise absolute lordship of creation with no recognized limitations; that is, "The freedom to determine his own goals: the freedom to dissolve the immediate reality of things, to employ its elements for the execution of his own ends. These things will be done without any consideration for what had been thought inviolate or untouchable in nature."[38] (Look around. Much that Guardini prognosticated is already with us.)

In this future, humanity will be ignorant of, or defiant toward, the religious sense "of the sacredness of nature which had endured within mankind's earlier vision of the world." Humankind might carry all of this "to the last consequence,"[39] says Guardini, by which I take him to mean the complete destruction of the world by human hands through a diabolic parody of God.

Guardini, however, presents an alternative that, because of his optimism (born of his Christian faith), he regards as the more likely possibility. "The faith of the Christian will . . . take on a new decisiveness, . . . strip itself of

37. Pieper, *Leisure*, 59.
38. Guardini, *End of the Modern World*, 73–74.
39. Guardini, *End of the Modern World*, 74, 73.

all secularism, all analogies with the secular world, all flabbiness and eclectic mixtures." Dogma and worship will also revive as Christians "are forced to distinguish [themselves] more sharply from a dominantly non-Christian ethos."[40] A new Christian culture might then arise from the renewed cult, although where it arises may be a surprise.

40. Guardini, *End of the Modern World*, 103–4, 106.

2

CONSTANTINE AND CHRISTENDOM

On May 21st of each year, the Orthodox Church commemorates the memories of Constantine the Great and his mother, Helena. The Byzantine liturgy declares them both "equal to the apostles." The thematic hymn for the Feast of Saint Constantine states the following:

> Having seen the figure of the Cross in the heavens,
> And like Paul not having received his call from men, O Lord, Thy
>   apostle among rulers, the Emperor Constantine,
> Was set by thy hand as ruler over the Imperial City that he preserved in
>   peace for many years,
> Through the prayers of the Theotokos, O Only Lover of Mankind.[1]

To the mind of some, this memorial for the first Christian emperor seems misplaced, if not downright wrongheaded. Leave aside the deaths of several family members, including a wife and son, for which some historians have suspected Constantine was responsible; over the centuries, there also have arisen several interpretations of Constantine's character and career that do not lend themselves to the appellation "saint."

An earlier version of this chapter originally appeared as "Does It Matter That Constantine Ended Sacrifice?," in *Life Amid the Principalities: Identifying, Understanding, and Engaging Created, Fallen, and Disarmed Powers Today*, ed. Michael Root and James J. Buckley, 38–50 (Eugene, OR: Cascade Books, 2016). Used by permission.

1. Various translations of this text are available on the internet. This translation is based on several of these.

For example, the view was once widely held that Constantine was a prag-matist or political opportunist who feigned conversion to Christianity in his ambitions for power. Another more generous interpretation is that, while a religious or superstitious individual, Constantine never genuinely embraced the Christian deity—in other words, that Constantine practiced religious syncretism suited to his goal of unifying and strengthening the empire. Even if, in the end, he adhered to an overarching monotheism, the god of this monotheistic faith might just as easily have been the solar deity, to which Constantine in his early years paid homage, as the Christian God, to whom he offered worship later on.[2]

In addition to these speculations about Constantine's "true" religion, some voice an uncomplimentary argument that Constantine was the founder of a Christian form of oriental theocracy in which the king stands above the law, and the church is subordinate and servile to the state. This form of rule has been named caesaropapism.

Reformed and Protestant thinkers from Luther on have espoused versions of church history in which the original purity of the New Testament church and the apostolic era was corrupted by an unholy alliance of ecclesiastics and political rulers that radically compromised the gospel. Constantine, whose life spanned the late third through the mid-fourth century, is regarded as among the first to have poisoned the water. The Radical Reformation spun the narrative of a pacifist church hijacked and turned against Jesus's own nonviolent convictions by the likes of Constantine. In our day, the late John Howard Yoder adroitly brought this narrative and its underlying thesis up to date. As I mention in the introduction, Yoder labeled this story of church compromise, corruption, and even apostasy "Constantinianism" after the emperor Constantine (AD 272–337).

In his book *Defending Constantine: The Twilight of an Empire and the Dawn of Christendom*, Peter Leithart summarizes the several meanings that Yoder invested in this moniker: (1) Constantinianism is "a wedding of piety to power"; (2) Constantinianism is a harmful "merger" of church and state in which the movement to God in history is identified with empire, nation, or ruler; (3) Constantinianism denotes "a set of mental, spiritual, and institu-tional habits" that deviates from the original gospel of the kingdom of God and the nonviolent teachings of Jesus.[3]

But does Constantine actually merit Yoder's criticism and condemnation? Leithart insists that he does not. In the course of his defense of Constantine,

2. See Charles Matson Odahl, *Constantine and the Christian Empire*, 2nd ed. (London: Routledge, 2010), 285.

3. Peter J. Leithart, *Defending Constantine: The Twilight of an Empire and the Dawn Chris-tendom* (Downers Grove, IL: IVP Academic, 2010), 176, 287, 310.

he argues that through a series of actions in which Constantine set himself against pagan sacrifice, he not only ended Rome as it had been known but also opened vital space for the Christian faith to prosper and become the foundation of a new order. In other words, Constantine granted the church the freedom to build its culture out into the public realm, a culture we even today refer to as Christendom.

Leithart names and discusses two actions in particular to support his argument: (1) Constantine refused to offer the customary animal sacrifice after his military victory at the Milvian Bridge in 312, and (2) in the Edict on Religion of 325, Constantine mandated that Roman officials refrain from making animal sacrifices. Leithart persuasively demonstrates that what Constantine accomplished and set in motion through actions such as these is theologically and politically significant, while also controverting Yoder's thesis about Constantinianism.

Before I discuss the end of sacrifice and desacrification of the empire under Constantine, I am going to lodge a criticism of Leithart's *Defending Constantine* that applies also to much of what has been written on Constantine and his relationship to the church. Leithart, like so many who have spoken on the subject, neglects to consult Orthodox historians and theologians in his assessment of Constantine's political theology. The result is that the historical mind of the Eastern church is virtually absent from *Defending Constantine*, excepting the absolutely obligatory discussion and analysis of the fourth-century church historian Eusebius of Caesarea. Yet one must ask: How can we consider Constantine's legacy without at least some discussion of the course of the Byzantine Empire and its worldview?

Some years ago, at a symposium on *Defending Constantine*, I raised the question of what kind of book Leithart's might have been had he not decided to spar with Yoder. For as it stands, Yoder is the ever-present shadow in the chiaroscuro of Leithart's portrait of Constantine. This, in my view, limits and weakens the book; Leithart fails to break wholly free from the false narratives and misleading historical constructs about Constantine and his legacy that dominate in the academy even today.

Does it matter in our estimate of the kind of political order and relationship of church and state that Constantine brought into existence that he brought sacrifice to an end and was finally baptized? The Orthodox Church's response is yes, it does. The hymn I cited at the start of this chapter supplies an important clue to how Orthodoxy has interpreted Constantine and his legacy. Among recent Orthodox writers, Alexander Schmemann, John Meyendorff, and John McGuckin have assessed Constantine and Byzantium, and their views represent a broad consensus of Orthodox scholarship. All three are aware of the standard Western criticism. Yet in the final analysis they work out of an Orthodox memory and ecclesiology. This amounts to a view on the church's relationship to the world that neither Leithart nor Yoder presents, or for that matter Gibbon, Burkhart, or Harnack before them.

Contemporary Interpretations of the Constantinian "Revolution"

In his early work *The Historical Road of Eastern Orthodoxy* (English edition published in 1963), and once again in his later collection of essays *Church, World, Mission* (published in 1979), Schmemann pauses to interpret the thematic hymn of the Feast of Saints Constantine and Helena. He asks his readers to take note of the proclamation that Constantine, "like Paul," received his call not "from men" but directly from God and Christ. This conviction of the church, he maintains, must be taken into account in order to rightly understand what made Byzantium tick and what kind of political theology it had.

"In the eyes of the Eastern tradition," Schmemann explains, Christ directly elected and called Constantine, and "not . . . through the Church." Nor was he called to the service of God "as an individual, but rather as emperor." Thus, in the mind of the church, Constantine's conversion was not merely personal. It was a translation, rather, of the office of emperor itself into a service to Christ and his kingdom. Schmemann adds that in the hagiography and memory of the church, Constantine's election occurs "at a crucial moment of his imperial career" when in a dream "the acceptance of Christ" is presented to him as "the condition of his victory"[4] over Maxentius and his army at the Milvian Bridge (in October 312) and over all the empire's enemies.

Henceforth, there is the understanding that through the emperor, the empire comes under the lordship of Jesus Christ. The church's hymns celebrate, and its hagiography describes, this transformation of emperor and empire as a triumph of the cross, an exorcism of the world order that places the empire in service to the kingdom of God. The empire is not the realization of the kingdom on earth. The church, not the state, is the true sign and symbol of the kingdom of God in this world. Christ alone is its ruler, not the emperor. This is not the caesaropapism of the familiar literature on Byzantium. More important—and pertinent to our discussion—there should be no presumption that Constantine inaugurated such a caesaropapism.[5]

4. Alexander Schmemann, *Church, World, Mission: Reflections on Orthodoxy in the West* (Crestwood, NY: St. Vladimir's Seminary Press, 1979), 35.
5. My argument is about the nature of the political theology that we find in the church's worship and hagiography, not about the historical realities, where emperors often transgressed this vision.

The Justinian *Symphonia*

Similarly, in his book *Imperial Unity and Christian Divisions* (1989), John Meyendorff maintains that "by allying itself to the Empire, the Church ceased to be a sect accessible to only a few. "It assumed 'catholic' responsibility for society as a whole"—without renouncing "its eschatological calling."[6] In the sixth century, Justinian gave a name to this alliance. He called it *symphonia*. Meyendorff explains that in its best representations, the Justinian *symphonia* did not expect a complete transfiguration of the social, economic, and political realm. Instead, *symphonia* was prescribed for bringing about a Christian order and culture in a still fallen world, with a mind that the kingdom of God, while at hand, belongs not to this aeon but to that which is yet to come. Meyendorff does concede, however, that at times, utopian expectations and aspirations supplanted this eschatology and ultimately contributed to the demise of Byzantium itself.

Schmemann holds that the mistake Western observers often make when assessing the Byzantine relationship of church and empire is interpreting this arrangement in fundamentally legal or juridical terms, which is to say as a relationship between "two *institutions*, two *powers*, two *governments*."[7] To the contrary, he insists the relationship that was worked out over centuries and evolved was premised in a shared faith. This relationship commenced when Constantine stunned a persecuted church by granting it freedom and giving it his imperial favor in 313 with the Edict of Milan. With the background of past persecutions deeply lodged in its memory, the church interpreted this course of events as providential, the fulfillment of the story of Israel in the Old Testament.

Unlike the debate in the Latin West, an argument did not ensue in Byzantium over whether the imperial throne or the church was superior. In his important essay "The Legacy of the 13th Apostle," John McGuckin explains: "The biblical doctrine of the 'conditional' blessing from God upon his people for their political stability" comes to play in such a way that the monarchy is bounded and limited by God's covenant with it and by God's law. He explains that this inherited biblical interpretation decisively modified the classical model of absolute sacral kingship.[8]

On this basis, McGuckin criticizes arguments that the Byzantine synthesis either persisted to be patently pagan or evolved into caesaropapism. Byzantium

6. John Meyendorff, *Imperial Unity and Christian Divisions: The Church AD 450–680* (Crestwood, NY: St. Vladimir's Seminary Press, 1989), 19.

7. Schmemann, *Church, World, Mission*, 34 (emphasis original).

8. John McGuckin, "The Legacy of the 13th Apostle: Origins of the East Christian Conceptions of Church and State Relation," *St. Vladimir's Theological Quarterly* 47 (2003), 285.

was neither. Rather, "the concept of *symphonia* . . . [was] fundamentally faithful to the biblical witness that 'salvation' is first and foremost . . . the gracious restoration and renewal of a people." This "witness" allows that salvation in this world is not perfect, and that the people of God must continually overcome "numerous failures" to approximate the "socio-political and moral dimensions of life"[9] to which God has called them.

Furthermore, Byzantine political theology fundamentally altered the Roman understandings of *potestas*, the effective administrative exercise of political and military power, and *auctoritas*, moral authority with the power to judge. These were reinterpreted within a new framework under the lordship of Jesus Christ. The horizon of Christ's rule on earth, the eschatological kingdom of God, set the parameters for what might be claimed by imperial power *or* ecclesiastical authority. McGuckin describes "the practical working-out" of the Byzantine *symphonia* in the following manner:

> [In] the Byzantine concept of *symphonia*, no one ever denied the emperor's right to command the allegiance of clergy, and their obedience, in all state matters. . . . No one in Byzantium (at least no one who ever got far enough from the capital to express the matter freely) ever doubted, equally, that if the emperor strayed too far in matters relating to conscience and orthodoxy (if he transgressed the limits of orthodoxy, that is, which was carefully regulated by the written and synodical tradition) his authority was rendered void, and his throne was endangered by the very fact that he had demonstrated that he no longer had sacral protection as the defender of the true faith.[10]

He concludes that the Byzantine political theology was dialectical. On the one hand, the state understood that the church's alliance with it was conditional. God's investment of the emperor with power of sacral dimension also placed limits on the autocracy. On the other hand, the church did not claim any power (i.e., *potestas*) over the imperial rule. We mustn't forget that this was an age in which our modern distinction between religious and secular political power is not imagined. Even within this Christian universe, political power is invested with sacral meaning. The political authority, however, must respect the "fundamental biblical teaching that the kingdom of God is not to be identified with the concern of the powers of this world."[11] Only the church is the sacramental body of Christ that gives access to the kingdom of heaven.

9. McGuckin, "Legacy of the 13th Apostle," 285.
10. McGuckin, "Legacy of the 13th Apostle," 286.
11. McGuckin, "Legacy of the 13th Apostle," 287.

The Role That Sacrifice Played

I have suggested that the genius of Peter Leithart's *Defending Constantine* belongs to his thesis that the revolution Constantine commenced is traceable back to the empire's desacrification, which Constantine initiated. This, Leithart rightly insists, is a fact to which the labels of caesaropapism and Constantinianism are both blind. We must recall that Constantine commenced his revolution immediately on the heels of his victory over Maxentius at the Milvian Bridge. The practice of the emperors who preceded him was to offer a public sacrifice to Jupiter upon entering the city. On this occasion, however, Constantine withheld from doing just that. "Diocletian's empire was built on sacrifice," Leithart explains, but Constantine, whether he realized it at the time or not, "made it clear that a new theology was coming to be, a political theology without sacrifice."[12] Leithart continues: "By eliminating the civic sacrifice that founded Rome and protecting and promoting the Eucharistic *civitas*, Constantine was, in effect, if not in intent, acknowledging the church's superiority as a community of justice and peace."[13]

No doubt, Constantine's refusal to make public sacrifices to the pagan deity did amount to something profound and revolutionary. I agree with Leithart's judgment that "when Constantine began to end sacrifice, he began to end Rome as he knew it."[14] Nonetheless, I do not think Leithart argues his case as strongly as he might. Constantine's action entailed more than merely the desacrification of the empire: by refusing the pagan sacrifice, Constantine also laid aside his lawful claim to divinity. And by so doing, he gave to the church complete and exclusive authority to offer the eucharistic sacrifice instead. Thus—and this alone is ever so significant—*Constantine granted the church the room and permission to freely constitute itself within the empire as the unique eschatological "polity" of the kingdom of God.*

Again, whether or not he initially intended it, when Constantine refused to perform public sacrifices and conceded that it was not his function to serve the eucharistic sacrifice, he guaranteed that the Hellenic concept of emperor as absolute ruler over one human and divine commonwealth would be fundamentally altered. There came into being a new commonwealth that, while ruled temporally by the emperor, was under the eternal lordship of Jesus Christ, whose body in this world was the church, not the empire.

The Eastern church's understanding of its relationship to the empire was and remains consistent with this interpretation. The church, Schmemann

12. Leithart, *Defending Constantine*, 66–67.
13. Leithart, *Defending Constantine*, 331.
14. Leithart, *Defending Constantine*, 328.

explains, viewed itself primarily as a "sacramental organism" whose function it was "to reveal, manifest, and communicate the Kingdom of God, to
communicate it as Truth, Grace, and Communion with God. . . . The Church
claim[ed] no 'power' in this world and ha[d] no 'earthly' interests to defend."[15]
Thus, it was not difficult for the church to leave to the state even the "man-
agement of her earthly life, the care and administration of her earthly needs
. . . as long as the empire placed itself under Christ's judgment and in the
perspective, essential for the Church, of the Kingdom of God." Last, "the
Church saw no reason to claim any 'juridical' independence from it [the em-
pire], and, in fact gladly put the reins of ecclesiastical government and policy
in the hands of the emperor." In this respect, the church's attitude toward the
state was the same before Constantine as after him, rooted "precisely in the
same 'eschatological ecclesiology.'"[16]

The Dangers in the Byzantine Political Theology

In *The Historical Road of Eastern Orthodoxy*, Schmemann pauses again to
note that lamentably the Justinian ideology of *symphonia* also permitted, if
indeed it did not invite, a serious misconstruing of the church's essence and
presence. This is exemplified in the famous analogy of body and soul, such
that the state is recognized as the body of the empire and the church as its
soul. By overly spiritualizing the church, this analogy threatened to undermine
the church's claim to being a separate and independent polity. "The early
Church felt it was itself a body," Schmemann argues.[17] The lurking danger in
the *symphonia* theory was that the state would refuse to recognize the church
as a distinct community apart from the empire.[18]

In other words, inherent in the Byzantine political theology was a tendency
to leave little or no room for the church to be something more than merely a
spiritual or mystical organ or entity in service to the empire. And in this respect,
there is more than a smidgeon of truth in Gerhardt Ladner's observation that
from the late fourth century onward the emperors increasingly asserted "a

15. Schmemann, *Church, World, Mission*, 38, 39.
16. Schmemann, *Church, World, Mission*, 40.
17. Alexander Schmemann, *The Historical Road of Eastern Orthodoxy*, English ed. (New
York: Holt, Rinehart and Winston, 1963), 150.
18. In this early work, Schmemann is quite negative about the Justinian theory of *symphonia*. He judged that this theory threatened to dissolve the church into the empire. When
he returned to this subject in *Church, World, Mission*, his mind shifted to a more positive
view of the Justinian synthesis, though it also is clear he did not entirely abandon his earlier
criticisms.

quasi-sacerdotal position in the Church" as the balance of influence tipped from the ascetic and mystic toward the ruler.[19]

Schmemann, no less than Meyendorff and McGuckin, is aware of this. So was the church, such that the church from the start "opposed the empire . . . not because of any political or social principles, not for the sake of any political doctrine of the state, but uniquely in the name of Christ whom God made the *kyrios* of creation. In other terms, she [the Church] opposed the demonic 'misuse' of the state by the 'prince of this world,' [while] her very refusal to acknowledge the emperor as *kyrios* implied . . . a positive attitude towards the state, faith in the possibility for the Messiah to be accepted by the entire 'house of Israel.'"[20]

Schmemann reminds his readers that exorcism was a crucial language of the early church and a way of thinking about and articulating its presence in the world. This helps to understand how the church interpreted the conversion of the emperor and the empire. "The power of the Cross—the Church's essential weapon against the demons—liberated the empire from the power of the 'prince of this world.' By crushing the idols, it made the empire 'open' to the Kingdom, available as its servant and instrument."[21] One can add that every baptism that the church performed would hereafter be a visible sign of this liberation.[22]

Likewise, McGuckin explains that even chapter 13 of the book of Revelation, which is so often referenced as a condemnation of kingship and empire, is not quite that at all. "Revelation demonizes the earthly king who stands against the will of God and refuses to align himself with the royal King's policies for the world and the Kingdom of God. It is abundantly clear, however, that the idea the earthly ruler is *either* the agent of God *or* the servant of the beast is prevalent throughout the entire book, and underlies its notion of Kingship."[23]

In summary, Schmemann, Meyendorff, and McGuckin share a distinctive Orthodox ecclesiology that shapes their respective analyses, an ecclesiology that they maintain is an inheritance from Byzantium. "The Church, to be sure, is *institution*"—note the absence of the article "a"—but of *sacramental*, and not *juridical*, nature," Schmemann explains.[24] The church exists as institution

19. Gerhardt B. Ladner, *The Idea of Reform: Its Impact on Christian Thought and Action in the Age of the Fathers*, rev. ed. (New York: Harper and Row, 1967), 124–25.

20. Schmemann, *Church, World, Mission*, 36.

21. Schmemann, *Church, World, Mission*, 36.

22. There are several lengthy prayers of exorcism at the beginning of the Byzantine baptismal rite.

23. McGuckin, "Legacy of the 13th Apostle," 263 (emphasis mine).

24. Schmemann, *Church, World, Mission*, 39 (emphasis original).

not to wield power but to be a *presence*, the presence of the kingdom of God, in order "to assure the Church's 'passage' from 'this world' into 'the world to come,' as the sign constantly to be fulfilled, as the 'means' by which the Church becomes all the time 'that which she is.'"[25]

But just how does this work out under the Byzantine doctrine of *symphonia*? It is essential for the church "as *sign* and *sacrament* to be an institution," Schmemann explains. Nevertheless, its institutional features are not its *esse*, its very being. As *institution*, the church belongs to and participates in this world. As *fulfillment*, however—which is to say in its sacramental and eschatological expression and fulfillment—the church is "the world to come." This ecclesiology does not allow for a division or for a distinction to be made between the church as "institution" and the church as "fulfillment," or between the "visible" and "invisible" church because the entire purpose of the institution is precisely to make fulfillment possible, to reveal as present that which is "to come."[26]

Thus if we are to speak of two realms or kingdoms within this Byzantine political theology, we must be careful not to confuse this distinction between two realms with Gelasius's theory of two swords, especially in its later form as developed by the scholastics. Christ testifies to two realms when, in response to Pilate, he proclaims that his kingdom is not of this world (John 18:36). But that is just it. These two realms are not comparable; one is on a strictly temporal plane and the other on an eschatological plane. Clearly, there is an earthly institution that rules over this world. That is the empire. The church makes no claim whatsoever to fill that role. To reiterate, the church's calling is "to witness to the anticipated presence" (i.e., the inbreaking) of the eschatological kingdom of God "in the midst of a fallen world."[27]

Thus from the standpoint of this ecclesiology, so stated, the standard description of the Byzantine system as caesaropapism is misleading. Leithart is correct to reject this terminology, and he argues persuasively that Constantine did not intend to establish such a regime. In my view, it would be more accurate to say that caesaropapism is the perversely inverted image of the relationship of church and empire that developed in the West. I say this because the charge of caesaropapism assumes that church and state both behave and define themselves in terms of power, whether sacerdotal or secular.

---

25. Schmemann, *Church, World, Mission*, 39.
26. Schmemann, *Church, World, Mission*, 39 (emphasis original).
27. Meyendorff, *Imperial Unity and Christian Divisions*, 20.

Conclusion

Leithart closes *Defending Constantine* with a provocative chapter titled "Rome Baptized." The metaphor may be misleading, but the point he is making is crucial. In order to explain what he means, it helps to cite another Orthodox hymn, this from the Christmas cycle:

> When Augustus reigned alone upon earth, the many kingdoms of men came to an end: and when Thou wast made man of the Pure Virgin, the many gods of idolatry were destroyed. The cities of the world passed under one single rule; and the nations came to believe in one sovereign Godhead. The peoples were enrolled by the decree of Caesar; and we, the faithful, were enrolled in the Name of the Godhead, when Thou, our God, was made man. Great is Thy mercy; glory to Thee.[28]

In light of this text, the importance of Constantine's baptism for the Byzantine imagination and political theology is clarified. By his baptism, by being "enrolled in in the Name of the Godhead," the emperor joins all those who denounce the prince of this world and "the many gods of idolatry." By virtue of his baptism, the emperor also becomes a participant in the eucharistic sacrifice. This means that those "enrolled in the Name of the Godhead" henceforward have as their earthly monarch someone who owes his first allegiance to the true Lord of the cosmos and founder of the *Pax Romana*. The hymn proclaims, "The cities of the world passed under one single rule; and the nations came to believe in one sovereign Godhead."

As told by Eusebius, Constantine received baptism on his deathbed. Deliberately, he set aside his purple vestment for good and donned a white baptismal gown. In his final speech to Eusebius and the other bishops, Constantine stated that should his life continue, he would "associate with the people of God and unite with them in prayer as member of his church," and follow "such a course of life as befits . . . service to God."[29] Constantine died on Pentecost in May 337. Symbolically, he died as a Christian neophyte, not as emperor. Later on, this symbolism was continued in the monastic tonsure that dying emperors received. Meyendorff comments that from the church's point of view "with Constantine, the emperor fulfilled his mission with a full understanding of the ultimate goal of creation which was anticipated in the mysteries of the Church."[30]

28. Translation of this text is available in various forms from many sources on the internet. This translation is based on several English texts.
29. Eusebius, *Life of Constantine*, bk. 4, chap. 62, newadvent.org/fathers/25024.htm.
30. Meyendorff, *Imperial Unity and Christian Divisions*, 30.

Thus, according to both contemporary Orthodox writers and Byzantine festal hymnody, Constantine's baptism signifies that the title of *kyrios* unambiguously belongs to Christ and that his kingdom is not interchangeable with the empire. In spite of Eusebius's idealized portrait of the office of emperor and of Constantine himself, the church more often than not accepted the practical reality that this "fallen world could not be changed overnight by imperial legislation," Meyendorff writes. Yet the church also took great hope from Constantine's baptism that "the ultimate goal—the Kingdom of God—was . . . common to both the Empire and the Church."[31]

In other words, in the mind of the Byzantine Church, the empire (through Constantine's baptism) was itself called to accept Christ and became the wardrobe of Christ's *politeuma* (polity or commonwealth) in this world. This is how the Orthodox Church has understood the conversion of Constantine and the new world, the new *ecumene* (civilization), that he brought into existence. This belief did not produce a theory of separation of church and state, with which we are so familiar in America and almost instinctively accept as a given for how these bodies ought to relate to one another. Rather, the Byzantine political theology rests in an eschatological vision that, far from being limited to the salvation of the individual soul, embraces the whole of the *politeuma*. There should be no suspicion here of pietism, either.

Leithart writes that Constantine may well have believed that "he was erecting a new civic cult, a new more effective priestly college, a patriotic religious institution that would secure the *pax Dei* for Rome," but that in this "he was wrong, because the church is not a cult but a polis." Despite the church's "very real peccability and fallibility," Leithart continues, the church remains "*Christ's city, his body. . . . Therefore it cannot finally be co-opted.*"[32] Once again, this sort of explanation, while approaching the truth of the matter, echoes a Western debate that simply does not arise in the East and that should not be thought of as a key to solving the puzzle of Constantine and Christendom.

The sharp distinction Leithart draws between cult and polity makes no sense within an Orthodox context. Isn't the church really something of both? This certainly is how Byzantine theology conceives the matter. The church is a special kind of "cult," as well as a special form of "polity." Serving God's redemptive purpose, the Byzantine Church adopted secular institutional forms, such as diocese, eparchy, and exarchate, so that it might merge itself into one politico-ecclesiastical organism over which the emperor was head, yet in no manner of speaking a priest. I reiterate, in this vision of Christendom, the

31. Meyendorff, *Imperial Unity and Christian Divisions*, 30.
32. Leithart, *Defending Constantine*, 331.

church as "polity," as institutional structure, is a presence, not a *potestas*, or a power.

The first act of the church is to constitute itself, its *esse* or being, through a cultic act of worship. The church is a "cult," the cult of the lordship of Jesus Christ, which manifests and testifies to the presence of the heavenly "polity" of the kingdom of God in the person of Jesus Christ. It is under this same person's lordship that the emperor places himself and his realm as well. Nevertheless, the "cult's" worship is not limited to a single place or time; its worship reaches all places and times. "Jesus said to her, 'Woman, believe Me, the hour is coming when you will neither on this mountain, nor in Jerusalem, worship the Father. . . . The hour is coming, and now is, when the true worshipers will worship the Father in spirit and truth; for the Father is seeking such to worship Him'" (John 4:21, 23). In the Byzantine vision, Christ called Constantine, and through him the empire, into the church's service (*leiturgia*), and by virtue of the church's continuing worship of the Lord Jesus Christ, the empire itself became a "location" of the presence of the eschatological *politeuma*, the kingdom of heaven.

In Philippians, Paul announces, "But our commonwealth [*politeuma*] is in heaven, and from it we await a Savior, the Lord Jesus Christ, who will change our lowly body to be like his glorious body, by the power which enables him even to subject all things to himself" (Phil. 3:20–21 RSV). Byzantine political theology, for which the Orthodox Church gives Constantine credit, rests itself in this truth.

If this account is accurate, then the Byzantine Church took a different path from the Roman Catholic Church and the churches of the Reformation. Its path was lit by an eschatological and sacramental vision for which the chief terms are *church* and *world*, not *church* and *state*. While the Western error lies in a juridicism that articulates a dyad of institutions, two powers in uneasy alliance, the East's error lies in an overestimation of its eschatological hope that the church through its worship can not only reveal the presence of the kingdom of God in the midst of the earthly kingdom, but also bring about a transformation of the worldly instrumentalities of the state into ligaments of the kingdom of God. If we must cling to the metaphor, the latter is the true Constantinianism.

PART 2

ORTHODOXY IN THE MODERN WORLD

3

HERESY, ANCIENT AND MODERN

Alexander Schmemann constantly lamented that whenever Orthodox theologians were invited to participate in ecumenical gatherings, their role was typecast by Western prejudices. He often told the story of an early ecumenical experience at the first assembly of the World Council of Churches in 1948. When he arrived at the Amsterdam meeting, the young Orthodox theologian was greeted by a dignitary who informed Schmemann that he had been seated at the right of the assembly hall next to representatives of the Western "high churches," such as the Swedish Lutherans, Old Catholics, and Polish Nationals.

Schmemann asked the "high ecumenical dignitary" who escorted him how this seating arrangement had been decided. The individual told him that it "reflected the 'ecclesiological' makeup of the conference, one of whose main themes would be precisely the dichotomy of the 'horizontal' and 'vertical' ideas of the Church. And [that] obviously the Orthodox belong (don't they?) to the 'horizontal' type." Schmemann remarked "half-jokingly" that in his "studies of Orthodox theology he had never heard of such distinctions." He added that had the choice been left up to him he might have assigned himself to "the extreme left of the hall with the Quakers, whose emphasis on the Holy Spirit we Orthodox certainly share."[1]

An earlier version of this chapter originally appeared as "An Orthodox View of Orthodoxy and Heresy: An Appreciation of Alexander Schmemann," *Pro Ecclesia* 4, no. 1 (Winter 1995): 79–91. Used by permission.

1. Alexander Schmemann, *Church, World, Mission: Reflections on Orthodoxy in the West* (Crestwood, NY: St. Vladimir's Seminary Press, 1979), 199–200. The text of the Hartford appeal,

This chapter was prepared initially as a paper that I delivered in 1994 at an annual meeting of the American Theological Society in Princeton, New Jersey. I had been asked to address the topic of heresy from an Orthodox perspective. I confessed to my colleagues that initially I greeted the invitation to write it with a reflex much like Schmemann's. Had I been chosen to fill the stereotypical Orthodox role of defending Nicene Christianity, nuanced with liturgical sensibilities and a broad interpretation of tradition encompassing Scripture and the church fathers? Should I conscientiously attend to this assignment?

I turned to Schmemann's writing and, in particular, to an essay that he contributed to a volume on the Hartford appeal.[2] The Hartford appeal was issued in 1975 with the signatures of some seventeen theologians and churchmen, Schmemann among them, who represented a broad spectrum of American Christianity. The Hartford appeal listed and responded to roughly a dozen theological issues that a new breed of radical theologians had raised. These "young Turks" had advanced the "death of God" thesis and urged the churches to commit themselves to a new form of secular Christianity.

Schmemann chose to make this an opportunity to explain why he was skeptical about the venture. He turned to the preface of the document in which the authors concerned themselves with several religious and cultural trends that they thought were especially troubling in light of the challenge of the "death of God" exponents. It read in part: "The renewal of Christian witness and mission requires constant examination of the assumptions shaping the church's life. Today an apparent loss of a sense of the transcendent is undermining the church's ability to address with clarity and courage the urgent tasks to which God calls it in the world."[3]

Schmemann recognized that this argument for a renewed emphasis on transcendence was in Western theological parlance a rallying cry to return to Christian orthodoxy. Nevertheless, he judged the appeal more a symptom than a solution to the contemporary crisis in Christian theology. Despite the best intentions of his colleagues, he doubted that this strategy could retrieve and reinvigorate Christian orthodoxy.

He praised the appeal's endeavor to correct theological vision on the themes of mission, Christology, worship, and strategies of Christian engagement with

which I discuss below, is included in this volume. It is followed by an essay, from which I draw, that Schmemann wrote on the appeal. The original title of Schmemann's essay was "That East and West May Yet Meet," changed to "The Ecumenical Agony."

2. The title of that volume was *Against the World for the World: The Hartford Appeal and the Future of American Religion*, ed. Peter L. Berger and Richard John Neuhaus (New York: Seabury, 1979).

3. Schmemann, *Church, World, Mission*, 194.

the world, but he strongly questioned reliance on the twentieth-century Protestant neo-orthodoxies of Karl Barth and Reinhold Niebuhr. Neo-orthodoxy
in its various forms relies on an immanence and transcendence dialectic that
Schmemann judged to be at the heart of the crisis they sought to answer.
This was because this dialectic was itself a symptom of the loss of a classical
vision of Christian orthodoxy.

Schmemann viewed his task as threefold. First, and most important, to
challenge in a constructive way the appeal's reliance on the problem of transcendence. Second, to explain why his fellow Eastern Orthodox would likely
ignore the appeal. And third, to indicate what the groundwork might be for a
serious Orthodox response to the damaging effects of secularism, from which
the Orthodox themselves mistakenly assumed their theology and ecclesiology
insulated them.

Thus, Schmemann excoriated the efforts of Orthodox to "justify their *de
facto* noninvolvement in this theological debate." These efforts were bound
to fail and bring trouble on the church. The "theological conservatism" of the
Orthodox churches and their "adamant faithfulness not only to the content
but also to the very form of . . . [their] doctrinal tradition," concealed "from
them their own . . . tragic surrender to that 'very "culture"' from which they
claimed their faith immuniz[ed] them."[4] For despite their prevarications, the
West's deviation from the ancient church's sacramental vision and experience
of the world had become an Orthodox legacy as well. The Orthodox Church
might claim purity of doctrine and consistency with ancient tradition. But its
behavior belied this rhetoric and showed it to be every bit as compromised
to secularism as the Western forms of Christianity that it criticized. What
was left of the Byzantine synthesis in the mother countries of the Orthodox
churches in Eastern Europe and Russia had been weakened immeasurably
by atheistic ideology and totalitarianism. In the West as well as the East,
Christendom was ended, and Orthodox Christians were no less affected by
that reality than their Western co-religionists.

Schmemann explained that the strategy of returning to the language of
transcendence in order to overcome the deracinating and hollowing effects of
secularism was a mistake bound to be futile. For, in fact, secularism can ac-
commodate transcendence language. As long as a "feeling" for transcendence
does not impinge on the autonomy of a world that has "come of age," that
has left behind Christendom, secularism embraces the idea of transcendence.
Secularism is an essentially dualistic view of the world. It assigns transcendence to a place far away from the ordinary (empirical) world yet leaves

4. Schmemann, *Church, World, Mission*, 204.

room for individuals to experience the transcendent through a proliferating variety of personal spiritualities and mysticisms. These begin to transform the churches themselves into hosts of new "religions" that look less and less like traditional Christianity.

Secularism: A Christian Heresy

Though the opposite of secularism is not transcendence, secularism is the opposite of a sacramental view of the world, argues Schmemann in his best-known book, *For the Life of the World*. It is a "new" heresy hatched from inside a decaying Christendom. "Heresy is always the distortion, the exaggeration, and therefore the mutilation of something true, the affirmation of one 'choice' [in Greek *hairesis*, from which our English word *heresy* derives], one element at the expense of others, the breaking up of the catholicity of Truth."[5]

Like all the great heresies, Schmemann continues, secularism makes claim to just enough of the Christian truth so that its worldview is plausible. Biblical revelation de-divinized the world, and Christian orthodoxy worked out the implications for an understanding of the biblical God, creation, and salvation. Secularism, however, seizes upon this de-divinization to declare the complete autonomy of the world. Secularism rejects the classical Christian experience of an antinomy of church and world within the unifying sacramental vision of a theonomous creation. Thus it is entirely capable of absorbing theological critiques like the Hartford appeal, which assume as fundamental to a Christian worldview that very dualism of immanence and transcendence on which secularism founds its vision of an autonomous world and with which it is very comfortable.

Not in his observations on the Hartford appeal or anywhere else that I know of did Alexander Schmemann deepen this analysis and critique of the relationship of neo-orthodoxy to secularism. This much, however, can be said. Schmemann saw neo-orthodoxy's reliance on a dialectic of immanence and transcendence as the theological legacy of a much larger problem. For example, while Orthodox Christians might be in fundamental agreement with Karl Barth on any number of distinct dogmatic themes, his rejection of the classical Roman Catholic formulation of the nature and grace relationship (i.e., the *via affirmativa*, the *via negationis*, and the *via eminentiae*) in favor of "dialecticism" contributed to the breakup of the catholic vision.

---

5. Alexander Schmemann, *For the Life of the World* (Crestwood, NY: St. Vladimir's Seminary Press, 1973), 127.

Orthodox theologians who kept track of theological debates in the 1960s and 1970s were not surprised that the principal advocates of a new radical theology were the "children" of neo-orthodoxy who rejected the dialectical theology of their forebears. For these younger theologians, the absence of God amounted to his "death," traditional God-talk was profitless, and the secular maturity and pluralism of a "world come of age" demanded a complete overhaul of Christian encounter with the world. Neo-orthodox dialecticism was not capable of resurrecting orthodoxy. This is because it inherited a doctrine of God that had developed in the West after its divorce from the East, and that by its own inner logic led to deism in many quarters. For example, in America a deistic and unitarian civic faith overarches the three major expressions of biblical faith.

Western theology excelled early at objectivizing the divine essence and the sacraments with metaphysical proofs, later became proficient at manipulating the god "thing," and in much of contemporary academic theology became obsessed with deconstructing and reconstructing "god metaphors." Schmemann dug back historically in order to understand and to lend a critique of the modern crisis of Christian orthodoxy. He concluded that all attempts since the Reformation to repair the deep rupture in the catholic consciousness of Western Christianity have failed and follow some distinct patterns.

The Demise of Sacramental Realism

One important benchmark of this long historical road of Western Christianity is the gradual reduction in the West of the early patristic church's sacramental realism and mystical theology. This mystical sacramentalism was replaced with metaphysical explanations for the efficacy of the sacraments. The patristic church had held to a theology and experience of the sacraments as divine mystery and eschatological hope. The key to this was an understanding of symbol as *pointing to* the mystery of God while simultaneously also *drawing persons into* the life and community of the triune God.

The Eucharist serves as an example. Even after their consecration, the bread and wine remain bread and wine and continue as natural symbols of the Creator Word's[6] presence in the world. The invocation of the Holy Spirit in the *epiclesis* completes the church's *mimesis* or remembrance of the Word's identification of himself with the bread and wine. Their translation into the body and blood of Christ is a disclosure of their true origin, nature,

6. "All things were made through Him, and without him nothing was made that was made" (John 1:3).

and *telos*. For instance, the natural *telos* of grain, and the bread into which it is made, is to become *living body*. Thus, it is seen that bread carries within itself a symbolism that is appropriately fulfilled when Christ identifies himself with the bread that becomes the spiritual *flesh* of his risen body. Within the patristic understanding of the transformation of the bread and wine into the body and blood of Christ, therefore, the elements retain their creaturely integrity while also manifesting the new creation in Christ. When the human being, who is created in the image of God, consumes in faith the body and blood of Christ, he or she is assimilated into the divine life by the very image of God the Father, his Son, who himself has worn our flesh and identified himself with bread and wine.

Schmemann maintained that later medieval Latin sacramental theologians were attracted to a causal definition of the relationship of grace and symbol and attempted to supply a metaphysical explanation for the efficacy of the Eucharist. This metaphysical speculation about the Eucharist, he judged, inevitably pushed in the direction of a nature and grace dualism that weakened, and in some sectors entirely supplanted, the ancient understanding of the relation of symbol and sacrament. Even Aquinas, who was not forgetful of the deeper ontological and eschatological relation of symbol and sacrament, failed to provide strong guidance for an understanding of the sacraments as enacted liturgy and experienced grace. Later, others even suggested that the substance of the bread and wine, understood primarily as causal "symbols," are annihilated in the process of transformation into the body and blood of Christ.[7]

Although the latter never became the official teaching of the Roman Catholic Church, a dangerous distinction and separation between symbol and reality is evidenced as early as 1086 when the Council of Lateran of 1059 rebuked Berengar of Tours for rejecting the real presence but, ironically, did so with the same distinction between symbol and reality implied by Berengar's own position. Schmemann describes this irony: "If for him [Berengar] the Body and Blood of Christ in the Eucharist are not real because they are symbolical, for the Council of Lateran they are real precisely because they are not symbol."[8] Thus Schmemann concludes that "between the Carolingian Renaissance and Reformation, and in spite of all controversies between rival theological schools," the "incompatibility between symbol and reality," between "*figura et Veritas*,"[9]

---

7. Schmemann drew broad strokes in his critique. He identified large and dominant trends that in historical retrospect bore real and damaging consequences for Christian orthodoxy. Not all that took place in the West under Roman Catholicism or historic Protestantism was bad, just as not all that took place in the East was good.

8. Schmemann, *For the Life of the World*, 143.

9. Schmemann, *For the Life of the World*, 138.

gained impetus. While these trends reached into the East, never did they obtain so pervasive an influence in theology or popular piety as in the West.

Later, of course, influenced by philosophical nominalism, Zwinglian Protestantism went one last step when it described the Lord's Supper as a simple remembrance and symbol as an arbitrary sign. These developments deepened the crisis in the Western experience and understanding of the relation of nature and grace and cut to the very quick of Christian orthodoxy. The ancient church had always retained an antinomy of created and uncreated and finite and infinite. This was very different, however, from later dualisms of natural and supernatural, immanent and transcendent, or secular and religious that took hold in the Western religious imagination. The latter distinction between secular and religious betokens a radical discontinuity of nature and grace that the antinomical theology of the East finds unacceptable. Under the influence of this dualism, the catholic vision of the church dimmed and the experience of God narrowed in Roman Catholicism and especially in Protestantism.

These developments paved the way for the rise of the secular worldview and modern atheism, Schmemann argues. In the modern world, a catholic understanding of the world as theonomous falls to a view of it as autonomous. Personal salvation may remain anthropologically interesting but also loses its theonomous meaning. In modernity, the centralization of authority in the papacy and the magisterium and the late doctrine of papal infallibility makes up the bulwark against these forces in the Roman Catholic Church, while classical Protestantism asserts the doctrine of *sola Scriptura*, and contemporary fundamentalism clings to a rigid notion of the inerrancy of Scripture.

Schmemann does not maintain that the West bears sole responsibility for this momentous shift in the sacramental vision of the church. And, certainly, Western patristic writers such as John Cassian, Vincent of Lérins, and Caesaris of Arles tried early on to correct some of the more troublesome tendencies toward dualism. More recently, Roman Catholic theologians such as Henri de Lubac and Hans Urs von Balthasar have remembered this tradition and influenced positively their church's sacramental theology.

Differences in a Doctrine of God

Still, the histories of Western and Eastern Christianity differ significantly. In the East, well into the fifteenth century a continuity in sacramental theology persisted from the Cappadocian fathers through Maximus the Confessor, John of Damascus, Simeon the New Theologian, Gregory Palamas, and Nicholas Cabasilas. The main thread of this continuity was a doctrine of the Trinity that carries a very different understanding of the relation of nature and grace than later trends in Roman Catholicism and Protestantism. An understanding of the *lex credendi* developed in the East that included not only a strong doctrine of creation founded in the earlier trinitarian teaching of Nicaea but also a theology of God's uncreated energies that are distinguished from the divine essence while equal in divinity.

In the fourteenth century, Gregory of Palamas put the finishing touches on this doctrine of the divine energies in his argument with the monk Barlaam of Calabria and the theologian Gregory Akindynos who, quoting Aquinas's *Summa Theologiae* in the Greek translation, argued that a direct vision of God was not possible for human beings.[10] Palamas responded to the Latin-influenced theologians of his time by demonstrating that the doctrine of the Trinity is not compromised by the claim that human beings are able to participate in the life of God (2 Pet. 1:3–4)—or to "see" God—so long as the utterly transcendent and unknowable divine essence is carefully distinguished from the uncreated divine energies. Palamas insisted that these energies thoroughly interpenetrate creation and draw human beings into the life of God.

According to Palamas, the divine energies are not mere emanations of God in the Platonic sense either. They are nothing less than the divine life itself manifested in and penetrating creation. They were present in Jesus Christ, whose humanity was thoroughly infused with the divinity of his pre-existent sonship. Jesus's transfiguration, which the three disciples witnessed and experienced as their share in the divine glory, proved the most significant biblical source for this doctrine. Palamas's doctrine of God certainly entailed both an existential and an ecclesial antinomy of nature and grace. But it did not permit the sort of discontinuities between nature and grace implied, if not explicitly expressed, by dominant theological, sacramental, and ecclesiastical developments in the West.

Modern Developments

Alexander Schmemann is not alone among Orthodox theologians who, in the latter half of the twentieth century and in this century, have judged that the outworkings of Western trends since the Middle Ages about the nature and grace relationship undermined and eviscerated classical Christian sacramentology and soteriology. Among the Russian Orthodox, Georges Florovsky

10. Later Western scholasticism drew the distinction between a "natural" vision of God and a "supernatural" comprehension of God reserved for the saints in heaven.

and John Meyendorff, and among the Greek Orthodox, John Romanides and John Zizioulas, reach similar conclusions. But Schmemann is undoubtedly the harshest self-critic among Orthodox theologians of his time. Mercilessly he chastises Orthodox Christians for remaining ignorant of what they are up against and criticizes the Orthodox escape into ethnic separatism and sectarian spiritualism. Indeed in his mind this behavior is the surest sign that the Orthodox have succumbed to the very secularity that they criticize. Nor did Schmemann let pass some Orthodox theologians' attempts to depict Orthodox Christians as the victims of a Western virus. No. Orthodoxy, which after the fall of Byzantium became divided into ethnic and national churches, brought this mindset with it into its Western diaspora under the influence of nationalism and other modern ideologies. More, much more, self-criticism was required from the Orthodox.

In *For the Life of the World*, Schmemann advises: "To condemn heresy is relatively easy. What is much more difficult is to *detect* the question it implies, and to give this question an adequate answer. But this was how "the church historically had dealt with 'heresies'—they always provoked an effort of creativity within the church so that the condemnation became ultimately a widening and deepening of Christian faith itself."[11]

A year before his death, in the winter of 1983, Alexander Schmemann spoke at Loyola College in Baltimore, Maryland, where I was teaching at the time. I still vividly recall one moment in his remarks when Schmemann described the impending "crack up" of Western secularism. Little did Schmemann realize how soon and dramatically its Eastern counterpart would crack up. Nevertheless, on this occasion Schmemann pondered out loud whether the church would be prepared to answer the genuine religious needs of modern people in the breach as they looked for something to believe in and hope for after the collapse of secularism's "religious" hegemony. Was enough of Christian orthodoxy still alive in the churches to make sense out of the debacle in order to counteract the dark forces already pushing through the cracks? He warned that if these forces are not answered by the church, then new and far more potent forms of denial of biblical faith would ensue.

Schmemann always insisted that the modern crisis is tied historically to the course that Christianity itself has taken since at least the Enlightenment. Yet he also thought it important to recognize that whereas the outbreaks of heresy that challenged the early church resulted from encounters of Christianity with Hellenism, modern secularity was gestated from within the historic Christian churches themselves and the weakened body of Christendom itself.

11. Schmemann, *For the Life of the World*, 127–28.

In this light, it is not surprising, he concluded, that Christian orthodoxy has become frail and dissipated.

The Rise of Old Heresies Anew

More than two decades ago I participated in a meeting of prominent North American theologians to discuss a paper in which the author argued that H. Richard Niebuhr's thesis about radical monotheism and his Christology, in particular, were especially helpful resources for ecumenical and interreligious dialogue. The author maintained that Niebuhr refused to equate Jesus with God or identify the church as the special locus of God's presence in order to safeguard God's utter transcendence. Christ represents transcendence, he explained, because he does not claim for himself absolute truth about God or sole faithfulness to God. His argument can be summed up in this way: Niebuhr's Christology relativizes every exclusive claim to religious truth, including Christian exclusivism.

I responded that the Christ so described resembled an Arian Christ and that by a logical extension, this rendered Christian baptism meaningless since orthodox Christianity maintains that through baptism we are bound[12] to a Person through whom salvation is possible precisely because that Person is God. The speaker found nothing particularly objectionable in describing Niebuhr's Christology as Arian, nor did he reject my suggestion that if all that he was saying about God and Christ were true, then Niebuhr might also be described as a modalist (the heresy that denies that the Trinity is a unity of three personal subsistences or hypostases in one indivisible divine essence). He added that such stipulations, distinctions, and controversies are no longer to be taken seriously in enlightened theological circles.

Over the years, I have remembered this exchange as exemplary of the "fall" from the Nicene understanding of the relationship between nature and grace that contemporary Orthodox theologians, like Schmemann, constantly argue is at the heart of the modern crisis of Christian faith and practice. For nothing less than a true trinitarianism, which rejects the Arian and modalist heresies, secures the salvific meaning of Christian baptism and of all the sacraments. Otherwise the sacraments are no more than anthropologically interesting examples of human initiation practices and rites of passage. For instance, every traditional Christian baptismal rite affirms the real presence

12. Here I am taking advantage of the multivocality of the English language. Soteriology is indicated by "bound" when it means "tied to." Eschatology is indicated when "bound" is used to mean "heading toward."

of the Trinity in the acts that are performed. This is a matter of cardinal importance. It is vital to the Christian belief in salvation from sin and death that the Father and Holy Spirit were truly present at Jesus's own baptism and, henceforth, every baptism the church performs. More than two decades after the exchange I have described, it is not so surprising that churches that once invited all present *who are baptized* to take communion no longer stipulate baptism as a precondition and simply invite all present to the table.

Today modalism exists rather comfortably in many churches alongside an Arian Christology. Like the Arianism of old, this new Arianism supplies a connection between nature and/or history and the transcendent deity while, at least implicitly, denying Christ's divinity. It is as if in this post-Christian time the churches are recapitulating inversely, as it were, the early church's refutation of the classical heresies. Thus, in our day we move from Arianism to modalism and unitarianism. While at present liberal American Protestantism generally retains traditional creedal formulas and trinitarian speech within its ecclesial boundaries, the shift to outright modalism is unmistakable. The adoption of so-called nonsexist language in liturgies and confessions of faith is a case in point. The vast majority of churchgoers today do not understand that the substitution of creator, redeemer, and sanctifier for Father, Son, and Holy Spirit—leave aside more radically divergent monikers—replaces the name of the triune God with the attributes (or the divine energies) that Christian orthodoxy ascribes to all three persons of the one holy and immortal God.

In public spaces, civic settings, and interreligious dialogue, representatives of the Christian churches regularly employ unitarian rhetoric in order to be "accommodating" to persons of diverse religious beliefs. This unitarian speech might well have begun as a practical strategy prompted by an encounter with pluralism and a respect for liberal canons of civility. But modalism and unitarianism—it is hard in present contexts to distinguish the two since new forms of each are constantly evolving—in our day have assumed a life of their own and invaded ecclesial space.

For many church-affiliated people, modalism and unitarianism are as near to what they can possibly imagine constitutes a unified and up-to-date Christianity. This modalism and unitarianism are, however, different from the radical monotheism of H. Richard Niebuhr's description that strives to be consistent with a Hebraic inheritance. For under the banners of "transcendence" and "spirituality" vast numbers of people within and outside the churches adopt a religious syncretism that blends biblical faith with elements of Eastern religions, therapeutic theories of wholeness and personal fulfillment, and New Age superstitions. I do not think it is farfetched to say that the trend is toward a neo-polytheism and that this polytheism and its many "gods" are quite able to abide comfortably under the canopy of a fairly vague and amorphous unitarian religion.

An Anecdotal Reflection on an Embattled Nicene Christianity

Some years ago, during an interview for a post at a Protestant seminary on the East Coast, I was asked to deliver a formal presentation to the faculty and students. My lecture analyzed the Orthodox experience in North America and the confusion of belief in the Orthodox churches. I was taken aback, however, when a member of the faculty raised the stakes by challenging me to describe my cosmology. I stated that I had not worked out a personal cosmology, at which point I began to recite the Nicene Creed. I did not get very far into that recitation before my inquisitor interrupted once more, this time exclaiming with more than a little rage in his voice, "Why, no one believes that neo-Platonic stuff anymore!"

It took me a while to understand fully the meaning of this encounter. The truth of the Creed is not primarily propositional. In its ecclesial setting the Creed is a dialogic and liturgical event, a prayer. My response that day was not only inappropriate but misleading. I have no doubt that the individual who interrupted me heard my recitation in strictly propositional terms and judged what I affirmed (perhaps it would be more accurate to say confessed) as intellectually inadequate.

A key piece of the puzzle surfaced the next day. During a roundtable discussion, this same person invited me to discuss Dostoevsky's *The Brothers Karamazov*, since I had mentioned it as a text in my courses. He solicited my interpretation of the section of the novel titled "Pro and Contra" that includes the famous Grand Inquisitor story. He explained his interpretation of the novel, especially the portion in which Ivan Karamazov passionately denies the Christian understanding of salvation. He argued that nowhere in the novel is Ivan's case against the Christian faith answered. And for that reason, he argued, as others have, that Ivan's point of view represents Dostoevsky's personal doubt and existential crisis of faith.

I answered that Ivan's "atheism" is answered in the novel but not in the way that so many Western readers anticipate. The novel, I stated, must not be read as a ledger of logical arguments and counterarguments about what constitutes truth in the upper case. Rather, as the twentieth century Russian literary scholar Mikhail Bakhtin demonstrates in his profound study, *Problems of Dostoevsky's Poetics*, Dostoevsky's novels are polyphonic. I said that we are obliged to imagine how the novel might have been received by its nineteenth-century Russian audience. For example, the section of the novel that immediately follows "Pro and Contra" is titled "The Life of a Russian Monk." Dostoevsky taps deeply into the milieu of Russian Orthodox piety through his portrayal of the monk, Father Zossima. Zossima is based on real holy figures that nineteenth-century Russians venerated. In the last analysis, Zossima's life, together with his teachings, answers Ivan's contention that forgiveness and love of neighbor are impossibilities in this world.

Ivan Karamazov embodies Western intellectualism, philosophical propositionalism, and individualism. His is one voice, and a prominent one at that, in the novel. Yet it is a mistake to equate his mind and ideas with Dostoevsky's own convictions or to conclude that the Russian reader in Dostoevsky's time would be so easily persuaded by Ivan's assault on the Christian faith.

Ivan tries his "atheist" credo on his younger brother Alyosha. Yet Dostoevsky positions Alyosha, the youngest Karamazov brother, as the hero of his novel. Alyosha is under the tutelage of Father Zossima, and Dostoevsky deliberately endows Alyosha with a deep Russian religious piety, the opposite of Ivan's atheism and intellectualism. Shortly before his death, Zossima sends Alyosha out of the monastery into the world, precisely in order to put to practice his teachings about forgiveness and love, compassionate care for one's fellow human beings, and *sorbonost* (communal togetherness). Throughout his own personal struggle with faith, Alyosha holds fast to Zossima's teaching, and he fulfills his mission by forming the quarrelsome young boys of the town into disciples of Christian forgiveness, love, and reconciliation. At the conclusion of the novel, Dostoevsky brushes in a literary icon of Alyosha and the boys gathered together at the great rock under which Ilyusha, their young friend, wished to be buried. The scene concludes with this chorus:

> "Karamazov," Kolya said suddenly, "can it be true, as our religion claims, that we shall all rise from the dead, come back to life, and meet again, Ilyusha too?"

> "We shall certainly rise and we shall certainly all meet again and tell each other happily and joyfully everything that has happened to us," Alyosha said.[13]

This is an image of the new and redeemed community, a new interiorized "worldly" monasticism that embodies Zossima's teaching and the example of his holy life. There aren't any formal arguments in the novel that answer the challenge of Ivan's "atheism." Dostoevsky, however, sets before his readers a

---

13. Fyodor Dostoevsky, *The Brothers Karamazov*, trans. Andrew H. MacAndrew (New York: Bantam, 1981), 936.

religious vision that refutes Ivan's assertion that the love that Christ taught is neither possible for human beings nor triumphant over evil and death.

Over the years, I have revisited the memory of this interview many times. It is a reminder to me of significant differences between Western and Eastern Christianity, especially between faith grounded in a propositional understanding of truth and faith that is dialogic and informed by an iconographic and sacramental religious imagination. For the Orthodox, the Christian faith is not some "thing" ensconced in a set of propositions located in texts from which religious truth may be extracted by the autonomous reader who is equipped with either the right exegetical tools or pious feelings. Rather, for the Orthodox, Christian orthodoxy is truth lived at a variety of levels of knowledge, worship, and good works. Truth is in the act as well as in tradition and shared memory.

The Orthodox understanding of Christian orthodoxy is, finally, liturgical. When Orthodox Christians recite or sing the Nicene Creed, this is not to assert a set of propositions, although the Creed may be said to contain propositions. Rather, the Creed is a communal act of prayer. It is dialogical and it is doxology.

If the Creed is a standard of orthodoxy, it is so only and totally as symbol of truth that is mystery. It is the speech act by which the catholic consciousness of the church comes into existence. This catholic consciousness must not be confused with idealist understandings of self-consciousness and transcendence, modern psychological notions of personality, or sociological concepts of community. Rather, it is and belongs to the polyhypostatic body of Christ in the world: the church itself. Within this body, this gathered fellowship, a duality of the immanent and the transcendent does not exist; only the real presence of the incarnate Word exists. For, "No one can say that Jesus is Lord except by the Holy Spirit" (1 Cor. 12:3).

In conclusion, catholicity is christological but also trinitarian, a pluralism in the unity of the *communio sanctorum*. Historicity also obtains. For the act of memory that draws together the many members of the church is the remembrance of a real and historical person. Even that supreme symbol of faith, the Nicene Creed, pauses to recall historical persons and events. Nevertheless, Christian orthodoxy is not merely a historical event. The grace that is in all the sacraments, especially the Eucharist, unites the church in communion with God. Christian orthodoxy, abiding in and expressed through liturgy, is the sign of the ever-present and future event of God's eschatological kingdom. All this is a far cry from the heresy that secularism is.

4

SECULARISM

In the previous chapter, I discussed secularism as a modern heresy gestated from within a decaying Christian order. Furthermore, I insisted that secularism is as much a spiritual problem for Orthodox Christians as for their Catholic and Protestant fellow believers. In this chapter, I am more specific about the Orthodox experience of and struggle with secularism, especially as this has played out in North America. I also describe and try to make sense of what I call the "secular pilgrimage" of Orthodoxy in America.

The newness to Orthodox Christianity of its cultural station in America cannot be gainsaid. With the notable exception of the Russian mission in Alaska, for the most part, the Orthodox Church did not arrive in America as mission but followed its people's departure from the homeland, often under the extremities of war, social upheaval, or natural disaster. There was no preparation for coming here. Whether Orthodox people arrived in America from Russia, Greece, the Middle East, or Armenia, in virtually every instance, the relocation was something akin to an out-of-body experience. These people left behind historical Orthodox cultures and became immersed immediately into a society that the Orthodox faith had no role in shaping, a secular society that bafflingly was also religious, though not in a familiar way.

Another version of this chapter also appears as "The Secular Pilgrimage of Orthodoxy in America," in *Tradition, Secularization, and Fundamentalism*, Orthodox Christianity and Contemporary Thought (New York: Fordham University Press, forthcoming). Used by permission.

Perhaps more than any other Orthodox theologian in America of his day, Alexander Schmemann, as I have already suggested, endeavored to make sense of America's secularism and religiosity: How is it that in America the churches themselves become carriers of secularism? Schmemann describes the Orthodox Church's encounter with American secularism as a crisis of faith "more radical and decisive than the one brought about by the fall of Byzantium in 1453." For even though "the Turkish conquest was a political and national catastrophe, it was not the end . . . of the 'Orthodox world' . . . of a culture, a way of life, a worldview integrating religion and life."[1] In America that culture, that integration of religion and life, was gone, no matter the imaginative and sometimes fantastical efforts to keep it alive in ethnic enclave or church building.

The anachronistic Orthodox adherence to regional and national identities in America parallels, ironically, Protestantism's fissiparousness. For in America both behaviors lend themselves to denominationalism, a phenomenon Orthodoxy has condemned as in conflict with the church's unity in Christ. Schmemann worries about the Orthodox Church's failure to resolve the canonical problem of overlapping dioceses in America, not just because rules are broken but also because this division fosters the perception, even among Orthodox, that Orthodoxy is itself denominational. "It is our betrayal of Orthodoxy, in our *reduction* of it to our petty selfish 'national identities,' 'cultural values,' 'parochial interests,'" Schmemann writes, "that makes it look like another denomination with limited scope and doubtful relevance."[2]

Preceding their arrival in America, Orthodox churches had experienced nothing comparable to the peculiarly American phenomenon in which a religious body is neither an established church nor a sect, but something in between. "Inside" the new denomination there might persist for a time the belief that in the new world it is still a church as it was in the old world; however, in view of an aggregate of other "churches," it can never aspire to be a national ecclesiastical institution as it was in Serbia or Bulgaria or Greece.[3]

Impressions grow into something akin to doctrine. The belief catches hold that a multiplicity of religious communities is good for America because each represents some part of the truth of Christianity, none the whole of it, or alternatively that each "religion" is true in its own fashion. In any case,

    1. Alexander Schmemann, *Church, World, Mission: Reflections on Orthodoxy in the West* (Crestwood, NY: St. Vladimir's Seminary Press, 1979), 9.
    2. Alexander Schmemann, "Problems of Orthodoxy in America III: The Spiritual Problem," *St. Vladimir's Seminary Quarterly* 8, no. 4 (1965): 193.
    3. See Will Herberg, *Protestant, Catholic, Jew* (Garden City, NY: Anchor/Doubleday, 1960), 85–86.

the result is that conviction in the catholicity of the church fades even among believers—a telling sign of secularization.

Religion in Secular America

Will Herberg's classic mid-twentieth-century study of religion, *Protestant, Catholic, Jew*, was among the first books of its kind to analyze the role of denominationalism in evacuating catholic convictions from churches and relativizing religious belief. Though Schmemann rarely cites Herberg, there can be little doubt that Schmemann learned from him.

Nor does Schmemann tell the entire story of the secular pilgrimage of Orthodoxy in America. How could he? Why would he? He was, after all, first and foremost a liturgical theologian. And though the theme of secularism appears frequently in his writings, Schmemann does not explore theories of secularization in detail. I cannot do much better in this brief space. Nonetheless, in order to understand the secular pilgrimage of Orthodoxy in America, something needs to be said about the meaning of such pivotal terms as secularization, secularity, and secularism.

Secularity versus Secularism: A Clarification

Some religionists and social scientists have argued that a distinction must be drawn between *secularity* and *secularism*. They maintain that the secularity of America is neutral about religion and affords space for religious belief and practice without intrusive state interference within a religiously pluralistic environment, and that this is a good thing. They argue that secularism is, by contrast, an ideology opposed to religion or belief in anything transcendent.

I do not think that social reality bears out this distinction. Rather, secularity and secularism go hand in glove; there is no such thing as a secularity that is neutral about religion, whether here in America or anywhere else. Nevertheless, secularism is not always antireligious. American secularism, unlike some European varieties, is not antireligious, at least not in the hard sense of that term.

This is another way of saying that secularity is inevitably ideational. I do not see how it could be otherwise. Wherever one finds it, secularity makes claims about the structure of the world and meaning within it, which may or may not be reflected in law and social arrangements. A philosophy of life inevitably accompanies secularity. The "ism" belongs to secularity as the germ to the grain. The "ism" in secular is "a worldview, and consequently a way of life, which attributes to the basic aspects of human existence, such as family, education, science, profession, art,"[4] and the like, an autonomy that may or may not leave room for organized religion.

Talcott Parsons: About Secularization and Modern Religion

The 1960s were rich in reflection on secularism and religion. The twentieth-century sociologist Talcott Parsons was an important contributor to this study. In the mid-sixties, Parsons penned an influential essay titled "Christianity and Modern Industrial Society." In it he dissented from a view commonly held then and now that secularization indicates a decline of religious belief. He argued, instead, that secularization can be, as in America, a process by which religious values become "differentiated" from their core, original communities and spread into society at various levels where they gain autonomy, an independence from the sanction of traditional religious authority. On this basis, Parsons confidently asserted that in "a variety of respects modern society is more in accord with Christian values than its forbearers have been."[5]

I first read Parsons as an undergraduate at the University of Virginia. I was not persuaded by his arguments, though my professors seemed to be. Perhaps this was because like Parsons they were Protestants. To begin, the title of Parsons's essay misleads. "Christianity and Modern Industrial Society" is not about Christianity in general. Parsons's perspective is distinctively Protestant; his suppositions about what a church is are also distinctively Protestant. To my mind, Parsons sets out to reconstruct Protestantism in order to account for secularity and make a case for Christianity's continued influence, even in the wake of the receding role of the churches in society. His method and analysis reduce the Christian faith to morality. He assumes that a Christian ethos can thrive unloosed and separated from the ecclesial body, its sacraments, and the worship that the body offers to God. But then again, I doubt Parsons had these things foremost in his mind when writing. Liberal Protestants like Parsons might be content with the emulsification of Christianity, even the church itself, into the secularist order; Orthodoxy, at least in its classical expression, cannot be.

I have paused to consider Parsons because today one still hears distinct echoes of his argument among church people and from within the academy. More important, Schmemann and Orthodox theology have a very different

4. Schmemann, "Problems of Orthodoxy in America III," 173.
5. Talcott Parsons, "Christianity and Modern Industrial Society," in *Secularization and the Protestant Prospect*, ed. James F. Childress and David Harned (Philadelphia: Westminster, 1970), 64.

view on the matter. With all due respect to Parsons, Schmemann does not argue that secularization is a measure of the decline of religion or morality, but he does insist that secularization is incompatible with the Christian vision of life. He maintains that Christian identity originates from and is sustained by worship, in the *lex orandi*, and that secularism is quite simply the *negation* of worship.

This, however, does not mean that secular people are ipso facto irreligious or that they are not attracted to religious ritual. Many are religious and belong to churches. Some are highly attracted to religious ritual and even dedicate themselves to creating new, more "relevant" forms of worship. Yet if one digs deeper, says Schmemann, more often than not one finds that these same persons cling to an understanding of what it means to be human that precludes any need to pray and that worship becomes not much more than a form of audiovisual assistance to comprehension of religious ideas.

A secularist, on one level, may ascribe to the idea of God, that God exists, even that God is the creator and that God governs the world, yet on another level, share with nonreligious, secular counterparts a complete confidence in the autonomy of human existence and the self-sufficiency of the world. A secularist of religious belonging might even believe in life after death, allowing that this belief has little or nothing to do with worldly projects of care for the sick or material assistance to the poor. Nor will one find this kind of religious secularist praying for the dead, unless perhaps as prescribed by liturgical forms that he or she is likely to believe are antiquated and need revision.

The secularist might say, "Why, you see, all that I know, I know through my senses. I can see the hungry child in front of me. I know what hunger is like. I am connected to the hungry person in front of me by my own experience of the same. I can feed this person. The dead I don't know about." I have heard just this sort of sentiment expressed in a church that prays for the dead at every liturgy.

The opposite of autonomy is *theonomy*. This is the belief that the fulfillment of human existence, while it begins in this world, is nonetheless entirely dependent on grace and communion with God. Genuine worship, Schmemann constantly reminds his reader, is not a mere referral of ourselves and the world to God. Secular people who often define themselves as "spiritual" think of worship as an aid to success in their aspirations for worldly happiness and prosperity and their efforts to make this a more just and peaceful world. American religion and secularism both frequently affirm the serviceableness of religion and prayer.

Rather, worship is the action by which human beings freely submit and dedicate their lives and the life of the world to God. The perfection of our humanity is holiness, the holiness of God, which God communicates to us through the sacraments of baptism, penance, and the Eucharist, especially. Holiness transcends the values of tolerance, social justice, and brotherhood held so high by secular America. Secularists and religious people alike will support these values with no need or thought to invoke divinity. Holiness and union with God, which are worship's true aim, are alien to the secular person.

Stated somewhat differently, secularity is the negation, the evacuation from life, of the experience of the world as sacred reality, as "participant" in divine reality and "participated in" by the divine. This is the full meaning of what Schmemann intends when he says that secularism is "the *negation of worship.*" Orthodox anthropology defines a person "as a worshipping being, as *homo adorans*: the one for whom worship 'posits' his [or her] humanity and fulfills it."[6] Only through prayer that affirms and establishes our and the whole world's relationship to God is theonomy restored and renewed. Only in this theonomy, which by very definition secularism denies, is human nature completed or perfected.

The name for this completion or perfection is deification, *theosis* in the Greek. From this high standard and goal, one can see how the secular pilgrimage of Orthodoxy is as great a challenge to the church as was its struggle in antiquity to define right belief over against the classical heresies that threatened the truth of salvation. That struggle was not just about being linguistically correct. It was about ensuring that the church be of right mind, be properly prepared to receive and accept the gift of salvation through Jesus Christ. As Flannery O'Connor, that gifted Roman Catholic writer of the deep South, liked to point out through her stories, it is possible to be "good" but not "right" or holy. In other words, "good" is not the same as holy. So much that is taken for goodness in the world falls dreadfully short of the goodness the church ascribes to God and to the lives of saints. One must be "right" about God and "right" in relation to God to be truly good and genuinely holy.[7]

As I have intimated in the preceding chapter, Schmemann, for these reasons, insists that "secularism is . . . the greatest heresy of our time, [and] requires from the Church not mere anathemas, and certainly not compromises, but above all an effort of understanding so it may ultimately be overcome by truth."[8] And as we have already heard him say, "The uniqueness of secular-

6. Alexander Schmemann, *For the Life of the World* (Crestwood, NY: St. Vladimir's Seminary Press, 1973), 118 (emphasis original).
7. As the outrageous vandal and miscreant youth Rufus Johnson, who, nonetheless, believes in God and the Devil, says of the atheist social worker Sheppard, "I don't care if he's good or not. He ain't *right.*" "The Lame Shall Enter First," in *Flannery O'Connor: Collected Works* (New York: Library of America, 1988), 604.
8. Schmemann, *For the Life of the World*, 128.

ism, its difference from the great heresies of the patristic age, is that the latter were provoked by the encounter of Christianity with Hellenism, whereas the former is the result of the 'breakdown' within Christianity itself."[9] In other words, secularism is a "stepchild" of Christianity.[10] It imitates the Christian virtues. But this is *just* an imitation. This is because the virtues have been stripped from the ascetical and spiritual disciplines that remind those who exercise them of their complete dependence on God and need to repent that they may become holy.

Secularism in a religious mode misinterprets Christ's promise to his disciples, "Peace I leave with you, My peace I give to you" (John 14:27), as a *plan* for peace in this world. It forgets, or overlooks, Christ's admonition that the peace he gives is "not as the world gives" (John 14:27). The progressivisms of our day owe their inspiration to Christianity. Christians hope for perfection by their participation in God's holiness. In a secular age, this hope is translated into the expectation that by human effort alone perfection is possible and peace can be achieved. A belief in history and progress replaces a belief in God and providence.

In *For the Life of the World*, Schmemann advises, "It is indeed one of the grave errors of religious anti-secularism that it does not see that secularism is made up of *veritas chretiennes devenues folles*, of Christian truths gone mad, and that in simply rejecting secularism, it in fact rejects certain fundamental Christian aspirations and hopes."[11] Or as G. K. Chesterton put it in his best-known book, *Orthodoxy*: "The modern world is not evil; in some ways the modern world is far too good. It is full of wild and wasted virtues. When a religious scheme is shattered (as Christianity was shattered at the Reformation), it is not merely the vices that are let loose. The vices are, indeed, let loose, and they wander and do damage. But the virtues are let loose also; and the virtues wander more wildly, and the virtues do more terrible damage. The modern world is full of the old Christian virtues gone mad."[12]

Will Herberg's "The American Way of Life"

In *Protestant, Catholic, Jew*, Will Herberg famously introduces the locution "American Way of Life." This is his shorthand way for speaking of the secular religiosity or, viewed from a somewhat different perspective, the religious

9. Schmemann, *For the Life of the World*, 128.
10. Schmemann, *For the Life of the World*, 127.
11. Schmemann, *For the Life of the World*, 111.
12. G. K. Chesterton, *Orthodoxy* (Garden City, NY: Image, 1959), 30.

secularity of America. Herberg's aphorism "America is at once the most religious and secular of nations" has been cited countless times since he first
spoke it almost seventy years ago. Herberg explains that the American Way
of Life is "not an overt philosophy; it is an underlying, often unconscious,
orientation of life and thought. [It] is essentially . . . thinking and living in
terms of a framework of reality and value remote from the religious beliefs
simultaneously professed."[13] Nor, according to Herberg, is the American Way
of Life a "'common denominator' religion; it is not a synthetic" or syncretistic
system, not a composite of beliefs drawn or selected from the major religions
in America. It is, rather, "an organic structure of ideas, values, and beliefs
that constitutes a faith common to Americans."[14] This "common faith" is the
default position of many if not most Americans when they are challenged
to describe what in religion they believe. "Nor can there be much doubt,"
Herberg posits, "that, by and large, the religion which actually prevails among
Americans today has lost much of its authentic Christian (or Jewish) content."[15]

The god of the American Way of Life is "unknown," so it may take many
names. There are many idols in the land. The god of the American Way of
Life is not the God of historic Judaism or the trinitarian God of Christian
orthodoxy. In its advanced state, the faith of the American Way of Life is a
"faith in faith itself." Herberg adds, "Of course religious Americans [may]
speak of God and Christ, but what they seem to regard as really redemptive
is primarily religion, the 'positive' attitude of *believing*."[16] Herberg maintains
that this is secularism and that the churches in America carry it in their very
bones.

As I have said, Herberg helped Schmemann to understand the Orthodox
experience in America. And yet, Orthodox Christianity is virtually absent in
Protestant, Catholic, Jew. In 1973, as a graduate student in theology at Drew
University, I asked Will about this. He responded that when, in the 1950s, he
was putting together *Protestant, Catholic, Jew*, he judged that the Orthodox
had not as yet drawn fully under the aegis of the American Way of Life. They
remained in most essentials still an immigrant church not yet integrated into
the familiar American religious panoply.

Herberg refers but once to Orthodoxy in *Protestant, Catholic, Jew*. This is
in a footnote that cites an article whose author, Fred Lewis, is Russian Orthodox. The writer protests: "'We Orthodox . . . are indignant each time we hear
of Three Great Faiths. We know it should be Four, and individually we have

13. Herberg, *Protestant, Catholic, Jew*, 2.
14. Herberg, *Protestant, Catholic, Jew*, 77.
15. Herberg, *Protestant, Catholic, Jew*, 3.
16. Herberg, *Protestant, Catholic, Jew*, 265 (emphasis mine).

tried to convince our fellow-Americans of this. But we have gotten nowhere.'"
Herberg interjects: "It would be interesting to discover how Mr. Lewis knows
that Orthodoxy 'should be "Four"'; obviously he takes the American scheme
of the three great faiths for granted, and merely wants to add his own as the
fourth."[17] Evidently, even as he was writing *Protestant, Catholic, Jew*, Herberg
had detected in this writer's frustration a next-to-certain sign that Orthodox
Americans had begun to conceive of their faith as a worthy adjutant to the
American Way of Life. He might easily have added that Lewis's statement
demonstrates how exactly the American Way of Life transforms historical
religious identity into its own idolatrous image.

Herberg also told me on this occasion that were he to write a second edition
of *Protestant, Catholic, Jew*, he would include Orthodoxy in it much more
prominently. Yet he was quite clear, speaking as teacher to student, that this
would not be an honor the author bestowed but rather an objectively obligatory amendment to his thesis about how the secularism of the American Way
dissipates the confessional muscle of the great religious traditions, Orthodoxy
now included.

Peter Berger's "Heretical Imperative"

During the 1980s as I set out to record some of my own thoughts on the subject
of religion and secularity in America, I happened upon a small book in the
Alderman Library of the University of Virginia by the late religious sociologist
Peter Berger. It bore the intriguing title *The Heretical Imperative*. Like virtu-
ally all notable books about religious belonging in America since *Protestant,
Catholic, Jew*, the book *The Heretical Imperative* says hardly a word about
Orthodoxy; well, just one paragraph. In that paragraph, Berger muses,

> One can only speculate at this point what will happen to . . . Orthodox Chris-
> tians as they move, with their icons and vestments, onto the center stage
> of American religion. [But] one will be on safe ground if one assumes that
> they will encounter . . . what their predecessors, from Puritans to Jews, have
> encountered—pluralization and *ipso facto* the existential as well as cognitive
> dilemmas of the Protestant paradigm.[18]

Berger already has told the reader that the Protestant paradigm *is* the
"heretical imperative" and explained that he is not using the word *heretical*

17. Herberg, *Protestant, Catholic, Jew*, 45.
18. Peter L. Berger, *The Heretical Imperative* (Garden City, NY: Anchor/Doubleday, 1980),
54–55.

pejoratively or negatively as in historical and dogmatic theology. He points out to the reader that the core meaning of *heresy* is "to choose," taken from the Greek verb *hairein*. He then proceeds to demonstrate on historical grounds, which I will not enumerate here, that Protestantism, much more so than Roman Catholicism, has had to confront straight-on modernity's pressure to deviate from tradition in making *choices* that best serve the prospering of individuals and the religious community.

Indeed, according to Berger, the heretical imperative arose within the historical circumstances that gestated Protestantism in Europe during the fifteenth and sixteenth centuries. These decisions to deviate from standing tradition and authority were made in a landscape filled with churches, monuments, and memories of the saints, memories that were in no way abstract but, rather, constantly confirmed by geography and history. America, however, is a very different landscape. In America religion lacks the supports of the old world. In America traditions are experienced not as "destiny," as they were in the old world, but as the products of necessary choices. Thus according to Berger, in America the heretical imperative is "normalized"; to choose what to believe, to choose one's religion, becomes almost the instinctive thing to do.

In America, Berger further explains, religious traditions lose their hold on both institutions and human consciousness. In the past, people could feel secure within a religious tradition because there was little that ordinarily competed with it. Modernity is different because modern people—he means those who live in advanced industrial societies—are faced with a plethora of competing "plausibility structures." "Heresy," which is to say "picking and choosing" from these "plausibility structures . . . becomes a necessity."[19] Before modernity, the normal condition was faith; in modernity, the normal condition is religious uncertainty or, at the very least, instability of religious belief and belonging. Before modernity, secularization was unlikely because traditional authority stood up. In modernity, religious traditions succumb to skepticism and voluntarism. There is a "pluralization" of religious beliefs and institutions. As no one "plausibility structure" is able to legitimate the social order, secularity (though not necessarily religious disbelief) takes hold.

Berger rightly warns against misdirected objections to pluralization and secularization—objections that seek cover under hardened neo-orthodoxies or rigid fundamentalisms. A pluralism of religions existed in the past, and people made choices. The story of St. Paul speaking on Mars Hill and addressing people of many different religious and philosophical persuasions testifies to this. His speech about the unknown or unnamed God reminds us,

19. Berger, *Heretical Imperative*, 25.

however, that he lived in an age in which religious belief was the norm. It is not that religious pluralism is new but that secularization also brings about the cognitive possibility of choosing not to believe in a god. More recently Charles Taylor has gone to great lengths in order to make a similar argument in his book *The Secular Age*.

But of course on the other side of this is the possibility of adhering to a belief in God. When Schmemann pleaded for a conscientious effort to understand the nature of secularism, he was calling on the Orthodox to fully comprehend and intelligently confront the novelty of the Orthodox Church's situation in America. Berger's *The Heretical Imperative* troubled me on first encounter because I found its analysis of modernity plausible (pun intended), and his speculation that Orthodoxy would eventually come under the influence of the heretical imperative persuasive as well. I also was reminded of Herberg's profound insight about the hegemony of the American Way of Life over even the much-celebrated religious pluralism that proliferates beneath its broad and encompassing sacred canopy.

The Secular Pilgrimage of Orthodoxy

In this chapter I have several times spoken of the Orthodox experience in America as a secular pilgrimage. This locution is brazenly borrowed from an essay titled "A Secular Pilgrimage" in Wendell Berry's *A Continuous Harmony*, published in 1970. I have thought that this locution and the proposal Berry makes in his essay about the path taken by several contemporary American poets might light a way beyond Berger's perplexing "heretical imperative." I, however, am sufficiently chastened by the several writers cited in the course of my analysis not to propose what the exact outcome of Orthodoxy's secular pilgrimage will be.

In "A Secular Pilgrimage," Berry defines "secular" and "pilgrimage" within his discussion and analysis of the "nature poets" Gary Snyder, Denise Levertov, and A. R. Ammons. These poets endeavor to articulate a positive vision of humanity's relationship with nature. In their work, pilgrimage is secular "because it takes place outside of, or without reference to, the institutions of religion."[20] No shrines or holy places populate their poetry. Yet, ironically, their quest may be described also as religious, for through their reflection on nature, these poets reclaim a sense of "wonder or awe or humility," a "presence

20. Wendell Berry, *A Continuous Harmony: Essays Cultural and Agricultural* (New York: Harcourt, Brace, 1970), 6.

of mystery and divinity."[21] They do not discover "a world of inert materiality
... [as] postulated both by the heaven-oriented churches and the exploitative
industries," but rather a "*created* world in which the creator, the formative
and quickening spirit, is still imminent and at work."[22]

There is something profoundly Orthodox, indeed, deeply sacramental,
in Berry's observations. For Berry, like Schmemann and Herberg, secularity
and secularism amount to one and the same thing. These terms connote
an absence of the kind of experience that human beings require in order to
truly thrive, not merely as animals but also as spiritual beings. Berry does
not name secularism a heresy, but were he to adopt theological speech, he
might. He insists that secularism misrepresents the world as an autonomous
one in which spirit is absent. This misleads us about the nature of the world
and our human condition. Its dualism of the sacred and the profane denies
the incarnation. It is void of a vision in which God heals a world wounded
by sin. In other words, Berry admires the nature poets for piercing through
secularism's false vision of a creation in which God is not present or active.

Berry is not about the business of reclaiming institutions and religious sites
that often are, in his view, anachronisms. Nonetheless, he recognizes that there
is a disadvantage in their absence. How can an incarnational Christian faith
be plausible without them? In summary, I find the situation of the Orthodox
churches in America analogous to Berry's description of the nature poet's
secular pilgrimage.

Having left behind "organic" Orthodox worlds that were filled with reminders of sacred reality, having entered a culture in which those reminders do not
exist for them, Orthodox Christians are indeed on a kind of secular pilgrimage, like the nature poets Berry admires. America's secularity is subtler than
its European counterparts but more disorienting, disordering, and disarming
precisely because of the relative absence of venerated holy places, churches, ancient shrines, and monasteries long associated with the Christian faith. Absent
are not only these markers of God's presence but also the geography, history,
and language by which Orthodox Christians identified themselves ethnically
or nationally as Orthodox Greek, Syrian, or Ukrainian. This helps to explain
the relentless efforts of Orthodox people to project the old world onto the new
American social reality, efforts that rather than renewing tradition, flag the slow
death of the religious community. This is because these efforts do not open up
but instead everywhere hinder a life-giving and redemptive comprehension of
what it means to be Orthodox in America and a mission for it in a new world.

21. Berry, *Continuous Harmony*, 5.
22. Berry, *Continuous Harmony*, 6 (emphasis mine).

The secular pilgrimage of Orthodoxy commences with this dislocation, this separation, from the geography, culture, and "material" history with which it has identified for millennia. Yet, obviously, that is not all. Whereas in Greece, Russia, or Romania the Orthodox faith was coextensive with the people, the nation, in America this is not possible. It is not simply a matter of religious pluralism or of the sheer diversity of American life that blocks the way. More important, the people *interpret* pluralism as the norm of religious life, much as they *interpret* the separation of church and state as virtually a divine mandate, an eleventh commandment.

For the first time in its history—*histories* is more accurate a description—Orthodoxy lives in a secular culture where free expression of religion is protected but religion is not permitted to claim the whole of life. In Armenia, Serbia, Ukraine, and so on, Orthodoxy was the symbol of the unity of the people. But here, "the American Way of Life is the symbol by which Americans define themselves and establish their unity,"[23] Herberg tells us.

Schmemann observes that "in spite of all formal rectitude of dogma and liturgy," Orthodoxy in America has lost something essential from its past, a "living interrelation with culture, a claim to the *whole* of life." He conjectures that "this explains the instinctive attachment of so many Orthodox, even American born, to arcane 'national' forms of Orthodoxy, their resistance, however narrow-minded and 'nationalistic,' to a complete divorce between Orthodoxy and its various nationalistic expressions."[24]

This behavior, may be understandable, yet it holds little promise for a future in which Orthodoxy prospers and the truth of the gospel on which it stands becomes attractive to fellow Americans. Nor is it possible, Schmemann rightly maintains, "simply to 'transpose' Orthodoxy onto American cultural categories."[25] To strive to be the "fourth major faith" of the American Way of Life amounts to a rejection of the freedom that American culture and polity give the church to dissent where dissent is called for, to criticize where the truth about God and humanity is jeopardized, and to proclaim God's saving grace in a public square where there remain few reminders of the kingdom of God that was for millennia the unifying symbol of Western culture.

Can Orthodoxy, so habituated to legitimating culture, act counterculturally? That is a big question. If, as Berger muses in *The Heretical Imperative*, the Orthodox were to move their icons out beyond the church building into

23. Herberg, *Protestant, Catholic, Jew*, 78.

24. Schmemann, "Problems of Orthodoxy in America II: The Canonical Problem," *St. Vladimir's Seminary Quarterly* 8, no. 2 (1964): 78.

25. Schmemann, "Problems of Orthodoxy in America III," 192.

the culture, is it possible that the power of Christ and the Holy Spirit within the icons could not only lay bare the idols of commerce and advertising, entertainment, celebrity, and politics that hold captive the imaginations of people, but also awaken those who hold up the icons to a new religious mission in a post-Christian America?

5

Orthodoxy and American Religion

As I mentioned in the previous chapter, while in graduate school at Drew University during the 1970s, I asked my teacher, the late Will Herberg, author of *Protestant, Catholic, Jew*, why he did not include Orthodox Christianity in that book. He answered that in 1955, when the book was published, Orthodoxy was not yet on the radar screen. It had not settled securely beneath the broad religious and cultural canopy that Herberg called the "American Way of Life."

Habits of the Heart (1985) and *The Naked Public Square* (1984) were, arguably, the two most influential books of the eighties that follow from Herberg's seminal study on the religious situation in America. Yet they also say little or nothing about Orthodox Christians or their churches. Robert Bellah and his collaborators apparently did not interview Orthodox Christians or at least did not see the need to report on them in *Habits of the Heart*. And only in the final pages of *The Naked Public Square* did Richard John Neuhaus raise the subject. In a disclaimer, he opined that he saw no need to mention Orthodoxy. "In the context of the present discussion," Neuhaus wrote, "[it] is almost possible to pass over the Orthodox completely." This was because Orthodox Christians remained "uncertain about whether" they constitute

An earlier version of this chapter originally appeared as "The Orthodox Presence in America: Its Meaning and Its Prospects," *St. Vladimir's Seminary Quarterly* 58, no. 1 (Summer 2016): 25–40. Used by permission.

"the *church* in America, an American denomination, or the Eastern Orthodox Church in Exile."[1] A decade after my conversation with Will Herberg,
Neuhaus essentially was repeating what Herberg had said.

In the early nineties, James Davison Hunter's *Culture Wars: The Struggle to
Define America* (1991) came on the scene. Once more, the Orthodox were not
present but for a cryptic comment that "the Greek Orthodox [had] threatened
to withdraw from the National Council of Churches because the council opposed both Bible reading and prayer in public schools,"[2] which, in any case,
was certainly not the whole story.

What explains this silence about Orthodox Christianity in these important,
influential books on religion and American life? The academy's ignorance of
Orthodoxy and indifference toward it played no small part. Forty years in the
profession has demonstrated to me firsthand how little attention is given to
Eastern Christianity in seminaries and theological schools, as well as departments of theology and religious studies, and what little will there is to correct
that situation. Yet this ignorance alone does not account for the silence and
near invisibility of the Orthodox churches in these studies.

There is more than a smidgeon of truth in Neuhaus's disclaimer. Even today,
the Orthodox have not articulated a clear, public vision of their identity and
purpose vis-à-vis the other major religions and American culture at large. Meanwhile, many Orthodox Christians have begun to view themselves as members
of a denomination, much like vast numbers of those in America who identify
themselves as Protestant or Roman Catholic. As Herberg would have said, this
is the American Way. It is the nomenclature by which followers of religious
faiths in America have for a long time distinguished themselves from others
in the great American grab bag of religions. This kind of speech and religious
self-perception of course contradicts the high "churchly" ecclesiology that Orthodox Christianity has held up ever so proudly as an earmark of its community.

Of late, fourth- and fifth-generation Orthodox and a growing number
of converts have even begun dropping the habitual ethnic nomenclature to
describe their faith to others. When asked about their religion, they simply
respond Orthodox, minus the Russian or Greek prefix. For better or for worse,
this development also fits the pattern of American religious identity Herberg
chronicled and described in *Protestant, Catholic, Jew*. This does not mean that
most contemporary Orthodox parishes have shed completely their Ukrainian,
Greek, Syrian, or Serbian identities or that major jurisdictions have stopped

---

1. Richard John Neuhaus, *The Naked Public Square* (Grand Rapids: Eerdmans, 1984), 263
(emphasis original).
2. James Davison Hunter, *Culture Wars* (New York: Basic Books, 1991), 270.

using national and ethnic tags. Many parishes stubbornly retain an immigrant church mindset, owing in part to the impact of new immigrations from the Middle East and the former Soviet Union. Nevertheless, even within the "ethnic" parish, the social imperative to define one's faith in contradistinction to Presbyterians, Pentecostals, or Roman Catholics down the street is a constant of everyday life. The Orthodox have not demonstrated that they are an exception to the rule that denominational identification is next to an inevitability in American religious life.

The Heresy of Denominationalism

During the entire span of their participation in the modern ecumenical movement since the turn of the twentieth century, Orthodox spokespersons have strenuously denounced denominationalism. They have maintained that it contradicts the fundamental unity of the church. The Orthodox report at the third Assembly of the World Council of Churches, held in New Delhi in 1961, is an example. The delegates declared that "the Orthodox Church, by her inner conviction and consciousness, has a special and exceptional position in the divided Christendom, as bearer of, and witness to, the tradition of the ancient, undivided Church, from which all existing denominations stem, by the way of reduction and separation." They insisted that under no circumstances anywhere or at any time would the Orthodox accept "the idea of a 'parity' of denomination" or any sort of "interdenominational adjustment"[3] as the basis for church unity. They drew this argument from Orthodox Christology, trinitarian theology, and sacramental theology.

This is in all respects faithful to the ancient understanding of what the church is, that the mystical unity of the church in Christ must be expressed in a tangible, visible unity. In other words, merely declaring unity of belief, while remaining institutionally divided into denominations, even with a high level of cooperation, is no real unity. I have no quarrel with this stance. Indeed, I affirm it wholeheartedly. My quarrel—as I suggested already in the two preceding chapters and shall suggest again in the next chapter as well—is that Orthodox churches have not adequately scrutinized their own behavior in pluralistic societies and measured that against theory.

A conscientious Orthodox exercise in self-criticism is long overdue. Here I can only suggest the foundation from which this self-criticism might proceed and conclusions to which it might lead. Frequently, Orthodox spokespersons

3. Gennadios Limouris, ed., *Orthodox Visions of Ecumenism: Statements, Messages and Reports on the Ecumenical Movement, 1902–1992* (Geneva: WCC, 1994), 30.

insist that their church is unique in avoiding the denominational and sectarian traps into which Protestants and Roman Catholics have stumbled. They maintain that Orthodox Christians have lived more successfully by the church's high standards of catholicity and unity than other groups have. And these spokespersons are confident that Orthodox ecclesiology guards against division and fragmentation. It is debatable whether the latter holds true. Certainly there is no "vaccine" against denominationalism.

The ironic, nearly tragic, reality is that Orthodox Christians in North America live and work *together* as citizens but are ecclesially divided, not by national boundaries but rather by transported jurisdictional structures, ethnic identities, and rivalries as well as diverse cultural practices. These institutions, identities, and practices have positive value. National origin and ethnic identity, language, and culture help to bind the religious community together, at least for a time. That which is binding, however, may also keep apart religious communities who share the same faith and may contribute to the growth of separate and distinct denominations.

H. Richard Niebuhr observes something like this in *The Social Sources of Denominationalism* (1929). "The cultural quality of nationalism . . . rather than [simply] its ethnic character must be considered as one of the probable sources of denominationalism," Niebuhr writes. Denominations, like the transplanted national churches from which they originate, "are separated and kept distinct by differences of language and of habitual modes of thought" more than by "physical traits, and the former are only incidentally rooted in the latter,"[4] he concludes. In sociological terms, therefore, the situation of the Russian, Greek, or Armenian churches in North America is comparable to the German and Swedish Lutheran churches or the Dutch Reformed of an earlier era.

The Problem of the Orthodox Ethnic Denominations

During the first great wave of immigration at the start of the twentieth century, Orthodox Christians brought with them to America a mixed and weighty baggage of traditional cultural and ethnic identity. Something similar continues with the new immigration from the former Soviet Union and the Middle East.

In America an instrumentalism, which in the homeland placed the church in service to nation, gradually and quite "naturally" transmutes the ethnic parish into what is functionally speaking a denomination. Under the American Way of Life, old-world national identity evolves into a distinctively American

---

4. H. Richard Niebuhr, *The Social Sources of Denominationalism* (New York: World Publishing Company, 1968), 110.

form of ethnicity and cultural religion that within ecclesial bodies establishes a mindset that measures ecclesial life not by the great marks of the church as "one, holy, catholic, and apostolic church," but over and against other churches that occupy the same space and time.

A state of multiple jurisdictions, dioceses, or bishops in a single location, as exist in America, is not canonical—at least according to historical norms and practices. This division, this obstacle to unity, is an important, perhaps the most important, backdrop to the principal questions raised in this chapter. At center in this chapter, however, is the question of what the meaning is of the Orthodox presence in America. This question of meaning transcends the historical and sociological discussion in which I have been engaging and becomes a profoundly theological and ecclesial concern. Even when the ethnic factor dissipates, even when Orthodox people of Greek, Russian, or Ukrainian background let go the national or ethnic nomenclature, the denominational mentality continues to grow. In fact, the American denomination is frequently the "religious" residue of the disappearing ethnic church.

No amount of historical and sociological analysis of Orthodoxy's place in this society or its relationship with other churches or denominations can yield the internal ecclesiological criteria by which the North American status of the Orthodox churches must be theologically evaluated. These criteria of catholicity, apostolicity (evangelism and mission), and unity are located in creed and confession, liturgy and sacrament. Thus while at any given historical moment or in any physical location the church may fall short, these norms remain relevant and binding. Historical miscalculation and accident do not override the norm of catholicity. Sociological "law" does not negate the freedom of the church.

Orthodox leadership has deliberated over how to unite the various transplanted churches administratively in America. Such jurisdictional regularity would help to halt the slide into denominationalism. But after a half century of serious engagement on this matter, that vision has not become reality. Orthodox canon law calls for this. The problem of unity underlies all other questions about belonging, identity, and meaning I raise in this chapter. These other questions transcend the historical and sociological discussion in which I have been engaging: they are profoundly about ecclesiology and religious meaning in the American order.

The Orthodox Diaspora

In order to address the question of Orthodox presence in America and its meaning for believers, however, one last factor in the American odyssey of Orthodoxy calls for attention. This is the belief, widely shared by the Orthodox, that their presence, even as church, constitutes a diaspora. More often than not in the minds of those who inject the term, *diaspora* means the forced removal of Orthodox peoples from their homelands. Diaspora assumes the character of a powerful myth, which suggests that Orthodox religion in the diaspora is derivative and inferior to what it was in the old country.

This notion of a diaspora is theologically mistaken: it misconstrues what it means to be the church. For Judaism, diaspora carries legitimate religious significance. The dispersion and exile of Jews from the promised land is not only part of secular history; it belongs to salvation history. God means to reverse the diaspora by returning the chosen people to their land. The Christian faith construes dispersion differently. Jesus says to the Samaritan woman, "The hour is coming when neither on this mountain nor in Jerusalem will you worship the Father" (John 4:21 RSV). And at the close of Matthew's Gospel, Jesus commands the eleven disciples to leave the mountain in Galilee and "make disciples of all nations, baptizing them in the name of the Father and of the Son and of the Holy Spirit" (Matt. 28:19 RSV). The church is not restricted to a single holy place, city, or nation. Indeed, God commands the church to disperse and spread throughout the known world, to be a mission of salvation to all peoples. This stands on its head the concept of diaspora as accident or misfortune. It affirms the church's universal and evangelical character. The church is catholic and apostolic and its mission is to all humankind or it is not truly the church.

However, there is a legitimate sociological meaning that may attach to diaspora. *Diaspora* may be used to identify and describe the removal, often forced, of ethnic groups from their indigenous homelands to other, unfamiliar locations. Ukrainians, Greeks, and Russians came to America as dispersed immigrant ethnic communities. The source of theological error and misuse of diaspora is that Orthodox people conflate ethnic identity with church and religion. The American "melting pot" actually reinforces this confusion.

Yet this religio-ethnic diasporic mindset cannot endure over the long term. It is at best transitional and will pass, whereas the presence of Ukrainians, Greeks, and Russians in America is permanent. The diasporic imagination belongs to just one phase in the inexorable process of acculturation and ecclesiastical adjustment in North America. Sociologically speaking, Orthodoxy is bound to cease being identified principally with the historic places and peoples to which it once gave a Christian character and to become increasingly "American" in a sense yet to be seen.

The "Americanization" of Orthodoxy

During the mid- and late twentieth century, the two most noteworthy voices
on the American situation of Orthodoxy were Alexander Schmemann, with
whom we are already familiar, and his colleague at St. Vladimir's Orthodox
Seminary, John Meyendorff. Both were prompted to address this subject leading up to the establishment in 1970 of the autocephalous Orthodox Church
of America, a jurisdiction that traces its origins to the Russian Church's Si-
berian and Alaskan missions of the nineteenth century. In books and articles,
Schmemann and Meyendorff inquired into the meaning and purpose of the
Orthodox presence in America and emphatically rejected the notion that the
Orthodox churches could or should continue as churches in exile or diaspora.

The name of the new autocephalous church, the Orthodox Church in
America, did itself indicate a "solution" to the identity issue: in the future,
there would be not an American Orthodoxy but rather the Orthodox Church
with a presence in and a mission to America. And it would be of America, in
so much as the church's principal service was to America; not an Orthodox
church that is Russian, Serbian, or the like, but the Orthodox Church in its
universal and catholic character, permanently present in North America and
actively engaged as a formative force within the culture. Schmemann and
Meyendorff hoped that the Orthodox Church in America, with its founding
claim as a mission to America (and the sole Orthodox jurisdiction in North
America until 1922), would be the agent of a restored unity among the various
Orthodox churches.

In an article published one month before the autocephalous status of the
Orthodox Church in America was formally established, Meyendorff urged,

> In restoring unity . . . we will not create a new "denomination," called "American
> Orthodox," but we will be at one in the "Orthodox Church of America."
> This Church will undoubtedly preserve, wherever necessary, various liturgical
> languages and traditions, . . . and it will, of course, welcome Americans, who
> do not desire to identify themselves by any national adjectives. The canons of
> the Church actually ignore "national" churches: they only require that in each
> area the essential Oneness of the Church be visibly realized so that our confes-
> sion of faith in the Creed—"I believe in One, Holy, Catholic and Apostolic
> Church"—may not sound like empty words.[5]

Thus Meyendorff insisted that the Orthodox Church in America not be
thought of as a new Orthodox denomination. He allowed for the continuation

5. John Meyendorff, *The Vision of Unity* (Crestwood, NY: SVS, 1987), 36.

of the use of "national adjectives" for the foreseeable future. But he invoked the Nicene Creed to remind his readers that the central norms of the faith require unity rather than division and mission rather than self-service.

Schmemann, likewise, tackled these issues of identity and ecclesial existence. And in closing, I give you his analysis in an endeavor to clarify his important seminal insights. In an essay published in 1964, Schmemann insists, "There is not and there cannot be a religion of America in the sense in which Orthodoxy is [or was] the religion of Greece or Russia," and so also there cannot be an American Orthodoxy that is like Greek or Russian Orthodoxy. The reason is that in Greece and Russia and other Orthodox lands the Orthodox faith was "coextensive with the national culture" and in some real and substantial way was even "the national culture."[6]

In the old country, the alternative to being Greek and Orthodox or Russian and Orthodox was to adopt a "cosmopolitanism" that might simply be described as modern or "liberal"—in other words, the culture of Western Europe that grew from the Renaissance and the Enlightenment. This "liberal" Western culture was an alien intellectual tradition in virtually all the Orthodox lands. In America, however, it is the overarching culture, and when the Orthodox arrived in large numbers to America, this culture was already turning markedly secular. This secular culture would permit space for religion but was more or less impervious to religion (or any one religion) as a singular or dominant formative force.[7]

"For the first time in its whole history," Schmemann explains, Orthodoxy was obliged to "live within a secular culture"[8] and not a culture that it birthed, shaped, and permeated in which religion, culture, society, and the nation had been highly integrated. Even today, the residue of the old Christendom in Greece, Russia, or Serbia is of a different character than what remains of American Christendom. That is because American Christendom was formed within the environment of the Enlightenment. This means that the *modus operandi* of the Orthodox churches in America must be different from in the homelands where, to be clear, Christendom is also at its close.

Yet many Orthodox, here and abroad, barely understand or take the circumstances Schmemann describes into account. In the old Orthodox countries (as mentioned in chap. 4), the church is still able to call on a strong memory of Orthodox Greece, Orthodox Russia, or Orthodox Serbia. This may or may not

6. Alexander Schmemann, "Problems of Orthodoxy in America I: The Canonical Problem," *St. Vladimir's Theological Quarterly* 8, no. 2 (1964): 77.

7. I have given this greater attention in chap. 4, citing with a somewhat different purpose the statements by Schmemann that belong to the following paragraphs.

8. Schmemann, "Problems of Orthodoxy in America I," 78.

serve a positive or useful purpose for the church or the nation. Nevertheless, the strategy is possible and may be viable. Many Orthodox mistakenly think this strategy is a real option in America. When adopted, however, it fuels the ethnic religious cult and misses the mark in the culture. It renders Orthodox churches irrelevant to American life at large.

"Deprived of [its] living interrelation with culture, of this claim to the *whole* of life," Schmemann warns, Orthodoxy in America is in jeopardy of betraying and losing "something absolutely essential" to its identity as a historical church. He opines that this is why so many Orthodox, even those who are American born and converts, remain instinctively attached to the "'national' forms of Orthodoxy, . . . however narrow-minded and 'nationalistic'" these may be.[9] They fear the wholesale abandonment of the old and familiar forms in which the faith was culturally embodied. That fear is not irrational but neither is it helpful. The truth of this situation is that "Americanization," carried out like "a surgical operation" to extract from the Russian or Greek Orthodox body a pure Orthodox spirit, is doomed to disconnect the spirit "from its flesh and blood, making it a lifeless form."[10] Yet if the Orthodox completely resist "Americanization" and cling to old national identities and nationalistic ideas, there is a high likelihood of one of two undesirable results. The first is that the church will diminish to nothing but an ethnic and nationalistic enclave. Ironically, this feeds into the American denominationalist pattern that H. Richard Niebuhr identified. The other possibility is that the ethnic church will simply atrophy and disappear.

Schmemann insists that the task of Orthodoxy in America is not "to perpetuate and 'preserve' the . . . national identity." For "'national' here has value not in itself, but only inasmuch as it is 'catholic,' i.e. capable of conveying and communicating the living truth of Orthodoxy."[11] Nor should this identity be immediately abandoned. Instead, a delicate balance needs to be struck wherein the church takes advantage of "the organic continuity" of the old national culture while assimilation progresses and a canonical solution to unity is worked out.

The real challenge is not about what to call the Orthodox presence in America. The appropriate nomenclature will emerge over time. The real challenge is, rather, to navigate a course that avoids a complete reduction to ethnic sect or denomination and to meanwhile retain a lively sense of the catholicity of the Orthodox Church. The challenge is to pave a way beyond the ethnic

9. Schmemann, "Problems of Orthodoxy in America I," 78.
10. Schmemann, "Problems of Orthodoxy in America I," 78.
11. Schmemann, "Problems of Orthodoxy in America I," 79.

and jurisdictional division that came of the passage to America. That way must lead to a true unity, however, not mere "cooperation *among* the various national 'jurisdictions.'"[12] Schmemann would have been the first to admit that this task is a difficult one.

Conclusion

During the closing decades of the past century and into this century, an unprecedented trend of large numbers of converts to Orthodoxy is presenting a fresh opportunity to renew the sense of mission and evangelism in the church and to emphasize anew the need for unity. The pace of growth in new, largely convert parishes marks a historical watershed. This may be a *kairos* moment in Orthodox Christianity. But the new influx of converts may also work against catholicity and unity. Disaffected, disillusioned, or embittered Protestants and Roman Catholics are seeking retreat and cover in Orthodoxy. This brings into parishes and Orthodox dioceses strong strains of voluntarism and an impulse among converts to transform their "new" church into an enclave opposed to the secular culture. The old, atrophying ethnic identity is pushed aside, even forgotten, and there is formed either a sectarian refuge or a fortress from which to wage the culture wars in the broader society.

Such happenings would be the very worst possible sort of "Americanization" of Orthodoxy. Orthodoxy in America would become an inverted "conservative" image of mainline Protestantism and liberal Roman Catholicism, another kind of religious lobby. This is how in America churches become adjutants to the state, whether they endorse or oppose the state's policies and whether they hold high or dismiss the banner of separation of church and state.

Until now, Orthodoxy in North America has struggled unsuccessfully to correct the rise of "overlapping" or "competing" jurisdictions (i.e., multiple primacies, or bishops of national churches, in one "place" whether city or region), and this contradicts canonical norms. But I suggest another outrageous (unthinkable?) possibility. With the exponential growth of predominantly convert parishes, religious history in America rises to haunt Orthodoxy with the specter of entirely new break-off denominations. I mean that there could come a time when primarily convert parishes view themselves (across competing Orthodox jurisdictions) as having more in common with one another than with their own ethnic diocese. They might then seek to form their own independent dioceses cleansed of ethnic proclivities and laxities that inhibit

12. Schmemann, "Problems of Orthodoxy in America I," 79.

serious Christian living and the will to combat the secular culture or to separate from it. The marked appeal of monastic asceticism to many of these converts can be an appropriate response to the moral laxity prevalent in our society. But it might also inspire a form of religious separatism not uncommon in the formation of American denominations. Such an orthodoxy in America might view itself as pure and untangled from ethnic culture religion while not recognizing just how much it has accommodated itself to American realities and adopted habits that are just as compromising to the Orthodox Christian faith as was the old ethnocentrism.

Ironically, these possibilities arise in large measure because the ethnic parish did not learn how to catechize effectively, having not thought of itself as a mission—that is, not until others came knocking at the door. Such catechizing would require much more than bringing together religious educators to create new curriculums. It would demand a thorough examination and analysis by the churches of the American situation. It would require courses in Orthodox seminaries not yet imagined, leave aside taught.

Whether Orthodox adopt the peculiarly American form of religious denomination or make a successful transition to a united Orthodoxy lies in the balance. I like to think that God in his providence swept all the Orthodox churches together to North America for a new Pentecost of mission, renewal, and unity. What I know for certain is that Will Herberg was right in *Protestant, Catholic, Jew* when he argued that over several generations, persons gradually shed the "foreign" or ethnic character of the religious community and adopt a distinctly American form of religious self-identification as Protestant, Catholic, Jew, and now, we may add with trepidation, Orthodox.

PART 3

Ecumenical Theology

6

THE AGONY OF
ORTHODOX ECCLESIOLOGY

This chapter continues a concern of chapters 4 and 5, namely, the contradiction between the high "churchly" theology of unity in Christ by which Orthodox define what is to be church and the actual organization and conduct of their churches in everyday life. In ecumenical settings, the Orthodox vision of the one, holy, catholic, and apostolic church has sailed up into the heavens. Rarely in ecumenical settings, however, have Orthodox spokespersons stepped down from their heaven-bound ladder to acknowledge candidly and self-critically how short they come of that vision on *terra firma*. Having said this, I still affirm the truth of Orthodox ecclesiology. In modern times, Orthodox Christianity has rendered a valuable service to all the Christian confessions with its vision of a church in which unity is the precondition of fruitful mission to the world.

I mentioned in chapter 5 the proceedings of the Third Assembly of the World Council of Churches held in New Delhi in 1961. At the New Delhi assembly, the Orthodox members of the Section on Unity submitted a response to the advance report of the Commission on Faith and Order. In that report, they praised Faith and Order's declaration that "'ecumenism in faith with all ages' [is] one of the normative prerequisites of unity."[1] Ultimately, New

An earlier version of this chapter originally appeared as "The Crisis of Orthodox Ecclesiology," in *The Ecumenical Future*, ed. Carl E. Braaten and Robert W. Jenson, 162–75 (Grand Rapids: Eerdmans, 2004). Reprinted by permission of the publisher; all rights reserved.

1. Gennadios Limouris, ed., *Orthodox Visions of Ecumenism: Statements, Messages and Reports on the Ecumenical Movement, 1902–1992* (Geneva: WCC, 1994), 31.

Delhi embraced this gem of ecclesiological wisdom and with only minor revisions ensconced it as the centerpiece of the assembly's famous prescription for church unity. The New Delhi assembly declared that genuine unity, "which is both God's will and his gift to his church," must be necessarily a fellowship "made visible as all in each place who are baptized in Jesus Christ and confess him as Lord and Savior." Christian fellowship, the church, occupies both space and time in unity and continuity. It is the same church "in all places and in all ages."[2]

In his address to the assembly, Greek Orthodox theologian Nikos Nissiotis not only summarized the Orthodox position but also summed up the spirit of the New Delhi assembly. He argued that the unity of the church is neither "a 'spiritualized,' sentimental, humanistic expression of good will" nor merely the product of "human agreement." Rather, the ground of this unity is God in his triune being. Jesus declares that the telos of those who believe in him is "that they may be one, even as we are one" (John 17:22–23 RSV). Nissiotis continues, "Unity among men in the Church" is nothing less than "the result, the reflection, of the event of the Father's union with Christ by his Spirit realized in the historical Church on the day of Pentecost." God has proffered this Pentecostal unity to humankind as a gift that they must themselves willingly accept in faith. "Unity is not an *attribute* of the Church, but it is its very *life*." And he insists "it [unity] is the divine-human interpenetration realized once and for all in the Communion between Word and Flesh in Christ."[3] He concludes, "The Church does not move toward unity through comparison of conceptions of unity, but lives out the union between God and man realized in the communion of the Church as a union of men in the Son of Man. We are not here to create unity, but to recapture its vast universal dimensions."[4]

In the years since the New Delhi assembly, Orthodox have consistently argued for this christological and trinitarian vision of unity—much as they have also rejected every form of incrementalism that ignores or denies the truth that the church can be whole only if there is a visible unity. They have vociferously objected to proposals that by the shared witness, cooperation, and service of otherwise divided denominations and confessions, a spiritual and invisible unity is achievable and that this is adequate. On the one hand, unity is not a goal that human organizations or schemes of denominational

---

2. https://www.oikoumene.org/en/resources/documents/assembly/1961-new-delhi/new-delhi -statement-on-unity, para. 116.

3. Constantin G. Patelos, ed., *The Orthodox Church in the Ecumenical Movement: Documents and Statements, 1902–1975* (Geneva: WCC, 1978), 231–32.

4. Patelos, *Orthodox Church in the Ecumenical Movement*, 232.

merger can accomplish, and, on the other hand, neither is unity a vague spirituality that can exist without a visible concord. Rather, unity is God's gift in Jesus Christ bestowed on all who call on him, worship him as Lord, and are committed to living out that unity in a love that binds them together in communion as one mystical and sacramental body in Christ.

Schism and Orthodox Responsibility

Together with this vision of unity, Orthodox have argued that their church "has a special and exceptional position in the divided Christendom as bearer of, and witness to, the tradition of the ancient undivided Church, from which all existing denominations stem, by the way of reduction and separation." They have maintained that the fundamental ecumenical problem is not even the many divisions within the one church of Jesus Christ but is instead "'schism' itself. . . . The unity [of the church] is broken and must be recovered."[5] As injurious as denominationalism is to unity, it is but a symptom of a far more detrimental and much deeper breach in the one, holy, catholic, and apostolic body of Christ.

Most of Protestantism has accepted implicitly, if not explicitly, the legitimacy or normalcy of this state of *schism* while not naming it for what it is; whereas, throughout the hundred or more years of modern ecumenism, the Orthodox Church has refused to retreat from its stance that schism is at the source of all the visible divisions within Christianity. There is nothing quaint or charming about this Orthodox conviction. It singes the souls of many of my colleagues in the religious academy. *Schism* is a word they would rather forget, much as they have expelled heresy from contemporary religious speech and relegated it to historical study, if it is even permitted to exist there.

But I believe with my church that schism *is* at the heart and center of the problem of unity. It needs to be named in order that it might be healed and overcome. Taking this position, however, imposes a heavy responsibility on Orthodox believers to strive strenuously toward living in accord with the high standard of unity that they uphold. Yet in the old Orthodox lands, much exists and persists that starkly contradicts this position; and the canonical mess of competing jurisdictions in North America and elsewhere is no less an egregious offence. My protestation, my confession, is this: If Protestants are guilty of dividing the one body of Christ into denominations and not being truly willing to let go of those separate and divisive identities, then the

5. Limouris, *Orthodox Visions of Ecumenism*, 30.

Orthodox are guilty of a comparable sin of dividing the one body of Christ into exclusivist national and ethnic enclaves that they will not let go of even when the opportunity arises, as it has in America.

New Delhi was brutally realistic about what the churches must do to reclaim genuine unity. The assembly declared that "nothing less than a death and rebirth of many forms of church life as we have known them" is required.[6] If Orthodoxy is to be a truly credible witness to the unity New Delhi affirmed, it must let go of old habits of ecclesial existence and ecclesiastical organization. But it has not, thus far, shown the capacity or willingness to do so.

The Rise of the Orthodox National Churches

The bitter pill that the Orthodox must swallow is that they have been complicit in that reduction and separation of the undivided church of which they accuse others. As I already have stated in the previous chapter, old forms of ethnocentrism, nationalism, triumphalism, and establishmentarianism continue to exist and divide the Orthodox churches, while very little is spoken about this in "mixed" company.

The issue is not localism or regionalism. Localism and regionalism are compatible with the essential unity of the church. As far back as at least "the fifth century, beyond the borders of the Roman empire, there were independent [Orthodox] churches."[7] John Meyendorff explains that in the Caucasus, the Armenian and Georgian churches were headed very early by primates who carried the title of patriarch or *catholicos*. The identity of these churches was defined along cultural or ethnic lines, often over and against Byzantine universalism and perceived threats of national and ecclesial absorption by the Greeks. Later on, in the medieval period, independent Orthodox patriarchal sees sprung up among Bulgarians, Serbs, and others. Meyendorff maintains that "the original ideology" of these churches "was Byzantine and therefore accepted the principle of a united universal Christian empire."[8] He continues, "The failure of Bulgarian and Serbian leaders, [however], to secure the imperial throne for themselves led in practice to the creation of monarchies and regional patriarchates." Yet in these instances "there were no canonical obstacles to the existence of . . . patriarchal pluralism. On the contrary,

---

6. https://www.oikoumene.org/en/resources/documents/assembly/1961-new-delhi/new-delhi -statement-on-unity, para. 117.

7. John Meyendorff, *The Byzantine Legacy* (Crestwood, NY: St. Vladimir's Seminary Press, 1982), 224.

8. Meyendorff, *Byzantine Legacy*, 224.

the ancient canons of Nicaea and subsequent councils were still serving as the backbone of Orthodox canon law, and these ancient rules sanctioned ecclesiastical regionalism within the framework of a universal unity of faith, secured by the councils."[9]

Nonetheless, later on, social, cultural, and ideological forces intruded to create environments inhospitable to unity and to further segregate the regional patriarchates. These forces were the dissolution of the Byzantine Empire, the invasion of the Turks, the creation and ultimate demise of the Ottoman Empire, the birth of imperial Russia, and the rise of nationalism and the modern nation-state. National Orthodox churches that were lending to and drawing from the identity of emergent geopolitical national entities came into their own as the Ottoman state and its hegemony disintegrated and as national movements rose up in the Balkans and Caucasus. These "national" churches consciously sought to cultivate Orthodox peoplehood.

Beginning in the nineteenth century, new "Orthodox" nation-states came into existence. Greece was the first in 1832. A modern "'notion' of autocephaly" or ecclesiastical independence took hold as Orthodox "national" jurisdictions found themselves no longer under an empire, Byzantine or Ottoman, but belonging instead to a nation-state, Greek, Serbian, or Bulgarian. From these conditions and circumstances "there emerged the idea of a *Christian nation*, with a national vocation, a kind of corporate 'identity' before God,"[10] Alexander Schmemann adds.

Schmemann argues that, though the idea of autocephaly was as much if not more a product of national feeling than ecclesiology, it is not necessary to think of this new form of national church in negative terms "as a 'deviation'" from the historical norm. "For in spite of all their deficiencies, tragedies and betrayals, there indeed were such realities as 'Holy Serbia' or 'Holy Russia.'"[11] Gradually, however, with the intensified march into modernity, these national churches became transformed into *nationalistic* churches, veritable handmaids to the state. Even before the modern era, Ottoman rule had narrowed and secularized the Orthodox Church's vision. Late forces of modernity finished gutting what remained in the national Orthodox churches of a sense of freedom and independence from the state. "The very essence of the church [its faith and mission]," Schmemann concludes, "began to be viewed in terms of ... nationalism and reduced to it."[12]

9. Meyendorff, *Byzantine Legacy*, 224–25.
10. Alexander Schmemann, *Church, World, Mission: Reflections on Orthodoxy in the West* (Crestwood, NY: St. Vladimir's, Seminary Press, 1979), 98.
11. Schmemann, *Church, World, Mission*, 99.
12. Schmemann, *Church, World, Mission*, 99.

Despite the discerning analyses of writers like Meyendorff and Schmemann, a habitual conflation of the church body with the ethnic community prevails in official Orthodox rhetoric and persists in the popular imagination. This mindset becomes that much more convoluted when ordinary people univocally identify the nation and nationhood with the nation-state. Consequently, they view the church as an organ of the state. Some see it as a functional organ of the state; other more secular sorts begin to view it as no longer useful to the state, as the human appendix is to the body. In either case, the stature of the church is diminished, its essence is misunderstood, and dysfunctions in its ecclesial existence set in.

The Sin of Phyletism and the Dividedness of Orthodoxy

There is precedent in Orthodox history for treating this "nationalization" of churches with as much concern as my account conveys. In 1872 an Orthodox council, held in Constantinople, condemned the so-called Bulgarian Schism. The council was not without blemish. It got nasty with its self-righteous invective against "the Bulgarians," as if they alone were guilty of ecclesiastical nationalism.[13] Nevertheless, as Meyendorff helpfully points out, the council is worth remembering for its condemnation of a "new" heresy, which it named *phyletism.*

The council of 1872 defined phyletism as "the establishment of particular churches [that accept] members of the same nationality and [refuse] the members of other nationalities, . . . [and that] are administered [exclusively] by pastors of the same nationality."[14] Phyletism is a heresy because in its attitude and behavior it practices an exclusivity that profoundly contradicts the unity, catholicity, and apostolicity of the church. Phyletism has evolved over time and migrates very often from the region or country in which it is most clearly attached by blood and soil to "alien" environs in which the phyletic national church is one among many churches in a religiously pluralistic environment. Today, for example, phyletism manifests itself as the "coexistence of nationally defined churches . . . within the same territory, city or village," that remain organizationally "independent from each other"[15] and even become competitive.

13. Meyendorff, *Byzantine Legacy*, 228. The Encyclical of the Holy and Great Council of the Orthodox Church of 2016 names the council as a forerunner to it and explicitly mentions its condemnation of "ethno-phyletism as an ecclesiological heresy." See https://www.holycouncil .org/-/encyclical-holy-council, I.3.
14. Quoted in Meyendorff, *Byzantine Legacy*, 228 (citing Metropolitan Maximus of Sardis).
15. Meyendorff, *Byzantine Legacy* (citing Metropolitan Maximus of Sardis), 228.

None of the Orthodox churches in North America would willingly accept the label. Yet whether by accident or intention (and it usually is something of both), their behavior and station in America has been phyletic. John McGuckin rightly judges that "the disease of phyletism has gained hold" in "America and Oceana." Regional churches that were once "located in the territorial comprehensiveness of the modern nation state"[16] have reestablished themselves in other countries alongside other churches that have had primates or metropolitanates for some length of time. The result is overlapping and competing jurisdictions, a state of existence that is completely contrary to the church's canons: *this is phyletism.*

The Case of the Holy and Great Council of 2016

In 2016, after many years of preparation, a pan-Orthodox council[17] was held in Kolymvari, Crete, under the presidency of Ecumenical Patriarch Bartholomew. In addition to an encyclical, the council produced eight documents addressing various subjects ranging from ecclesiology, mission, and the sacraments to relations with other churches. One hope was that the council would be an emblem of Orthodox unity in the modern world. This did not happen, as major constituencies absented themselves from the council.

That the council failed in this respect needn't detract from the aspirational symbolism of its convocation. Many councils in the history of the church have fallen short of their goals. Nonetheless, the council must also be seen as a symptom and glaring example of how short Orthodoxy comes of its claim not only to represent the ancient ecclesiological mind of the one, holy, catholic, and apostolic church but also to be its living embodiment.

In the end, four of the fourteen autocephalous churches refused to attend, and several of these churches, the Church of Antioch and the Russian Church (the Moscow Patriarchate) most notably, issued statements that though they affirmed the goals of the council, they refused to accept its documents as

16. John Anthony McGuckin, *The Orthodox Church* (Oxford: Blackwell, 2008), 26. In the preceding chapter I have spoken already of the inability or unwillingness of the leadership of the Orthodox churches in North America to resolve such jurisdictional issues and to unite under "one bishop in each city" (or under one common metropolitanate); and I said that this state of affairs has reinforced old-country ethnocentric habits among the laity, contributing to the secularization and hollowing out of the churches.

17. For the Encyclical of the Holy and Great Council and a list of its signatories, see https://www.holycouncil.org/-/encyclical-holy-council. Not present at the Council was the family of so-called Oriental Orthodox churches. This includes the Armenian, Coptic, Syrian, and Ethiopian Orthodox churches that do not accept the christological definition of the Council of Chalcedon (451).

binding on them. The Church of Antioch recognized the council as "a prelimi-nary gathering on the way to a Pan-Orthodox Council" and its documents as provisional and open to discussion. The Russian Church refused to recognize the council as pan-Orthodox or its documents as "reflecting Pan-Orthodox consensus."[18]

The stories behind the refusal of these several churches to attend the council are as or even more revealing than their statements about the shortcomings of the council and of the divisions within Orthodoxy. That background is much too complicated to discuss here, but suffice it to say that the sin of phyletism and other misuses of ecclesiastical authority came to roost in Kolymvari. Yet nowhere that I can find in the council's encyclical or in the criticisms of the dissenting Orthodox churches is there a call to repent for the failure of all to be, in that time and place, a visibly unified and catholic representation of the ancient faith that Orthodoxy propounds as the norm for all churches or communities that take the name of Christian.

In a group of essays submitted beforehand for the council's consideration, Orthodox theologian Will Cohen enjoined the council to approach the subject of ecumenism "humbly as an ascetical task."[19] This was apropos for churches that have from the inception of modern ecumenism insisted that the unity of the church must be a visible unity and that have at times and in many places not been the best example of this unity. The tension, if not outright contradiction, between claims about the unity of the church and the behavior of sinful humanity must not be attributed to others while the critics remain incapable of making their own confession: *We too have fallen far short of what God asks of us.*

Conclusion

Despite these shortcomings in Orthodox Christianity, I cling to the belief that the right ecclesiology makes a vital difference in the shape the church takes in the world. Ideas and dogmas have consequences. What those consequences will be, however, depends on human decisions freely reached and openness to the guidance of the Holy Spirit. Orthodoxy's most valuable gift to the modern

18. "Statement of the Secretariat of the Holy Synod of Antioch, Balamand, 27 June 2016," Greek Orthodox Patriarchate of Antioch and All the East, https://www.antiochpatriarchate.org/en/page/statement-of-the-secretariat-of-the-holy-synod-of-antioch-balamand-27-june-2016/1448/.

19. Will Cohen, "Orthodoxy and Ecumenism in View of the Upcoming Great and Holy Council," in *Toward the Holy and Great Council: Theological Reflections*, ed. Nathanael Symeonides (New York: Department of Inter-Orthodox, Ecumenical & Interfaith Relations, 2016), 3:18.

ecumenical movement has been itself, not a theory of the church but the *ancient, living* church that it is, yes, even with its blemishes and failures. There is no guarantee that Orthodoxy will be able to resist here in North America, or anywhere else, the same schismatic and divisive forces that afflict the other Christian confessions. The admonition and call of New Delhi that "nothing less [is required] than a death and rebirth of many forms of church life as we have known them," applies with a devastating immediacy to the Orthodox churches themselves.[20] New Delhi, in which the Orthodox churches played such a crucial role, still stands as a reminder that the Orthodox, too, must bravely follow the pioneer of their faith on a journey from old and familiar places and ways into God's unknowable future.

In recent times, that journey has taken a dramatic turn in the Orthodox Church's relations with the Roman Catholic Church, especially during the consecutive papacies of Pope John Paul II, Pope Benedict XVI, and the reigning Pope Francis. The following chapter does not entirely account for all that has happened over the encompassing years, but it does tell a story of renewed hope for reconciliation and reunion of the Roman Catholic Church and the Orthodox churches.

20. https://www.oikoumene.org/en/resources/documents/assembly/1961-new-delhi/new-delhi-statement-on-unity, para. 117.

7

The Problem of Papal Primacy

> The exchange of official visits . . . from our two Churches on the
> occasion of the feasts of their patron saints [the Apostles Peter
> and Paul] has become now an established tradition. It is a sign of
> our willingness to seek the restoration of our full unity. . . . For
> it is above all through our common saints that we can reach each
> other and foster our spiritual bonds.
>
> His Eminence Metropolitan John of Pergamon
> (John Zizioulas), representing Ecumenical Patriarch
> Bartholomew in Rome on June 30, 2005

In 1879, Malachia Ormanian (1841–1918) left the Armenian Uniate Catholic
Church and was received into the Armenian Orthodox Church as a celibate
priest. The next year he became primate of the city of Erzerum in Eastern
Turkey and in 1886 was consecrated bishop. Ormanian's scholarly career
also blossomed during this period. In 1887 he was appointed professor of
theology at the Seminary of Holy Etchmiadzin in Armenia. Two years hence,
he accepted the deanship of the Armash Seminary near Izmit, Turkey. In 1896
Ormanian was elected Armenian Patriarch of Constantinople.

An earlier version of this chapter originally appeared as "A Communion of Love and the Primacy
of Peter: Reflections from the Armenian Church," in *Ecumenism Today: The Universal Church
in the 21st Century*, ed. Francesca Aran Murphy and Christopher Asprey, 139–50 (New York:
Routledge, 2016). Used by permission.

Ormanian's story is of interest to us not just because of his conversion. Its background and circumstances are at least as significant, for Ormanian had been a committed Catholic. From 1863 to 1866, he served in Rome as Armenian teacher to The Sacred Congregation *de Propaganda Fide* and in 1870 he attended the First Vatican Council. The council's declaration of papal infallibility, however, shook Ormanian; perhaps it confirmed doubts he had already been harboring. In any case, he voiced his objections openly, and three months before the close of the council, Ormanian left Rome.

Over the ensuing decades, Ormanian made a scriptural and historical study of the primacy of Peter and published his findings.[1] His conclusions about the contested meaning of Matthew 16:18–20 ("I tell you, you are Peter, and on this rock I will build My church"), as well as other relevant New Testament passages, closely follow the standard Orthodox and Protestant interpretation and criticism. Ormanian discovered no conclusive proof in Scripture or in early church history for the bishop of Rome's claim to supreme headship over all Christians.

Thirty years after his reception into the Armenian Church, Malachia Ormanian still had not let go of his own hurtful memories of the First Vatican Council. In *The Church of Armenia*, originally published in 1910, he harshly criticizes Rome's imperious behavior: "The Roman Church alone deemed it necessary, in the second half of the nineteenth century, to take away [the] prerogative [of] the Councils and fix it on the person of the pope."[2] He adds, "The papacy continues arrogantly to assert its right to meddle in the intellectual domain, and to maintain its politico-administrative interference over those portions of the world which are dependent on its authority. It contrives indiscreetly to restrict more and more the administrative sphere of authorities which are subordinate to it, by annulling those ancient rights which still

1. I am indebted to Professor Abraham Terian, formally academic dean of St. Nersess Armenian Seminary in New Rochelle, New York. He has supplied me with the abstract of a lecture he delivered in Armenian at the Conference in Memory of Archbishop Malachia Ormanian, held in New York at the Eastern Diocese of the Armenian Church in America on October 31, 1998. The main body of the lecture, titled "Ormanian, The Primacy of Peter, and 'The Queen of Translations,'" was in Armenian in rough draft at the time. Professor Terian, however, generously discussed its contents and related matters with me. He also provided me with references to writings in which Ormanian examines scriptural texts and historical documents relevant to the issue of the primacy of Peter and the papacy's claim to universal jurisdiction over the whole of Christianity. These include the following: *Theological Loci* (in Armenian, *Teghik' Astuacabut'ean*) (Jerusalem: St. James Press, 1985; reprint of articles in *Sion*, 1967–1985), esp. 37–47; *Synopsis* (in Armenian, *Hamapatum*) (Antelias, Lebanon: Catholicosate of the Great House of Cilicia, 1983), esp. 229–31.

2. Malachia Ormanian, *The Church of Armenia*, 3rd ed., trans. C. Marcar Gregory (New York: St. Vartan Press, 1988), 99.

remained to the Gallican, Hungarian, Ambrosian, Mozarabic, and Eastern Churches; it reduces the ordinaries (bishops) of dioceses to the position of mere vicars."[3]

Ormanian traces the declarations of the First Vatican Council back to the Council of Trent (1545–63) and dismisses as disingenuous Rome's invitation to the other churches for dialogue. At Trent "every doctrinal opinion of the Church was defined, stereotyped, and enacted,"[4] he argues. When the Vatican council met, the Catholic Church did invite others, but this act was read by other churches as a "sheer matter of form . . . to save appearances." Nonetheless, "in order to be canonical, it was necessary, as a preliminary, to [contact] the other Churches concerning the points to be discussed, so as to pave the way for a common ground of understanding. But this writ to assemble was, properly speaking, but a summons to bow before her [the Roman Catholic Church's] pretensions."[5]

In the Armenian world, Malachia Ormanian is remembered as a liberal and ecumenical spirit of the modern church. In *The Church of Armenia*, he favored "*in necessariis unitas. . . , in dubiis libertas . . . , in omnibus caritas*" (unity in essentials, liberty in doubtful matters, charity in all things)[6] for the sake of amity among the churches and so that the universal church might flourish. What then moved Ormanian to speak so severely and bitterly of the Roman Catholic Church? How did his love for it turn to distrust and even scorn? A study has not yet been done to definitively answer these important questions. Nevertheless, it is instructive simply to let stand this sharp contrast between Ormanian's ecumenical ecclesial vision and his disenchantment with and alienation from Rome. This contrast neatly represents a division of mind regarding Rome and ecumenism common within the whole of Orthodox Christianity.

Recent Papal Overtures to the Orthodox Churches

In 1995 in his encyclical *Ut Unum Sint*, Pope John Paul II graciously invited theologians and church leaders to engage with him in "a patient and fraternal dialogue" about how the papacy might facilitate better relations among the churches, with the aim of full and visible church unity. The pope's eye was turned especially to the Orthodox churches. In his inaugural sermon on April

3. Ormanian, *Church of Armenia*, 129.
4. Ormanian, *Church of Armenia*, 119.
5. Ormanian, *Armenian Church*, 125–26.
6. Ormanian, *Armenian Church*, 109.

20, 2005, newly elected Pope Benedict XVI stated that he was entirely committed to John Paul II's ecumenical aims. "Theological dialogue is necessary," he insisted. "The current Successor of Peter feels himself to be personally implicated in this question and is disposed to do all in his power to promote the fundamental cause of ecumenism."[7]

Neither John Paul II nor Benedict XVI were naive about their aspirations for renewed communion between Rome and the Orthodox churches. Both recognized the deeply seated obstacles to full communion. How the primacy of Peter is defined lies at the heart of the matter. The issue is complicated by deeply seated Orthodox memories of offenses that Rome committed against Orthodox peoples in the past, for which John Paul II asked forgiveness. That, no doubt, is why in his inaugural homily Benedict XVI repeated his predecessor's plea for a "purification of memory."[8]

The Roman Journey of Karekin I

A century and one decade after Malachia Ormanian became Armenian Patriarch of Constantinople—that is, in December 1996—Karekin I, Catholicos of All Armenians, journeyed from Holy Etchmiadzin, the ancient and historic first see of the Armenian Church, to Vatican City. He arrived with political goals. The newly established sovereign Armenian nation was embroiled in a violent struggle with neighboring Azerbaijan. The Armenian population of the ancient region of Nagorno-Karabakh, which Stalin had treacherously incorporated into Azerbaijan, sought to be rejoined to the Armenian homeland. Armenia sought the support of the papacy, and in a Common Declaration issued by the pope and the catholicos on December 31, 1996, John Paul II gave that support.

This was not the only matter, however, that moved the Armenian catholicos to come to Rome. As a young priest and bishop, Karekin I had cut his ecclesial teeth in the World Council of Churches, and he remained deeply committed to ecumenism and the goal of church unity. He traveled to Rome in that spirit. Thus, in their Common Declaration, he and the pope also agreed on a christological formula that bridges the difference between the Armenian Church's preference for a Cyrillian miaphysite (this references Cyril of

7. Benedict XVI, "First Message of His Holiness Benedict XVI," April 20, 2005, Libreria Editrice Vaticana, https://w2.vatican.va/content/benedict-xvi/en/messages/urbi/documents/hf _ben-xvi_mes_20050420_missa-pro-ecclesia.html.

8. Benedict XVI, "First Message of His Holiness Benedict XVI," Libreria Editrice Vaticana, https://w2.vatican.va/content/benedict-xvi/en/messages/urbi/documents/hf_ben-xvi_mes_200 50420_missa-pro-ecclesia.html.

Alexandria [d. 444] and a particular christological formula named for him) manner of affirming the fullness of Christ's divinity and humanity and the dyophysite definition of the Council of Chalcedon (451) embraced by the Roman Catholic Church.[9]

This paragraph lit an acrimonious controversy within the Armenian Church, not just about the language employed but also about whether the catholicos had acted within his authority. I was drawn into the maelstrom. With the consent of the catholicos, I publicly defended his actions.[10] For that I too was roundly criticized. The controversy surrounding old suspicions about Rome's intentions resurfaced. There were dire admonitions about Rome's deviousness and imperial ambitions; some openly accused Karekin I of being duped.

The catholicos and the pope did not limit themselves, however, to dogmatic and political issues. In several key paragraphs, they declared their mutual desire for reconciliation between their churches. They mutually repented of old animosities and emphasized their personal determination to set these divisions aside to further dialogue and cooperation. Speaking in the third person, the catholicos and the pope expressed

> their sorrow for these controversies and dissensions and their determination to remove from the mind and memory of their Churches the bitterness, mutual recriminations, and even hatred which have sometimes manifested themselves in the past, and may even cast a shadow over the truly fraternal and genuinely Christian relations between leaders and the faithful of both Churches, especially as these have developed in recent times.

They continued,

> The spiritual communion already existing between the two Churches and the hope for and commitment to the recovery of full communion between them should become factors of motivation for further contact, more regular and

9. The text reads as follows: "They [the catholicos and the pope] welcome particularly the great advance that their churches have registered in the common search for their unity in Christ, the word of God made flesh. Perfect God, as to his divinity, perfect man, as to His humanity, His divinity is united in Him to His humanity in the Person of the Only-begotten Son of God, in a union which is real, perfect, without confusion, without alteration, without division, without any form of separation." "Common Declaration of John Paul II and Catholicos Karekin I," December 13, 1996, http://www.vatican.va/roman_curia/pontifical_councils/chrstuni/anc-orient-ch-docs/rc_pc_christuni_doc_19961213_jp-ii-karekin-i_en.html.

10. Vigen Guroian, "On the Controversy over the Joint Vatican Declaration," *The Armenian Reporter International* 30, no. 34 (May 24, 1997). Also published as "Fully God and Fully Man—Rome and Armenian Orthodox Settle War of Words," *National Catholic Register* 73, no. 27 (July 6, 1997).

substantial dialogue, leading to a greater degree of mutual understanding and recovery of the commonality of their faith and service.[11]

Eucharistic Ecclesiology versus Universalistic Ecclesiology

Karekin I's journey to Rome is, admittedly, a small chapter in the much larger story of modern ecumenism. Yet his and the pope's reconciliatory speech and their earnestness to resolve differences merit our attention. The catholicos and the pope spoke of "a deep spiritual communion which already unites them and the bishops, clergy and lay faithful of their Churches."[12] This choice of language was deliberate. It reflects the eucharistic ecclesiology (or communion ecclesiology) that the Orthodox churches have favored for some time in ecumenical settings.

Much of the remainder of this chapter explores the nature of this eucharistic ecclesiology and how it contrasts with what some have called universal or universalistic ecclesiology. I then extend this analysis briefly to the question of the primacy of Peter and the possibilities for full communion between the Roman Catholic and the Orthodox churches.

Eucharistic Ecclesiology

Eucharistic ecclesiology situates the unity of the church in the local celebration of the Supper presided over by the bishop, where love binds all who are present through the symbols of the shared gifts of bread and wine and the mystical manifestation of the gathered church as Christ's own body. Paul expressed a similar view of the church in his counsel to the Christians of Corinth who were dividing into contending parties. He impressed on them that "because there is one bread, we who are many are one body, for we all partake of the one bread" (1 Cor. 10:17 RSV). Clearly alluding to the liturgical formula "this is my body," that Christ spoke at the Last Supper, Paul insists, "You are the body of Christ" (1 Cor. 12:27 RSV)

Eucharistic ecclesiology declares that by love (*agape*), the Eucharist brings the church into existence. This is the kind of love about which Paul speaks in 1 Corinthians 13. There he expounds on the meaning of love in his famous

11. "Common Declaration of John Paul II and Catholicos Karekin I," December 13, 1996, http://www.vatican.va/roman_curia/pontifical_councils/chrstuni/anc-orient-ch-docs/rc_pc _christuni_doc_19961213_jp-ii-karekin-i_en.html.

12. "Common Declaration of John Paul II and Catholicos Karekin I," December 13, 1996, http://www.vatican.va/roman_curia/pontifical_councils/chrstuni/anc-orient-ch-docs/rc_pc _christuni_doc_19961213_jp-ii-karekin-i_en.html.

hymn: "Love is patient, love is kind . . ." When contemporary Christians cite this chapter, often they overlook the eucharistic context of the hymn. Three and one-half centuries after Paul recorded this hymn, John Chrysostom remembered this eucharistic context when he spoke of charity as "a sacrament [a mystery]" and exhorted his listeners to "shut your doors, so that no one can see the objects that you could not put on show without giving offence. For our sacraments are above all God's charity and love."[13]

Love is a sacrament. Love is fully revealed in the eucharistic service. It is embodied in the communion of those who have come together to worship Christ for the love of him and of all things. In doing so, the gathered church becomes perfectly identified with Christ's own body. According to eucharistic ecclesiology, the body of Christ can never be divided. The church is one because Christ is one. The real question concerns where communion is whole and where it is weakened or broken.

In 1963 the Russian Orthodox theologian Nicholas Afanasiev published "Una sancta," an essay on Vatican II dedicated to the memory of John XXIII. In it he argues the case for a eucharistic ecclesiology. He writes, "According to eucharistic ecclesiology, when we participate in the eucharistic assembly, we are united with all those who at that moment also participate in eucharistic assemblies—not only those of the orthodox church but also those of the catholic church—for everywhere there is only the one and the same Eucharist being celebrated."[14]

The church's catholicity is not the sum of the parts that make up the whole. Rather, every gathering around the eucharistic table is itself, and in communion with others, a mystical manifestation of the entire church. In this formulation, there is an analogy with the Trinity. The Holy Trinity is constituted of three divine persons, each of whom is not merely part God but wholly God. Gregory of Nyssa once described this perfect co-inherence of the Father, the Son, and the Holy Spirit as "a sort of continuous and indivisible community."[15] Likewise, the universal church is multiplicity in undivided communion.

13. This is Emilianos Timiadis's translation as it appears in his "Restoration and Liberation in and by the Community," *Greek Orthodox Theological Review* 19 (Autumn 1974): 54. See also John Chrysostom, *Homilies on the Gospel of St. Matthew*, in *A Select Library of Nicene and Post-Nicene Fathers of the Christian Church* (Grand Rapids: Eerdmans, 1956), 10:434–35 (homily 71).

14. Nicholas Afanasiev, "*Una sancta*," in *Tradition Alive: On the Church and the Christian Life in Our Time; Readings from the Eastern Church*, ed. Michael Plekon (New York: Rowman & Littlefield, 2003), 24.

15. Gregory of Nyssa, "On the Difference between *Ousia* and *Hypostasis* 1–4," in *Documents in Early Christian Thought*, ed. Maurice Wiles and Mark Santor (Cambridge, UK: Cambridge University Press, 1975), 34.

Universalistic Ecclesiology

Eucharistic ecclesiology sees the church as this communion of love, defined early on by the Apostle Paul and later by John Chrysostom; whereas, universalistic ecclesiology regards the church as a concord of individual parts organized by one principal and head. Universalistic ecclesiology is monarchical. Its conception of the one, holy, catholic, and apostolic church is comparable to a cone in which the local churches form the base. Above them resides the college of bishops, and the apex stands over all. Lines that radiate from the apex (for our purposes this is the pope) connect the apex, or pope, with the bishops and the bishops with the local congregations. Much as a cone without an apex is not a cone, the church without a single head is not the universal church.

The papacy, in its best representations, is by no means *merely* monarchical in its exercise of power over the subordinate parts. Contemporary Orthodoxy does not regard the papacy this way. It argues, however, that the ideology that has supported the claim of papal supremacy is quintessentially an expression of universalistic ecclesiology. The Orthodox churches, as they are presently constituted, however, are liable to a similar characterization. The ecclesiastical heads of these decidedly ethnic autocephalous churches often mimic a monarchical model of rule in their exercise of primacy. While it is not proper to speak of the Patriarch of Moscow as the Russian pope or the Catholicos of All Armenians as the Armenian pope, to one degree or another, persons in such positions within the largely ethnocentric autocephalous churches have exercised primacy in a jurisdictional and magisterial manner that is the earmark of universalistic ecclesiology. Lines become blurred.

Disunity or Broken Communion?

According to eucharistic ecclesiology, what is ordinarily called disunity is, in truth, a breach of fraternal communion—a frustrated and attenuated communion that, owing to sin, is prevented from reaching genuine harmony and oneness. Afanasiev explains, "Modern ecclesial consciousness, orthodox as well as catholic, considers, with few and rare exceptions, the separation of the churches as a pathological state, as a sin against Love."[16]

The title that John Paul II gave to his encyclical, *Ut Unum Sint*, echoes Jesus's prayer: "May [all] be one . . . that the world may believe that You sent Me" (John 17:21). And in the encyclical the pope takes into account the pathological sin that afflicts all parties, divides them, and acutely hampers

16. Afanasiev, "*Una sancta*," 24.

the church's witness to all humankind. Eucharistic love is the remedy for this broken communion. Yet ironically, the divided churches do not celebrate the Eucharist as the one body of Christ in the world. John Paul II exposes this irony and urges all the churches to overcome it through a mutually shared spirit of contrition, love, and forgiveness. He writes, "An imperative of charity is in question, an imperative which admits no exception. Ecumenism is not only an internal question of the Christian Communities. It is a matter of love which God in Jesus Christ has for all of humanity; to stand in the way of this love is an offence against him and his plan to gather all people in Christ."[17]

Over a gulf of thirty years, as if in intimate dialogue with John Paul II, Afanasiev responds, "To think that the annihilation of dogmatic divergences is the condition for the reunion of the churches would be simply to affirm their division. . . . By an effort in Love, the orthodox church *could* reestablish [full] communion with the catholic church, the dogmatic divergences notwithstanding."[18]

The Primacy of Peter in Armenian Liturgy

The personal sins of parties, who in the past issued recriminations, denunciations, and even anathemas against each other, have reified into collective habits and institutional bulwarks. The present moment calls for a form of ecclesial headship that inspires to overcome old divisions and dresses the wounds of sin with love. The present moment also cries out for a form of ecclesial headship that can speak for all Christians. Nevertheless, even Orthodox Christians like myself who believe that the bishop of Rome is in the most propitious and historically justifiable position to meet this need also believe that a reformulation of papal primacy is needed.

Now the case for a supreme papacy is complex, based on a particular reading of Scripture, especially of Matthew 16:18–20, and supported also by historical claims that Peter was bishop of Rome. There is not room here for a broad and extended historical analysis. Instead, I am going to describe briefly the Armenian interpretation of the primacy of Peter as it is ensconced especially in the liturgical practice of that church, keeping in mind that this liturgical interpretation is not a response to how the Roman Catholic Church defines the nature and role of the Roman see but rather that process by which the Armenian Church articulates itself as a church.

17. John Paul II, Ut Unum Sint, May 25, 1995, para. 99, http://w2.vatican.va/content/john -paul-ii/en/encyclicals/documents/hf_jp-ii_enc_25051995_ut-unum-sint.html.
18. Afanasiev, "*Una sancta*," 25.

It is by and through liturgy that the church constitutes itself and interprets what it is and what is its mission. The dialogue in which John Paul II called on the churches to engage one another cannot simply be about how the papacy is understood or understands itself; it must also be about how other churches define themselves as church. If we are going to get beyond the present impasse, it seems to me that this matter must be understood and respected by all parties.

The most relevant Armenian liturgical text belongs to the Feast of the Holy Apostles Peter and Paul, which the Armenian Church celebrates on December 27th. This is an important occasion on which the church remembers the origin of its faith and to what purpose God wants Christians to put that faith. The Gospel reading for this liturgy is John 21:15–22, "Simon, son of John, do you love Me? . . . Follow Me" (vv. 17, 19 RSV). The two epistle readings are from 2 Peter 1:12–19 and 2 Timothy 4:1–8, respectively. "For when he received honor and glory from God the Father . . . we were with him on the holy mountain. And we have the prophetic word made more sure" (2 Pet. 1:17–19 RSV). "For I am already on the point of being sacrificed. . . . I have fought the good fight, . . . I have kept the faith. Henceforth is laid up for me the crown of righteousness" (2 Tim. 4:6–8 RSV).

Matthew 16 is not in the readings. There is no need for it to be because the principle hymn takes up its content.

> Rejoice today at the memory of the Holy Apostles.
> O Church of God,
> founded on the rock of faith,
> adorned for the glory of the Word made flesh.

> The one [Peter] who through the revelation of the Father above
> confessed the existence of the indescribable Only-begotten,
> the renowned rock which is immovable by the gates of Hades.

> The one [Peter] who in earthly nature
> surpassed the assemblies of the fiery, incorporeal ranks
> and ascended to the heavenly tabernacles,
> was made worthy of the Word whom words cannot comprehend.

> You who named the blessed Peter
> to be more eminent than the ranks of the apostles,
> head of the holy faith—
> the foundation of the church.

> You established Your Church, O Christ
> through the two chosen enlighteners of the world.
> Through their intercessions take pity on us.

> You promised to give the keys of the kingdom of heaven
> to blessed Peter,
> who summoned us to the hope of eternal life.
> Through his prayers, save us,
> Lord God of our fathers.[19]

Peter is here given special honor; one might go so far as to say exceptional honor. Other Armenian sources support this approbation. Peter is head (the Armenian word is *glukh*, literally "head of the body") of the faith. He is head because he was the first of the disciples to confess Jesus as "the Christ, the Son of the living God" (Matt. 16:16 RSV) according to Matthew and "the indescribable Only-begotten" according to the hymn.

The twelfth-century Armenian catholicos, Nerses Klayet'i, elaborates: "Most glorious and venerable is the great throne of Peter the *Coryphaius* [head] of the Apostles and of the Church, immovable, built on the Cephaean rock, invincible against the gates of hell and seal of the keys of heaven."[20] Like the hymn, the church, according to Klayet'i, does not name Peter the Cephaean rock. Peter is, rather, "the rock of faith." This rock-solid faith is Christ's gift to the whole church, first exemplified in Peter. Likewise, it is Christ and faith in him, beginning with Peter, that prevails against the gates of Hades and the powers of death. This interpretation is embedded in the Resurrection icon of the Harrowing of Hades in which Christ knocks down Hades's gates on Holy Saturday, holds back the demons with his victorious cross, and draws Adam and Eve and all the fallen and repentant souls from the dark pit of death.

Archbishop Tiran Nersoyan (1904–89), one of the most respected of twentieth-century Armenian clergy, supports this interpretation in a discussion of the hymn. He points out the wordplay in Matthew 16:18: *Petros* (Peter) and *petra* (rock). "You are Peter, and on this rock I will build my church" (RSV). He argues that the sentence is "an ellipsis."[21] A sentence that is elliptical lacks a word or words that would complete its meaning. In this case, the metaphorical play on the Greek words *Petros* and *petra* needs clarification.

This clarification reduces to two possibilities according to Nersoyan. The first is that *petra* (rock) refers back reflexively to *Petros* (Peter), meaning that on Peter's steadfast personality, which is defined by his faith, God founds the church. The second is that Christ gives Simon, Son of John, the name *Petros*

---

19. Altered from an unpublished translation with no translator listed.
20. Cited by Tiran Nersoyan, *Armenian Church Historical Studies: Matters of Doctrine and Administration* (New York: St. Vartan Press, 1996), 206.
21. Nersoyan, *Armenian Church Historical Studies*, 203.

because of his confession of faith, and on the foundation of this rocklike faith, first seen in Peter, the church is secure.

Nersoyan judges that the first interpretation is questionable, although it has been well argued by apologists for the papacy. Nersoyan deems the second way of completing the structure and meaning of Matthew's sentence to be the more plausible. According to this second way, Peter's character is his alone. His preeminence among the apostles is relational and does not apply to the foundation or organization of the church in its extended institutional existence. The moment of New Testament record has long since passed when Peter alone made the confession and gave his life for it, sealing its truth with his freely given blood. The faith that Peter exhibited became the faith of all the apostles, as witnessed by Scripture, and in and by that faith all became founders of the universal church. Peter "was *chief* among the Apostles," but not chief "*over* the Apostles."[22] "In the Eastern view," concludes Nersoyan, "all the bishops who have the faith of Peter are the successors of Peter together with the other Apostles. All of them inherit the same faith and no one bishop could be considered the sole guardian of the Christian tradition."[23]

The fourth-century Armenian catechism *The Teaching of St. Gregory* refers to St. Gregory the Enlightener (ca. 240–332), the founder of the Armenian Church, and understands Matthew 16 according to the second of Nersoyan's interpretations. It also states, without equivocation, that the keys of the kingdom belong not just to Peter but to all the apostles. The catechism states, "And He [Christ] made him [Peter] the rock of establishment of all of the churches [Matt. 16:18; John 1:42]. And the apostles became the foundations [Eph. 2:20], and received the grace of priesthood, and prophecy and apostleship and the knowledge of the heavenly mystery. . . . And He [God] gave the keys of the kingdom into their hands [Matt. 16:19; 18:18], for the Son of God Himself was the gate for those who enter [John 10:7, 9]."[24]

Thus this primary text of the Armenian tradition interprets Matthew 16:18 in light of Matthew 18:18 in which Christ, who is addressing the disciples at Capernaum, declares, "Truly, I say to you, whatever you bind on earth shall be bound in heaven, and whatever you loose on earth shall be loosed in heaven" (RSV). As leader of the disciples, Peter surely had a special authority among the others. But as his confession of faith is ultimately attributable to all the apostles, the powers of teaching, the sacraments, and leadership also equally belong to them and to their successors in the universal episcopacy.

22. Nersoyan, *Armenian Church Historical Studies*, 204.
23. Nersoyan, *Armenian Church Historical Studies*, 205.
24. *The Teaching of St. Gregory: An Early Armenian Catechism*, trans. Robert W. Thomson (Cambridge, MA: Harvard University Press, 1970), 105–6, para. 467, 468.

However we interpret these texts, there is little room to doubt that within the Armenian tradition a primacy of honor is attributed to "the great throne of Peter." In this vein, I will cite one final text, some portions of a homily for the Feast of Peter and Paul contained in the Armenian *Synaxarion* of Grigor Vardapet Khlatetsi (d. 1425). It stands without commentary as segue to my closing remarks.

> We are saved . . . with the help of the rock of faith, the holy Apostle Peter, who confessed that the Son is of the nature of the Father. This Peter, who was pronounced blessed by Christ and became guarantor of the grace of blessedness; Peter, who was named Rock and was set for the foundation of the Church, Peter, who received power from Christ not to be overcome by the gates of hell; Peter, who was a fisherman and the key of the gates of heaven, Peter who was the ignorant and the wise; Peter, who was the stupid and the deep philosopher . . . ; Peter, who for his love of the Teacher was entrusted with pasturing His flock.[25]

Conclusion: The Primacy of the Bishop of Rome

Alexander Schmemann once wrote, and with great wisdom it seems to me, "The ecclesiological error of Rome lies not in the affirmation of her universal primacy. Rather, the error lies in the identification of this primacy with 'supreme power' which transforms Rome into the *principium radix et orgio* of the unity of the Church and of the Church herself."[26] There is no objection—indeed, there would seem to be a strong consensual affirmation within the Armenian tradition—that the Roman see ascended to universal primacy of honor and relationship to the rest of the church at a relatively early date and that this *primus inter pares* (first among equals) was widely recognized and may still be not only desirable for the good of all but "necessary" to the success of the mission of the church in our day.

In his seminal essay "The Church which Presides in Love," Afanasiev cites Ignatius of Antioch's famous greeting in his letter to the church of Rome: "Ignatius also named Theophoros, to the church which presides in the land of the Romans . . . which presides in (the) Charity (*agape*)." Again, Afanasiev reminds us that Ignatius's use of *agape* is eucharistic and that the phrase "which presides" is in the masculine form in the Greek and clearly means the bishop.

25. Abraham Terian, "Peter, Paul and Related Accounts in the Earliest Edition of the Armenian Synaxarion," *St. Nersess Theological Review* 5–6 (2000–2001): 9, 10.

26. Alexander Schmemann, "The Idea of Primacy in Orthodox Ecclesiology," in *The Primacy of Peter: Essays in Ecclesiology and the Early Church*, ed. John Meyendorff (Crestwood, NY: St. Vladimir's Seminary Press, 1992), 163.

"Each local church" with the bishop as its head, "is the Catholic Church and so manifests the Church of God in Christ."[27] Empirically, however, there may be among the churches, all of which are one body under the symbols of the bread and wine, one bishop who presides in love over all and represents, for all, the unity that they eucharistically share. Afanasiev prefers to call this act of presiding in love *priority*, not primacy. He does so because primacy in its historical accretions suggests juridical and magisterial governance and is an earmark of universalistic ecclesiology. However, "priority implies that every local church has fullness of ecclesial *esse*."[28] Not hierarchy or power but communion and equality are the essence of the church.

Aram I, Armenian Catholicos of the Great House of Cilicia, who has been prominent in the Word Council of Churches, distinguishes between several forms of primacy. There is the magisterial primacy to which Afanasiev rightly objects. But there is a primacy of honor to which the bishop of Rome, above all others, might be entitled. In his essay "The First Vatican Council and the Petrine Office," Aram I argues that in order for it to effectively lead in bringing church unity, "the Petrine office needs to be reinterpreted on pastoral rather than in juridical terms. It has to be conceived as a primacy of ministry (*primates pastoralis*) and service (*primates servitii*) and not authority."[29]

I have always thought that over the full course of his reign John Paul II was carefully redefining the papacy along these very lines. In *Ut Unum Sint*, he took up all the themes Aram I brings forward. He reiterated his declaration, first made in 1985, that the ecumenical task was "one of the pastoral priorities" of his pontificate. In the expression of Gregory the Great, he declared that his ministry was "that of *servus servorum Dei*" (para. 88). John Paul II offered himself in service as a bishop of Rome, willing to preside "in truth and love" (para. 97). He also went on to state that it was his responsibility to "continue in the Church . . . [as] her sole Head." As such, the bishop of Rome has authority to speak for the whole church while also respecting the authority of other primacies within their local churches, the same as Peter respected "the authority of James, the head of Jerusalem" (para. 97).[30]

To all these statements I believe my church could agree. Even to the last stipulation of authority, so long as it is understood in relational terms—that is, in terms of the pope's equality of relation as primate or bishop of Rome

27. Nicholas Afanasiev, "The Church Which Presides in Love," in Meyendorff, *Primacy of Peter*, 126.
28. Afanasiev, "Church Which Presides in Love," 142.
29. Catholicos Aram I Keshishian, *Orthodox Perspectives on Mission*, ed. Petros Vassiliadis (Oxford, UK: Regnum Books, 2013), 76.
30. John Paul II, *Ut Unum Sint*.

to the other local primacies, which, joined in communion, are the one, holy, catholic, and apostolic church over which he presides. More discussion and clarification is called for, however, about what "sole Head" of the church means, and more important, on what grounds the bishop of Rome has claim to this headship. Is this principally a right as a matter of succession from Peter, or is it a duty of love? Must it include the power of the bishop of Rome to speak *ex cathedra* (from the chair) not just for his own church but also for all of the churches?

In "*Una sancta*," Afanasiev proposes the following: "It should be clear after a series of less than fruitful attempts to bring back different confessions—orthodoxy above all—to the catholic church, such an objective is unattainable" under the presently prescribed conditions. "If, due to the sacrificial spirit of Love of the bishop of Rome, [however], the union-of-the-churches-joined-by Love were to be re-established, the church of Rome would be able to occupy in this union of the multiplicity of churches the same place she had in ancient time."[31]

In broad terms, what Afanasiev suggests is that the papacy not insist on imposing its magisterial authority, as defined by the Council of Trent and the First Vatican Council, over the other churches; and that the churches, in turn, not insist, as a condition for full communion, that the Roman Catholic Church revoke doctrines pertaining to the papacy and its governance over the Roman Catholic Church. But it does seem to me that this needn't and really shouldn't exclude a form of primacy and headship that is reflective of an ongoing consent of all other local primacies. John Zizioulas has described this as a primacy "exercised in *synodical context*. . . . [The bishop of Rome] would be the President of all the heads of churches and spokesman of the entire Church once the decisions announced are the result of consensus."[32]

Zizioulas's proposal reflects a view common in Orthodoxy of the pastoral and "presidential" or "presiding" role that the bishop of Rome played through

31. Afanasiev, "*Una sancta*," 27.

32. John D. Zizioulas, "Primacy in the Church: An Orthodox Approach," in *Petrine Ministry and the Unity of the Church*, ed. James F. Puglisi (Collegeville, MN: Liturgical Press, 1999), 125; as cited in Radu Bordeianu, "Primacies and Primacy According to John Zizioulas," *St. Vladimir's Quarterly Review* 58, no. 1 (2014): 19. I have not here discussed the issue of power. A presidential function in any real sense must include, in some measure, an exercise of power. Let me add that the issue of primacy cannot be discussed abstractly. Over their long histories, both the bishop of Constantinople and the bishop of Moscow have claimed that they inherited primacy above all others as the authority of the bishop of Rome was transferred to them when the center of Roman political power moved to the East. In any future agreement, a return of such authority to Rome as it once had, would require concessions to claims for primacy that Constantinople and Moscow in the past have not made. Likewise, "ranking" and roles of other Eastern bishops would need to be settled and agreed on.

the first millennium. However, it is not how the Roman Catholic Church has traditionally interpreted the matter. And yet we do have John Paul II's words in *Ut Unum Sint* that line up with such an interpretation. Would that the present pope, Pope Francis, could accept a title such as "Patriarch of the West," thereby strongly indicating a parity of the bishop of Rome with the patriarchs of the East.

When Pope Francis journeyed on pilgrimage to Jerusalem in May 2014 to meet with Patriarch Bartholomew, this was a significant gesture, but it was not in itself a concession to patriarchal parity. I believe that Francis made an even more powerful symbolic gesture at the time of his inauguration in March 2013. At the start of a private audience with Orthodox hierarchs, Francis stepped down from his throne and greeted the assemblage as "bishop of Rome," thus symbolizing a parity with the Orthodox bishops. Realistically, that is about as far as a pope can go to acknowledge parity, short of having the full weight of the Roman Catholic Church behind him. It is significant that in the week following his appointment, Pope Francis repeatedly identified himself as "bishop of Rome." And he reiterated Pope John Paul II's pronouncement that the person in his office must preside in charity and insisted in various company that the power of the papacy is the "power of service" as seen in Jesus's charge to Peter: "Feed my lambs. Feed my sheep" (John 21:15–19).[33]

These kinds of humble, genuinely kenotic papal gestures are what could enable the Armenian Church (and other Orthodox churches) to enter into full communion with Rome. These gestures must come from Rome, for in reality it is in the position of greatest authority with the greatest power. Yet even if the bishop of Rome proffers such humble gestures, there is no guarantee that the Orthodox churches will engage Rome in a reciprocal spirit of charity and humility. Sin of the collective and habitual sort is stubborn and not easily overcome. Nationalistic and particularistic proclivities, the desire to cling to power, and false pride and defensiveness can at any moment, and over the long haul, overwhelm all the good reasons for Orthodox churches to accept the pope's fraternal invitation. I am by nature a pessimist. I am by faith, however, an optimist. With God, all things *are* possible.

---

33. Cindy Wooden, "Table Time: Pope Discusses, Prays, Dines with Orthodox Representatives," *Catholic News Service*, March 21, 2013, http://www.catholicnews.com/services/english news/2013/table-time-pope-discusses-prays-dines-with-orthodox-representatives.cfm.

8

Love That Is Divine and Human

This chapter is in a somewhat different key from the two that precede it, although the theme of love that emerges so strongly in chapter 7 continues here in depth. Church unity is not a mechanical or bureaucratic "thing." Rather, first and foremost, unity is grounded in a love that is both divine and human. Here I explore the theological and ethical dimensions of Christian love. In other words, what the meaning of love is, what divine love is, how human love is an image of and participation in God's love. And, finally, how love that is divine and human unites humanity in a life-giving communion of being.

Love is personal and that which is personal is communal. God, the Holy Trinity, is perfect love. As Gregory of Nyssa observes, the Holy Trinity "is a sort of continuous and indivisible community,"[1] a perfect communion of the Father, the Son, and the Holy Spirit in which each gives love freely and perfectly to the others and each receives love in the same measure from the others so that the three are not several gods but three divine Persons (*hypostases*), one Being (*ousia*), one God (*theos*). The Father is the *arche*, the eternal originator of the triune Godhead and the love that unites them. From

---

An earlier version of this chapter originally appeared as "The Humanity of Divine Love: The Divinity of Human Love," in *Divine Love: Perspectives from the World's Religious Traditions*, ed. Jeff Levin and Stephen G. Post, 201–18 (West Conshohocken, PA: Templeton, 2010). Used by permission.

1. Gregory of Nyssa, "On the Difference between *Ousia* and *Hypostasis* 1–4," in *Documents in Early Christian Thought*, ed. Maurice Wiles and Mark Santor (Cambridge, UK: Cambridge University Press, 1975), 34. Although traditionally included among the letters of Basil, this work is now generally attributed to Gregory of Nyssa.

the ground of his absolute freedom and infinity the Father in an eternal act of love begets the Son and breathes forth (processes) the Holy Spirit, and the Father communicates in and through his love the divinity that is common to the Trinity. It is the Father, writes the twentieth-century Russian theologian Vladimir Lossky, "that distinguishes the hypostases 'in an eternal movement of love.'"[2] The Son, in whom the Father eternally forgets himself as his very own image, offers himself back to the Father in a sacrificial act of love that is for the salvation of the world and through this sacrifice also glorifies the Father. The Son sends the Spirit, who eternally processes as the life-giving "breath" of the Father into the world in a perfectly hidden and self-eclipsing manner in order to impart the gift of the knowledge of salvation and to sanctify all so that they may become participants in the divine life (2 Pet. 1:3–4).

The Personal Nature of Love

Love is freely given or it is not love at all. Love issues from persons, whether these persons are uncreated, as are the divine Persons of the Holy Trinity, or created, as are the multitude of human beings. "Personhood," writes Lossky, "is freedom in relation to nature."[3] Persons enact their own nature. Natures may be *what* they are (e.g., human, angelic, or divine), but the nature does not determine *who* these persons are. "A personal being," Lossky continues, "is capable of loving someone more than his own nature, more than his own life."[4] Freedom and love are thus the cardinal attributes of personhood. This freedom to enter into loving communion with others, this personhood, is the image of God in human beings. Personhood thrives and is perfected through mutual reciprocity, more still in and through communion. This deep reciprocity and intercourse of communion is not mere sociality. Human beings together with much of the rest of the animal kingdom exhibit sociality among their own kind. But sociality may be determinate, governed by the animal nature. Sociality need not entail freedom or love, whereas communion does.[5]

Among human beings, love appears to spring from feelings and emotions. Thus some mistakenly characterize love as irrational. But love transcends feeling

2. Vladimir Lossky, *The Mystical Theology of the Eastern Church* (Cambridge, UK: James Clark, 1975), 60.

3. Vladimir Lossky, *Orthodox Theology: An Introduction* (Crestwood, NY: St. Vladimir's Seminary Press, 1978), 42.

4. Lossky, *Orthodox Theology*, 72.

5. I have spoken of this already in chap. 1. Let me add that I have been a beekeeper, and I marvel at the complicated social organization of the beehive. It is accurate to say that bees have a society. Nonetheless, it is false to attribute communion to a beehive.

and reason. Love is not rationally justified nor is it just a "natural" affection. At its source, love is a divine reality. Love, as I have stated, is rooted in freedom, in the absolute freedom of God and, next, in the relative freedom of the creature.

"In perfect love persons do not merely engage in a reciprocal exchange of self," writes Romanian theologian Dumitru Staniloae. "They also affirm themselves reciprocally and personally and establish themselves in existence through giving and receiving."[6] Love that is at once wholly self-donative and perfectly reciprocal is divine. The love that is communicated between the Father, the Son, and the Holy Spirit, however, is not merely shared as between three individuals but binds an indissoluble triunity in which there is no "distance" between the three divine Persons, a perfect co-inherence and interpenetration of personal life as one being. The *telos* of love is union minus extinction of relation, complete intimacy without compromise of integrity.

Love within the Godhead is perfectly efficacious. In other words, within the Godhead, freedom and love and love given and love reciprocated are commensurate. Nor in the mutuality that the Persons share is there pause, interlude of expectation, distance, or diminishment of personal integrity either for lack of reciprocation or reason of self-absorption. The Father, the Son, and the Holy Spirit are one and yet "other" to one another. Within the Godhead, love that is virtue and love that is self-gift are one. This perfect love, this co-inherence in one another, is the *unity* of the Father and the Son and the Holy Spirit.

Communion is the ideal milieu of personal existence. Rather than reducing multiplicity and diversity to uniformity and sameness, it is the blossoming of multiplicity and diversity within an unreservedly and uninterruptedly shared life.

Human existence is similar to divine existence in that it is personal. Yet, even if we discount the divisive effects of sin, we must take into account that human beings are individuated physically and psychologically and are subject to biological death. Within human existence, there is a certain order and sequence of freedom and love, love gifted and love reciprocated. Love's movement is modified by expectation and waiting on reciprocation, which may or may not be forthcoming. Even when communion is joined, it lacks the uninterrupted immediacy of the relation of the Father, the Son, and the Holy Spirit. Love and communion are attendant to finitude within a spatiotemporal world. Human beings are always threatened by death. Nonetheless, human beings are capable of giving love without expectation of return, even in the face of the mortality that threatens to shatter communion. Human love and communion approximate divinity, but they also await salvation.

6. Dumitru Staniloae, *Orthodox Dogmatic Theology: The Experience of God*, trans. Ioan Ionita and Robert Barringer (Brookline, MA: Holy Cross Orthodox Press, 1994), 1:257.

Communion and Salvation

In a fallen and sinful world, love and communion are expectant on salvation. More than this, the imperfect communion that love achieves in such a world is an intimation of salvation, for there is no such thing as solitary salvation. The salvation and *theosis* (deification) of the human person is the process by which God graciously narrows the "gap" between freedom's movement and love's substantiation as communion. The Son brings the love of the Father into this world, and the Holy Spirit inspires this love and spreads it among all who believe in the Son. The gift of the Holy Spirit reduces not only the gap that sin and death have brought about between God and humanity but also remedies the division of humanity into selves who are existentially alienated from one another and die spiritually for want of love. The communion of the saints is the approximation of the triune life of God.

The gift of the Holy Spirit transfigures human persons through a holy communion. This is the meaning and aim of the prayer of *epiclesis*[7] in Orthodox liturgy. This prayer invokes and petitions the Holy Spirit not only to reveal the elements of the bread and wine as the body and blood of Christ but also to bring all who participate in the liturgy within a bond of love and togetherness. Thus, for example, the hymn of the Kiss of Peace in the Armenian Orthodox rite announces, "Christ in our midst is revealed; / . . . The Church has now become one soul, / The kiss is given for a full bond. / The enmity has been removed; / And love is spread over us all."[8]

Furthermore, absolute love, the love of the triune God, is ecstatic and effluent. It is an unceasing outgoing of the "self" to meet and embrace the other and give life to the other, joyfully affirming and uniting with the other. The character of God is not a necessary outcome of the divine nature—for if we must attribute a "nature" to God, this "nature" is the love itself of which we speak—but rather, as I have said, this character is grounded in God's absolute freedom. God the Father loves humankind no differently than he loves the Son and the Holy Spirit, as he draws us into the perfect communion of the divine life, all the while respectful of our creaturely freedom. Love "is the same and universal," writes Maximus the Confessor (d. 662). By and through love, God and humans come together in a single embrace. By and

---

7. The *epiclesis* in Orthodox rites is the invocation of the Holy Spirit over the elements of the bread and the wine not merely so that they are revealed as the body and blood of Christ but to bring about communion. The Armenian prayer of *epiclesis* states, "We bow down and beseech and ask thee, beneficent God, send upon us and upon these gifts set forth, thy co-eternal Holy Spirit." *The Divine Liturgy of the Armenian Apostolic Orthodox Church*, trans. Tiran Nersoyan (London: St. Sarkis Church, 1984), 79.

8. *Divine Liturgy*, 71.

through his Incarnation, the Son has consummated this "embrace." In him, divinity and humanity are joined forever so that we need not assign "one form of love to God and another to human beings."[9] Christ reveals that the norm of humanity is quite simply love, God himself.

God Is Love

John the apostle writes that "God is love" (1 John 4:8). But in this instance, he is not speaking of the divinity in general. He has in mind God the Father "who sent his Son" (1 John 4:14)—the Father whom "no one has seen" (1 John 4:20) and who "has given us of His Spirit" (1 John 4:13). This aligns with the church's teaching that the Father is the *arche* or "source" of the Godhead. God, the Father, however, is never alone Godself. To echo Greek Orthodox theologian John Zizioulas, it also is perfectly appropriate to say, "God is Love signifies that God subsists as Trinity."[10] There was never a time when the Trinity was not.

Love that is not shared is not love at all. A god who is a simple monad is neither person nor love. "Love, as God's mode of existence, 'hypostatizes' God"—that is, makes God person—"constitutes His being," Zizioulas continues. Love is God's eternal mode of existence. His existence as love and person are not contingent on creation. Love is not a quality, property, or characteristic of a simple divine substance but is, rather, "that which makes God who God is, the one God," who is three Persons in perfect union and communion. Love is *the supreme ontological predicate*."[11] It transcends all other forms of predication. Love is the absolute. God = Love. Love = God. In so much as human beings love, they grow into the likeness of God and they enter into communion with others.

The Trinitarian Structure of Love

As we already have seen, the structure of love is trinitarian. Even the love that two share is incomplete and imperfect. Even the most self-giving and self-communicating relation between two is inherently egocentric, limited in its horizons, and subject always to the erotic fixation of each on the other, an "absorption . . . [in] a mutual love that is indifferent towards the presence

9. Maximus the Confessor, "Letter 2: On Love," in *Maximus the Confessor*, ed. Andrew Louth, Early Church Fathers series (London: Routledge, 1996), 90.

10. John Zizioulas, *Being as Communion* (Crestwood, NY: St. Vladimir's Seminary Press, 1985), 46. Much of this discussion is drawn from Zizioulas.

11. Zizioulas, *Being as Communion*, 46.

of any other,"[12] Staniloae writes. He continues, "Communion between two does not open up an unlimited horizon" such as befits an infinite God. "A third enlarges the dimension of existence to in principle include all that can exist."[13]

Family as Image of Trinity

The Trinity exceeds our comprehension. The knowledge that divine revelation gives us of this mystery, however, opens to us a deeper understanding of God and love than might otherwise be possible. In his Letter to the Ephesians, Paul writes, "I bow my knees to the Father of our Lord Jesus Christ, from whom the whole family in heaven and earth is named, that He would grant you, according to the riches of his glory, . . . to know the love of Christ which passes knowledge; that you may be filled with all the fullness of God" (Eph. 3:14–16, 19). According to Paul, God the Father is the head of a single family—another way of saying communion—of whom Jesus Christ, the only begotten Son of the Father, "is the firstborn over all creation" (Col. 1:15). Reflecting on this Scripture, Dionysius the Areopagite (Pseudo-Dionysius, 6th c.) observes that "all fatherhood and all sonship are gifts bestowed by that supreme source of [divine] Fatherhood and Sonship on us."[14] Staniloae adds, "Only a God who is Father and Son explains the whole reality of earthly paternity and sonship. . . . The warmth of differentiated human relationships derives from the existence of a God who is no stranger to the affection of such relationships."[15]

The "fullness of God" that Paul invokes is trinitarian. It includes not only the Father and the Son but also the Holy Spirit. The entirety of Paul's writings justifies our saying so, even though he does not refer explicitly to the Spirit in the Ephesians passage. God would not be full and God would not be love without the Spirit. The Spirit is the third that completes the love bond of the Trinity. This third, however, is not reducible to a number within a sequence. The Trinity transcends counting and enumeration. Three is a symbol of ontological fullness, personal existence, and communion.

12. Dumitru Staniloae, *Theology and the Church*, trans. Robert Barringer (Crestwood, NY: St. Vladimir's Seminary Press, 1980), 93. This belongs to an original (or first) version of a chapter titled, "Holy Trinity: Structure of Supreme Love," revised for publication in vol. 1 of *Orthodox Dogmatic Theology: Experience of God*, such that this passage has been expurgated.
13. Staniloae, *Theology and the Church*, 93.
14. "The Divine Names," in *Pseudo-Dionysius: The Complete Works*, trans. Colm Luibheid, 47–132, Classics of Western Spirituality series (Mahwah, NJ: Paulist Press, 1987), here 64 (chap. 2, para. 8).
15. Staniloae, *Orthodox Dogmatic Theology*, 1:246.

Human love "finds its explanation in the fact that we are created in the image of the Holy Trinity, the origin of our love."[16] And within the Christian tradition this insight has directed theological eyes to marriage, and the family that marriage produces. God has inscribed the trinitarian structure of love on marriage and the family. Biblically speaking, the family is a community of the man (husband), the woman (wife), and the child (son or daughter) born of the love of husband and wife, attendant on the sexual nature and generative powers of male and female. Here then is the primordial three that mysteriously comprise the *imago Dei*. As the book of Genesis states, God "created man in his own image; in the image of God he created him; male and female he created them. Then God blessed them, and God said to them, 'Be fruitful and multiply'" (Gen. 1:27–28).

Marital Love as Model of Trinitarian Love

In the fourth century, John Chrysostom drew an important analogy between the marital bond and the unitive power of love in its trinitarian form. He described how love and being are the same in God and that within humankind we find an approximation of this. God, observes Chrysostom, created humankind male and female and providentially made their "fleshly" love union (with its procreative power) a manifestation of the mystery of God's own triune being.

In his homily on Colossians 4:18, Chrysostom poses the rhetorical question, "How is marriage a mystery?" And he answers, "The two have become one." He adds, "This is not an empty symbol. They have not become the image of anything on earth, but of God Himself. . . . They come to be made into one body. See the mystery of love."[17] Chrysostom, however, immediately points out that the human nature that male and female share in common does not in and of itself secure the trinitarian character of their sexual and procreative union. In all the animal species, males and females share a common nature, yet God does not call them or their union his image.[18] Something more is needed, and that something is the love that draws persons into communion.

In his homily on Ephesians 5:22–33, Chrysostom urges, "A man should love his spouse as much as he loves himself, not merely because they share the same nature; no, the obligation is far greater because there are no longer two bodies, but one. . . . I say that husband and wife are one body in the same way

16. Staniloae, *Orthodox Dogmatic Theology*, 1:245.
17. *St. John Chrysostom on Marriage and Family Life*, trans. Catherine P. Roth and David Anderson (Crestwood, NY: St. Vladimir's Seminary Press, 1986), 75 (homily 12 on Col. 4:18).
18. I want to add here that my statement, which for rhetorical reasons may lack nuance, does not discount that traces of the image of God and personality are present in other animal species.

as Christ and the Father are one."[19] In turn, the child that the lovemaking of husband and wife engenders is not just a visible sign of their one-flesh union but is their very flesh, the same nature as themselves. He likens the child to "a bridge connecting mother to father . . . [and] the bridge is formed from the substance of each." He continues, "That is why Scripture does not say, 'they shall be one flesh,' but that they shall be joined together 'into one flesh,' namely the child."[20] The three by virtue of not just the flesh but also of their love for one another constitute an image, an icon, of the Trinity. For this reason, as well, marriage is the preeminent sacrament of love.

Last, Chrysostom wisely does not identify the child with the Holy Spirit.[21] He does not advance the argument so often voiced, especially by later Western writers, that the Holy Spirit is the love shared between the Father and the Son. He is primarily interested in exploring the analogy of marriage with the divine triune love communion. Counting or designating numbers to the persons of the Trinity can mislead, and so the same can be said of the human family. The father or the mother can just as easily be counted as the third within the fluid communion of father, mother, and child. The child, who is a third for husband and wife in their mutual love, becomes a second for each in his or her relationship with the child. In this relationship, each spouse may experience the other as third whose love is born and reflected in the child. But the child also may experience mother or father as third in whom his love for him (or her) is perfected by the love he (or she) has for the other spouse (parent). The *imago Dei* is love as love can only be in its perfection, love perfectly shared, love unselfishly given and unselfishly reciprocated. Yet such unselfish love, given and received, is never mere exchange but rather gift of shared love, indivisible love that reaches to embrace yet another and another in communion.

Sin and Sacrifice

The Sinful Self

Human beings are individuated; God is not. This individuation, by reason of material and psychological existence, however, does not, in and of itself, frustrate the full blossoming of love. Rather, sin is the hindrance. Sin grows like a weed in the soil of personal existence, and the fruit of sin is the "detestable self." All the great ascetics of the Christian faith argue that this weed

19. *Chrysostom on Marriage and Family*, 52 (homily 20 on Eph. 5:22–33).
20. *Chrysostom on Marriage and Family*, 76 (homily 12 on Col. 4:18).
21. I have made this mistake in my book, *Incarnate Love: Essays in Orthodox Ethics*, 2nd ed. (Notre Dame, IN: University of Notre Dame Press, 2002), 30.

must be pulled and the sinful self be put to "death" in order that the image of God may grow in its place. The sinful self is distinguished by a "self-will" that sets up the individual as a small "god" that asserts itself over and against other selves, as it seeks to possess what it desires. Of course, sin also afflicts the family, so even this "icon" of divine communion becomes tarnished.

"In the creaturely, sinful world," writes Russian theologian Sergius Bulgakov, "love for one's own, that is, in essence love for oneself, acquires the character of self-love and prejudice in virtue of which this 'one's own' is prized not as its essential and true worth, but precisely as one's own." Bulgakov continues, "This is the egotistical admiration of one's own image."[22] Such self-love is the ruination of marriage and family.

Adam's first act earned divine condemnation not because he behaved in a self-determining manner. Rather, Adam and Eve chose to make themselves (i.e., self-gratification) the sole end of their self-determination. This transmuted their natural individuality into an instrument and expressivity of a newly born self-will or autonomous self, the self that makes itself its own law and is moved by a love of self to the exclusion rather than inclusion of others, most especially God.

"Self-love . . . separates[s] men from one another," writes Maximus the Confessor, "and splits the single nature (of those endowed with a single nature) into many parts."[23] Love corrupted into selfishness (or self-centeredness) shatters the unity of a single nature from which grows genuine communion. The biblical fall brings about the ruin of the original *imago Dei*. Henceforth, men and women are moved by an egocentric (self-possessive and self-assertive) principle that alienates the male from the female (Gen. 3) and pits brother against brother (Gen. 4). This principle spreads so that the human environment is charged with a contention of wills, alienation, and conflict of every sort.

Vocation and Self-Sacrifice

"Sacrifice is the most natural act of man,"[24] argues Alexander Schmemann. The "religious" vocation to which God has called every human being is priestly in character. We are to receive creation from God as the "food" of communion with God and return it to God as our very "body" with love and thanksgiving

22. Sergius Bulgakov, *The Lamb of God*, trans. Boris Jakim (Grand Rapids: Eerdmans, 2008), 105.

23. Maximus the Confessor, "Contemplative and Active Texts," in *Early Fathers from the Philokalia*, ed. R. Kadloubovsky and G. E. H. Palmer (London: Faber & Faber, 1954), 365.

24. Alexander Schmemann, *For the Life of the World* (Crestwood, NY: St. Vladimir's Seminary Press, 1973), 35.

(Rom. 12:1–2). In Adam, humankind has rejected this priestly vocation of sacrifice or, as the Orthodox Eucharist liturgies describe such sacrifice, rendering up "Holy things to the Holy." Instead, sacrifice in a fallen world has become of necessity self-sacrifice or in other words "the rejection of all selfishness in the very form of sin."[25] In paraphrasing Cyril of Alexandria, Staniloae states, "Wherever sin exists there no pure sacrifice is found."[26] Christ is the sole human being in whom sin is not found. Only his sacrifice is pure and completely efficacious for restoring complete communion with God. Christ reclaims and fulfills in his person the vocation that God gave to humankind at creation. The incarnation is the revelation that perfect human love is sacrificial, is sacrifice. Christ obediently, lovingly, and selflessly gives himself over to the Father even as he is put to death. He was destined to do this from all eternity. He is "the Lamb slain from the foundation of the world" (Rev. 13:8) and also "our High Priest who has passed through the heavens" (Heb. 4:14).

Moreover, Christ reveals to us that the love that is sacrifice and the love that seeks communion are not two loves but the same love. In baptism, new Christians gives themselves over to the Father as they allow their sinful selves to be put to death in order that Christ's pure self is born within them. In Orthodox worship, chrismation and first communion follow immediately after baptism in one continuous sacramental action. The gift of the Spirit, symbolized by anointing with oil, is freedom from the hold of sin that imprisons the self within itself. "Now the Lord is Spirit; and where the Spirit of the Lord is, there is liberty" (2 Cor. 3:17). This liberty is the "law of Christ" (Gal. 6:2). It is the image of God restored in the person. It is the person once again "rooted and grounded in love" (Eph. 3:17). It is the liberty—as love and freedom are the same in God—that enables persons to enter into communion with one another without the hindrance of the self that was born of sin. Yet baptism is not merely a sacrament of repentance and cleansing; it is also a sacrament of illumination, liberation, love, and communion. Paul, in speaking of baptism, writes that love "binds everything together in perfect harmony . . . in the one body" (Col. 3:14–15 RSV).

Thus through the incarnation, God and humanity are reconciled and communion is restored not according to a substitutionary formula or measure of infinite satisfaction for sin in God's mind but by the power of divine love, first in Christ the God-man and second in the creature. The love of God in Christ moves the human being to turn toward God (*metanoia*, or conversion) and then toward others in a manner that reflects that love of the Trinity in

---

25. Staniloae, *Theology and the Church*, 195.
26. Staniloae, *Theology and the Church*, 195.

which each divine person freely and fully turns to the others to form a perfect communion.

Incarnate Love: A Different Reading of the Parable of the Good Samaritan

Jesus's parable of the Good Samaritan (Luke 10:25–37) has often been a touchstone for reflection on the meanings of divine and human love. And to that end, I would like to turn to it briefly. I propose a reading, however, that differs from standard interpretations of Christian neighbor-love and the agape that modern Protestant theology, in particular, has espoused. According to this theology, Christian love is, preeminently, self-sacrificial love, so-called agapic love, that ideally is not motivated by the expectation of reciprocation. It is argued that the Good Samaritan story illustrates precisely such a pure benevolence that affirms the other person's humanity without prejudgment or precondition.

Let me begin by conceding, for the sake of discussion, that the Samaritan does respond to the plight of the wounded traveler from a profoundly disinterested regard for him as a fellow human being. Nonetheless, it is a mistake to restrict the intention or the meaning of the Samaritan's act to this alone. Luke states that the Samaritan "had compassion" (*splanchnizomai*) for the traveler (v. 33). This compassion is a basic, viscerally human response of pity or mercy toward another who suffers and is helpless. Empathy and compassion are necessary preconditions for human community. They pave a "natural" path to agape, though even my use of *agape* here is broader than benevolence or self-sacrificial love.

Luke introduces the story of the Good Samaritan with the question a certain lawyer asks: "Teacher, what shall I do to inherit eternal life?" (v. 25). Jesus turns the question back to the lawyer, who responds that the law says you are to "'Love the LORD your God with all your heart, with all your soul, with all your strength, and with all your mind,' and 'your neighbor as yourself'" (v. 27). Then the lawyer inquires, "And who is my neighbor?" (v. 29).

Despite the fact that it is often assumed (or claimed) that the neighbor in this story is the wounded traveler, this is not what Luke is reporting. Rather, he lets us know that the Samaritan has made *himself* a neighbor to the wounded man (vv. 36–37). This is no small difference. On the one hand, if the wounded traveler is the neighbor, he has become so by the Samaritan's unilateral action and remains a passive recipient of the Samaritan's kindness. But, on the other hand, if by his gesture of kindness and compassion the Samaritan has declared himself the neighbor of the wounded traveler, then a dynamic dimension is added to the equation. The Samaritan *acts* as a neighbor. He has made a clear gesture to establish a bond of friendship with a Jew, whose people are traditional enemies of the Samaritan people. The parable of the Good Samaritan should be seen not as concerned with disinterested love alone but also as indicating a path that may lead to friendship, neighborly relations, and even reconciliation between enemies.

I have been arguing that, contrary to how it has been described by some, agape is not merely sacrificial or self-donative love; it is also love that opens into reciprocity, intimacy, and communion with others. The parable of the Good Samaritan suggests just this. *Agape* is more like a gerund than a noun proper. It is a dynamic process that heads *toward* communion. It is no accident that the early church also used the word *agape* to connote the eucharistic fellowship itself, in particular the meal of fellowship shared at the liturgical gathering.

Luke does not tell us whether the traveler eventually befriends the Samaritan. There is no strong likelihood of this in the Palestine of Jesus's day. But this does not rule out the possibility. The parable certainly suggests that God desires this to be so and beckons the listener to act in that spirit. We need only recall Jesus's own gesture of forgiveness and kindness in John's story of Jesus's encounter with another Samaritan, the woman at Jacob's well (John 4:5–26). This story is a reminder that the one who told the parable of the Good Samaritan strove in his own encounters with strangers and enemies to establish a lasting bond of friendship. The Gospels as a whole invite us to imagine that the Samaritan's act of compassion is the initial movement of a love that establishes fellowship and communion.

The root error of the standard readings of the story of the Good Samaritan is that they view agape narrowly, through the crucifixion severed from the resurrection. The work of Incarnate Love does not end on the cross. It is finished only when all who are of goodwill toward God and others are gathered together in the resurrected life. Love's work is complete only when communion in the body of Christ supplants the sinful divisions that afflict humanity, when the trinitarian image of love is fully restored to human nature and death is overcome by eternal life.

Agape and Eros

Thus far, we have been concerned almost entirely with agape, the preeminent form of love. Agape most properly expresses love from a divine point of view. Agape knows and treats the other as "thou," as neighbor, and not as merely an object for selfish use or pleasure. Nevertheless, in closing I want to argue that agape does not stand alone, that the fullness of love includes the love that is called *eros*. Love of neighbor is not just a handshake; it is an embrace. If we see the face of God, the image of God, in the other, then we will *desire* communion with the other as we desire union with God. In the final analysis, agape and eros are one love; much as divine and human love are one. "Let us not fear this title of 'yearning' [*eros*] nor be upset by what anyone has to say about these two names [*agape* and *eros*], for, in my opinion, the sacred writers regard 'yearning' [*eros*] and 'love' [*agape*] as having the same meaning,"[27] writes Dionysius the Areopagite. And he sets the tone for the Orthodox Christian tradition to this very day.

In a fallen world, agape and eros do indeed break apart, and they become distortions of their true character in God. Eros, severed from agape, degenerates into carnal desire and finally a God-and-human-denying narcissism. Agape severed from eros narrows into mere benevolence, then altruism, and finally ethical egoism. Salvation entails the reintegration of agape and eros, much as it calls for the incarnation itself.

In Christ, agape and eros obtain "the same exact meaning" with respect to his divinity and with respect to his humanity. In him, eros signifies not selfishness, as some have suggested about eros, but "a capacity to effect a unity, an alliance, and a particular commingling in the Beautiful and the Good."[28] Without eros, God would not be Trinity nor would the Word have united with human nature. Without eros, God would not have brought creation into existence nor would God have redeemed it. "The divine yearning [*eros*] is Good seeking good for the sake of the Good,"[29] the Areopagite continues. For as God yearns for Godself—the Father, the Son, and the Holy Spirit—so also God yearns for the world in all of its original goodness and beauty, and especially for humankind whom God created in his very own image and likeness.

Likewise, love of neighbor, the beginning of divine love in this world, is inexplicable without the presence and pull of eros. Christ's dual love commandment makes no distinction between divine persons and human beings or between eros and agape. When we love properly, we love in God; and through God's love for us, we are inspired to act the same toward others. We recognize the face of God in human beings and are drawn to them because God has loved them even before we were moved to do the same.

27. "Divine Names," 81 (chap. 4, para. 12).
28. "Divine Names," 82 (chap. 4, para. 12).
29. "Divine Names," 79 (chap. 4, para. 10).

A Case Study: Rayber's Terrifying Love

In her novel *The Violent Bear It Away*, Flannery O'Connor, the twentieth-century Southern fiction writer, makes the case for eros as I have discussed it. The lesson is in the tragedy of Rayber, a secularist schoolteacher. Rayber has one son by his deceased wife and wants custody of his nephew, Francis Marion Tarwater, whom Mason Tarwater, his uncle and a backcountry religious fanatic, has kidnapped. Rayber looks on his own son, Bishop, as an "idiot" child. Although O'Connor does not name his condition, Bishop appears to be a child with Down's syndrome. Whereas Bishop cannot profit from his enlightened education, Rayber is confident that Francis will.

Rayber is outraged at the religious training that the old man has given Francis and repulsed by the boy's beliefs and behavior. Meanwhile, his love for Bishop frightens Rayber because it seems irrational and uncontrollable. "He was not afraid of love in general," O'Connor writes. Rayber feels he knows the value of love and how it can be used. But his love for Bishop "could not be used for the child's improvement or his own. . . . It was completely irrational and abnormal." Rayber believes that as long as this love for Bishop is focused on the child only, he can control it and it is safe. But if anything should happen to Bishop, "he would have to face it in itself. Then the whole world would become his idiot child."[30]

Rayber is comfortable with benevolence as a principle of life, as an educator, but he steers clear of deep and intimate relationships. His love for Bishop is a crack in Rayber's rational egoism and utilitarian ethos. This love, this eros, that moves Rayber to embrace Bishop with his whole heart, not just his mind or intellect, is the remedy for his egocentrism and loneliness. Nonetheless, he fights against it because it threatens to broaden and expand so that he might even embrace God, whose existence Rayber vehemently denies. Nor is Rayber able to disentangle his love for Bishop from the attraction he still feels, despite his resistance and denial, to the life he once lived as a child with Mason Tarwater, and especially to the old man's longing for the bread of life and his vision of a transfigured world. O'Connor vividly likens this longing to "an undertow in his blood dragging him backwards to what he knew to be madness."[31]

In self-defense, Rayber transfers to Bishop his self-hatred and denial of God. In defiance of his love for the boy, he thinks of him "as an x signifying the general hideousness of fate." This hideous fate is the severe and wrathful

---

30. Flannery O'Connor, *The Violent Bear It Away*, in *Collected Works* (New York: Library of America, 1988), 401.
31. O'Connor, *Violent Bear It Away*, 401.

God of Mason Tarwater's extreme religious imagination. And that twisted image blinds Rayber to the authentic image of God within himself and his son. "He did not believe that he himself was formed in the image and likeness of God," O'Connor writes, "but that Bishop was he had no doubt. The little boy was part of a simple equation that required no further solution, except at the moments when with little warning he would feel himself overwhelmed by the horrifying love."[32]

Here O'Connor has brought us face to face with eros in ourselves through Bishop's characterization of Rayber, just as the lesson of Rayber's resistance to it betrays how necessary eros is in our lives in order for love to blossom into communion. Within this milieu of love that eros sparks, we see beauty where before we might have seen ugliness, and we are attracted to it. We see goodness where before we might have seen evil, and we are drawn to it. We see integrity where before we might have seen corruption, and we desire it. We see a neighbor where before we might have seen a stranger or an enemy, and we love that person.

Had Rayber been able to surrender to his love for Bishop, the legitimate status of his son's humanity might have come into view, the image not of some hideous fate but of the God who is love and whose love for humankind (God's *philanthropia*) abides in every human being. Ironically, love is more alive in the "idiot child" than in the educated father. The hope and possibility for Rayber's salvation from the deadening entropy of his own egocentrism and isolation lies mysteriously in his afflicted son. Bishop is a sacramental sign of Christ's presence, Christ who draws us nearer and nearer to himself through our neighbor or through an "idiot child," like the pull of gravity itself.

As regards Rayber, eros's immediate object may be the "idiot child," but its final resting place is God. Eros beholds beauty even in difficult places and opens the human heart to the joy that is beyond all earthly suffering. Rayber is afraid of this and withdraws into himself. At the moment that he could rescue Bishop from drowning, he is unable to act to save the boy and, by extension, himself.

Conclusion: Eros and Agape United

Eros and agape united belong to the original image of God in human beings. As O'Connor demonstrates through her storytelling, benevolence alone cannot restore that image. Rather, a communion of love is necessary. This might

32. O'Connor, *Violent Bear It Away*, 401.

start with love of neighbor, love of spouse, or a mother's love for her child. It reaches out to embrace others. The love that is the Trinity is the exact same love that unites God and human in Jesus Christ. The love that restores the image of God in humanity is also this love that is both eros and agape. In Augustine's words, "The very same person is at once God and man, God our end, man our way"[33]—that is, Jesus Christ.

"God," writes the fourteenth-century Byzantine theologian Nicholas Cabasilas, "has emplanted [sic] the desire [eros] into our souls by which every need should lead to the attainment of that which is good, every thought to the attainment of truth. . . . For those who have tasted of the Savior, the Object of desire is present. From the beginning, human desire was made to be gauged and measured by the desire for Him, and is a treasury so great, so ample, that it is able to encompass God." In other words, eros's repose is in Christ, in whom it is translated into universal love. "Those, therefore, who attain to Him," Cabasilas continues, "are hindered by nothing from loving to the extent that love was implanted in our souls from the beginning."[34]

In Christ, humanity's natural, inner movement toward the Godhead is consummated, and the human capacity to reciprocate God's love is perfected as a complete communion of human and divine natures. In Christ, human love and divine love are commensurate: they are one in his person. The heart of the Christic human being has a "burning love [eros] of its charity [agape] for God," Maximus the Confessor writes.[35] Agape is the fullness of love, while in the creature, eros is the way to that fullness. When grace has purified it, eros in the creature is stripped of the selfishness that sin introduces and is elevated to agape. The human being is once more an unblemished reflection of the express image (karakter, or stamp) of God (Heb. 1:3), Jesus Christ himself.

33. Augustine, City of God (New York: Random House, 1950), 347 (bk. 11, chap. 2).

34. Nicholas Cabasilas, The Life in Christ (Crestwood, NY: St. Vladimir's Seminary Press, 1974), 96–97 (bk. 2).

35. Maximus the Confessor, "The Four Centuries on Charity," in St. Maximus the Confessor: The Ascetic Life, the Four Centuries on Charity, trans. Polycarp Sherwood, Ancient Christian Writers Series 21 (Mahwah, NJ: Newman Press, 1955), 138 (Century I, para. 10).

PART 4

THEOLOGICAL ETHICS

ON MARRIAGE AND FAMILY

9

MARRIAGE

In the preceding chapter, I discussed marriage and family within a framework of trinitarian love. Here I extend that discussion in a christological direction. Marriage is a sacrament of love. But the love to which the sacrament attests is not abstract. This love is grounded not only in the divine nature but also in our human nature. It even derives from natural and biological needs and necessities (e.g., sexual attraction that leads to offspring). All the sacraments belong to God's act of creation. This means they must not be spiritualized so that they are removed from their grounding in creation. This is the heresy (gnostic of a kind) in contemporary efforts to stretch the meaning of marriage so that the love of two persons of the same sex may be said to make a marriage. Our nature, however, is not unisex or androgynous; it is two-sexed. This chapter weighs in theologically against the cultural and legal contortions through which some have been seeking to redefine marriage into something it is not.

Chapters 10 and 11 are about parenthood and childhood, which in the Orthodox vision of marriage are among its highest goods. But in our day, these goods—like marriage itself—are being redefined to make same-sex marriage appear to possess a value identical to the consanguinity brought into existence by the sexual union of male and female and begetting children. It was not my thought or intention, when I first composed chapters 10 and 11 as essays for

An earlier version of this chapter originally appeared as "If Love Has Won, Has Marriage Lost? An Orthodox Response to *Obergefell v. Hodges,*" *Clarion Review* (March 6, 2016), http://www.clarionreview.org/2016/03/if-love-has-won-has-marriage-lost-an-orthodox-response-to-obergefell-v-hodges/. Used by permission.

edited volumes, to respond to the grave theological error in extending marriage to same-sex partnerships. Even as they stand here, these chapters do not address that error full on. But it is clear to me now that a full Orthodox Christian defense of marriage must of necessity clarify not only the meaning of marriage but also the meanings of parenthood and childhood. It is to this latter, more precise, end of defining these two goods of marriage, parenthood and childhood, that these chapters attend.

In recent decades, intense campaigns have been waged in the United States, Great Britain, and Western Europe to legalize same-sex marriage. In the United States, the argument has been cast principally as a civil liberties issue, and on June 26, 2015, this argument won the day. By a 5–4 decision in *Obergefell v. Hodges*, the Supreme Court declared that marriage is a constitutional right for all citizens and that laws banning same-sex marriages are unconstitutional.

The court's decision is the fruit of a ruinous juridical and legislative nominalism that twists the meaning of marriage beyond anything recognizable in our culture or in historical religion. This nominalism embraces the strange notion—strange to the Orthodox faith, certainly—that the desire or love that two persons have for one another constitutes a marriage even when they are of the same sex. In *Habits of the Heart* (1985), published over three decades ago, Robert Bellah described an ethos that he called "expressive individualism." According to Bellah, expressive individualism "holds that each person has a unique core of feelings" that should be allowed and enabled "to unfold or be expressed" without external limitation in order that an authentic and self-fulfilling "individuality is . . . realized."[1]

Increasing numbers of modern folk, Bellah argues, subscribe to this ethos. It would appear the Supreme Court now believes in it as well. It is this ethos that, apart from legal and constitutional embellishments, inspirits the majority opinion in *Obergefell v. Hodges*. Writing for the majority, Justice Anthony Kennedy repeatedly appeals to the "dignity" of the person—nine times by my count.[2] In Kennedy's hands, however, dignity acquires the meaning of a secularist "god-term"[3] (what Richard Weaver describes as any term perceived automatically as good), which is distinctly aligned with expressive individualism. Dignity, when wielded by Kennedy, stands for the belief that

1. Robert Bellah, Richard Madsen, William M. Sullivan, Ann Swidler, and Steven M. Tipton, *Habits of the Heart: Individualism and Commitment in American Life* (Berkeley: University of California Press, 1985), 333–34.

2. Obergefell v. Hodges, 576 U.S. 3, 6, 7, 10, 13, 21, 26 (2015), https://www.supremecourt.gov/opinions/14pdf/14-556_3204.pdf.

3. Richard Weaver, *The Ethics of Rhetoric* (1953; Brattleboro, VT: Echo Point, 2015), chap. 9.

self-expression and self-realization of personal desire are among the very most important values and ends that the law should serve and uphold. As Justice Clarence Thomas rightly observes in his dissenting opinion, this notion of dignity is not the dignity that biblical faith recognizes, a dignity that is grounded not in human desire, or even law, but rather in that creative act of God wherein he endows every human person with the *imago Dei*—the inviolable, dignified image of God.

In addition, Kennedy speaks of marriage as a "union"[4] of two individuals, yet he does not tell us how the two "become something greater than they once were."[5] He merely asserts that this is so. He does not explain how this union is deeper than the momentary feelings or desires that bring two persons together. In the end, Kennedy's embrace of expressive individualism is vague, imprecise, and incapable of distinguishing between a partnership of two persons of the same sex and the conjugal union of two persons of the opposite sex. Traditional jurisprudence never walked this path.

It is difficult to imagine how the Supreme Court's action can be interpreted as anything but a repudiation of millennia of divine and human wisdom about the nature and meaning of marriage. Until our day, our culture, informed by biblical religion, understood marriage strictly as a union of one man and one woman. Until our day, this conviction was reflected in common morality and embodied in civil law. Now this meaning is being exploded, vacated from the law as if two thousand years of history in which marriage was so understood never existed.

Of course, advocates of same-sex unions could argue that their judicial victory is nothing less than a revolutionary one that has to break from the past in order to set people free to be who they are. The very antiquity of the traditional view might heighten rather than deflate the exhilaration of the triumph over old prejudices as history advances. In response, much also might be said about the foundations of a politics of prudence and the role that inherited wisdom ought to play in any sort of reform, perhaps most especially about marriage since it concerns the very heart of our humanity.

Here, however, I wish to return to and examine for a moment the damaging semantic confusion that has been inflicted on the word *marriage*. Henceforth, it seems, marriage will mean something it did not mean for millennia, even up until a few years ago, in both religious and secular realms. This obliges the church to be much clearer than it ever has been about its theology of marriage,

4. Obergefell v. Hodges, 576 U.S. 13 (2015), https://www.supremecourt.gov/opinions/14 pdf/14-556_3204.pdf.
5. Obergefell v. Hodges, 576 U.S. 3 (2015), https://www.supremecourt.gov/opinions/14 pdf/14-556_3204.pdf.

what *it* means by marriage, and why a partnership—and partnership is the right term, not union or marriage—of any sort between persons of the same sex is not nuptial in character.

We must also recognize that under this "new order," many are bound to judge (a judgment the law now supports) the Orthodox Church's belief about marriage as an offensive totem of a backward religious tribe. This calls for serious soul searching about how, henceforth, Orthodox people and other Christians are to live their faith in society. I believe justice Samuel Alito was entirely sober and not being the least bit alarmist when he warned in his dissenting opinion, "The decision will also have other important consequences. It will be used to vilify Americans who are unwilling to assent to the new orthodoxy," as their nonconformity will be analogized to the denial of "equal treatment for African-Americans and women."[6]

History and Our Understandings of Marriage

What then does the church understand marriage to be? A little reflection on history proves helpful. In pagan Rome during the first centuries of the Christian era, marriage was one of several acceptable forms of cohabitation and family life and was available as a legal status only to free citizens. If two such persons, man and woman, lived together consensually in a regularized fashion and assumed the roles and responsibilities of husband and wife, then the law regarded them as married. Roman law stipulated that marriage in its essence was not about intercourse but rather about the free consent of the individuals entering into it. Marriage would exist, therefore, where there was the intention to form a household, and this did not require legal formalization, though that was available and enabled couples to benefit from the special privileges that Roman law accorded to married people. These privileges included passing down the family name to children and inheritance of the father's estate by the legitimate offspring of the marriage.

To one degree or another, the early church found its way to bless the civil marriages of couples. And, to one degree or another, in Roman Catholic and Protestant traditions alike, consent was "baptized" as the cardinal element of marriage, with the contract as its material representation. The Catholic Church eventually defined marriage as a sacrament, but the principle of consent and rule of contract have been at least as important in its theology of marriage and divorce. Consent and rule of contract stand behind the Catholic Church's

6. Obergefell v. Hodges, 576 U.S. 6 (2015), https://www.supremecourt.gov/opinions/14 pdf/14-556_3204.pdf.

belief that the bride and groom administer their marriage to one another, and they also are reflected in the way the Catholic Church justifies its denial of divorce. (I do not have the space here for a more nuanced discussion of Catholic theology of marriage, especially of the more recent emphasis on the "nuptial mystery" by some writers, including John Paul II, which is more compatible with Orthodox theology.)

In the Orthodox tradition, consent never was so pivotal in defining a marriage. The clerical officer (bishop or priest) representing the church blesses and marries the bride and groom, and the couple is by this act bonded as husband and wife to Christ and the church. The conjugal love union, and not consent or contract, is understood to be the very heart of marriage. Marriage is a sacrament of love but not just any sort of love. This love union is founded and grounded in God's will, in his creative act of making humankind as male and female so that, through their love for each other and their sexual union, they may be united "in one flesh." Consent and contract belong more properly to betrothal.[7]

The Logic of Consent Allied with Expressive Individualism

Many North Americans, even Orthodox Christians, assume that the couple's consent seals the marriage—that in a practical sense, the will and desire of the couple bring the marriage into existence, and that the withdrawal of the will and desire to be together is sufficient to terminate a marriage. This is what present secular marriage and divorce law reflects. The point is simply that the principle of consent has remained fixed as a cultural norm even as contemporary people have forgotten the sacred meaning and sacramental depths of marriage, while at the same time they embrace an ethos of expressive individualism.

The principle of consent, the logic supporting it, and a godless, anthropocentric understanding of love as personal desire are what today enable the advocates of gay marriage to make great headway in the legislature and the courts. Such advocates have even made progress within the churches, especially Protestant churches that lack a sacramental understanding of marriage. It should surprise no one that as these churches believe less and less that homosexual acts are sinful, unnatural, or psychopathically abnormal, the argument for gay marriage gains plausibility and persuasiveness among adherents. Thus today there prevails among many religious and secular people a belief that when two homosexual persons love each other and desire and freely consent

7. All Orthodox marriage rites include consent by inference—and in some cases explicitly, as in the Slavonic version of the Byzantine rite—but the latter is a late addition to the rite and does not change its emphasis on the conjugal love union.

to share their lives with one another as a domestic couple, the state should grant this partnership legal status as a marriage. The Supreme Court has now also embraced this view and made it the law of the land.

Since the logic of consent and contract as well as equal protection under the law are deeply embedded in our cultural ethos and in modern jurisprudence, it is easy to imagine that the sorts of changes in marriage law and tax codes that the supporters of same-sex marriage have won may eventually have to be extended to other same-sex households that are not homosexual. How can the state possibly discriminate—or even ask the questions needed to discriminate—between homosexual and heterosexual couples of the same sex that come to get licensed? How can the state differentiate one love from another? If marriage is no longer defined as strictly between a man and a woman, why shouldn't widows or widowers or brothers or sisters who live together for mutual assistance and economic reasons be granted licenses for domestic partnerships with all the legal benefits and protections now accorded to married couples?

It would make much more sense under present circumstances for the state to abandon the language of marriage altogether and issue simple contracts of cohabitation. Even before *Obergefell v. Hodges*, civil marriage had become virtually meaningless under a regime of unilateral and no-fault divorce in which the long-honored norm of permanence disappears. In *Obergefell v. Hodges*, the Supreme Court has shown that it does not even know what marriage is, since it no longer defines marriage as the union of one man and one woman with an intent for a lifetime together.

Two-Tiered Marriage: An Orthodox Response

This revolution profoundly challenges the traditional understanding of marriage. It is emblematic of the crossroads at which our society is poised on many fronts. And it places Orthodox and other Christians in an agonizing countercultural position. Careful navigation in the culture's tumultuous waters is required, at least as careful and considered as the course the church steered from the reigns of emperors Theodosius I and Theodosius II of the fourth and fifth centuries through Justinian in the sixth century. This was the period in which Christianity became the official religion of the empire and in which the great legal codes were promulgated that truly defined and shaped Christendom as a social realm. This has been our legacy up until now when the heart and spirit of Christendom are being banished from North American soil, and the last remnants of these codes, which privileged marriage, supported sanctions against abortion and suicide, and provided for public prayer and the observation of Christian holy days, are being erased.

For reasons that in this chapter I can only sketch, I believe that it is imperative for the Orthodox churches now to cease cooperation or collaboration with the government in civilly marrying persons, as they have done in one form or another within Christendom since the fifth and sixth centuries. Orthodox clergy should no longer act as agents of the state in signing (or in any way giving the impression of consecrating) civil contracts. This step would, for laity and clergy alike, expose the radical discontinuity between the state's definition of marriage and marriage as the church understands it.

It also would bring into existence a de facto two-tiered arrangement in which Orthodox Christians might come to the church to receive the sacrament or marital blessing and then obtain a civil contract to meet the legal requirement and qualify for married status before the state. Even under present arrangements, two marriage certificates are issued in most states, one religious and the other civil. By no longer assuming responsibility for consecration of civil contracts, the church would be lodging its profound disagreement with the state's unilateral and theologically erroneous redefinition of marriage.

My reasoning is that *Obergefell v. Hodges*, much like *Roe v. Wade*, is going to be debated and contended for a long time to come. The decision gives significant numbers of people the courage to demand that churches embrace same-sex marriage and offer some kind of blessing for these relationships. Perhaps also in the not too distant future, the federal government may even pressure churches to conform to the new order with punitive sanctions that would include denial of tax-exempt status. The abortion decision not only divided the nation—it split churches. Same-sex "marriage" is not just a moral issue; it is a sacramental matter. It affects how Christians envision themselves as church and may become an existential threat to how they envision and pursue the life of the family.

The Orthodox Theology of Marriage as Sacramental, Epiphanic Union

Under conditions like these, it is imperative that Christians be better instructed in the theology of marriage. According to the new wisdom, legal marriage is going to be defined as covering a broad range of consensual domestic relationships, both heterosexual and homosexual, so that all who enter into these arrangements may receive the benefits traditionally reserved for marriage between a man and a woman. Marriage will be defined strictly as a civil liberty under the law, irrespective of sex or procreative intent, and indifferent to sacrament.

By contrast, the Orthodox theology of marriage, as I have intimated, is grounded in the church's doctrines of God and creation. While an anthropological argument opposing same-sex "marriage" on biological or natural law grounds is not necessarily incompatible with the Orthodox faith, it is not sufficiently theological, nor is it ecclesial. And I do not think it can win the day. For the Orthodox Church, the primary argument *is* sacramental and ecclesial.

From the standpoint of Orthodox theology, whether or not the individuals who seek a same-sex union are homosexual or heterosexual is not what is theologically decisive. Neither is the argument from procreation decisive—in other words, that same-sex couples cannot produce offspring in the manner that heterosexual couples are able to do. While human beings, like other members of the animal kingdom, are sexually dimorphic, mate, and produce offspring, only human beings marry; birds and monkeys do not. A spiritual and sacramental dimension of human existence modifies human sexuality and transforms the human organism into something unique in the animal kingdom. Marriage is sign and symbol of this unique spiritual and sacramental dimension of human sexual coupling. This is what makes marriage a sacrament; and male and female are the essential and nonsubstitutable elements of that sacrament. Thus, the Orthodox object to same-sex unions and not same-sex "marriage" per se, though the latter is a subset of the former.

Marriage's Grounding in Creation

A profound doctrine of creation stands behind the Orthodox theology of marriage. Marriage's origin is in the act by which God created humankind as male and female.[8] According to Genesis (Gen. 1:27; 2:24) and Jesus (Matt. 19:5) the conjugality, the nuptiality, of man and woman is woven into the very fabric of our humanity.[9] The fall damaged this fabric, but it did not destroy

8. I regard this as the consensus and normative position of the church reflected by Augustine in the West and Chrysostom in the East. There are, however, those among the church fathers, Gregory of Nyssa being a chief example, who dissent from this view and regard marriage strictly as a remedy for the fall, instituted by God after Adam and Eve were expelled from paradise.

9. The Priestly account of the creation of humankind (*adam*) establishes that the full meaning of humanity includes both male and female. It describes the creation of male and female together, simultaneously, as the "image of God" (Gen. 1:26–27). The more ancient Jahwist myth of the creation of Adam and Eve (Gen. 2:4–25) also confirms a common human nature; however, juxtaposed to and following the Priestly account, it imaginatively establishes the distinction, within this one nature, of male and female. It presents us with the nuptial mystery of the spousal unity, complementarity, and reciprocity of the two sexes as "one flesh." Jesus reaffirms Genesis's meaning in his response to the Pharisees who question him as to whether divine law permits divorce: "Have you not read that He who made them at the beginning 'made them male and female,' and said, 'For this reason a man shall leave his father and mother and be joined to his wife, and the two shall become one flesh'?" (Matt. 19:4–5).

it. John Chrysostom argues, "When husband and wife cleave to each other in love, there is a remnant of paradise."[10] Russian theologian Paul Evdokimov adds that "conjugal union discovers again the origins of man, and the order of grace fulfills the order of creation."[11]

Genesis states that God observed Adam and considered it "not good for man to be alone." Thus God decided to "make him [Adam] a helper comparable to him" (Gen. 2:18 SAAS).[12] God brought a deep sleep (*tardemah*) over Adam and removed from him a rib, out of which he formed Eve. Then Adam awoke to a transformed consciousness. He was face to face with another like himself and declared, in a moment of joyful encounter with this intimate "other," "This is now bone of my bones / And flesh of my flesh; / She shall be called Woman." (Gen. 2:23). Pope John Paul II refers to this ecstatic exclamation as "the first wedding song."[13]

Ancient tradition interprets "bone of my bones" as an expression of the complementarity and reciprocity of the sexes. "Bone," *etsem* in the Hebrew, also connotes "self" or "being," so that "bone of my bones" may also be translated as "self of myself" or "being of my being." God creates humanity as Adam-Eve humanity, a perfectly reciprocal unit, one humanity, one nuptial being. Though each human individual is either a male or a female,[14] when united by love for one another and their love for God, male and female become one being. In Shakespeare's poem "The Phoenix and the Turtle," this is captured well:

> So they lov'd, as love in twain
> Had the essence but in one;
> Two distincts, division none:
> Number there in love was slain. . . .
> Either was the other's mine.[15]

10. Cited by John H. Erickson, *The Challenge of Our Past* (Crestwood, NY: St. Vladimir's Seminary Press, 1991), 40.

11. Paul Evdokimov, "Conjugal Priesthood," in *Marriage and Christian Tradition*, trans. Sr. Agnes Cunningham, SSCM (Techny, IL: Divine Word, 1968), 78.

12. SAAS denotes the St. Athanasius Academy Septuagint translation that belongs to the Orthodox Study Bible (Nashville: Thomas Nelson, 2008).

13. John Paul II, *Man and Woman He Created Them: A Theology of the Body*, trans. Michael Waldstein (Boston, MA: Pauline Books, 2006), 83n15.

14. There are known "exceptions" of persons for whom gender identity is highly ambiguous, though they are physiologically male or female: persons whom, in our day, we speak of as transgender. But these conditions, by the standard of Christian anthropology anomalies, are by no means within the range of normality.

15. William Shakespeare, "The Phoenix and the Turtle," https://www.poetryfoundation.org /poems/45085/the-phoenix-and-the-turtle-56d2246f86c06.

The Hebrew *ezer kenegdo* of Genesis 2:18 is commonly translated "helper" or "fitting companion." A better translation might be "another, an opposite, who is turned toward or facing" Adam. Nothing in this prelapsarian picture of humanity suggests that Eve originally is in a servile or subordinate relationship to Adam. "Bone of my bone" already is suggestive of an equality of the two. The servile or subordinate status of Eve is a consequence of the fall. The Lord says to Eve, "Your recourse will be to your husband" (Gen. 3:16 SAAS). And even this status is functional and does not abrogate the ontological equality that *etsem* suggests and is reinforced by *ezer kenegdo*. No being that is less than the equal of Adam would be suited to be joined with him nuptially.

When Adam awakens from his slumber, he sees not a slave or an inferior but rather a living person who is a reflection of himself, one who, unlike the animals Adam has seen and named, is his own flesh. We could say that Adam yearned for Eve even before he "knew" her and was united with her conjugally. Mysteriously, Adam's yearning for another like himself drew Eve out of him; for, without Eve, Adam was not just alone but was also unaware of the fullness of his humanity as a moral and social being.[16]

When Adam looks at Eve, it is as if in a mirror, not in reverse, however, but rather he sees an "other," the same nature as himself but also different from him. Adam completes his "wedding song" by naming this other being who is like him "woman," his wife. The Hebrew is *ishah*, the same as *ish*, man, excepting that it is in the feminine. This emphasizes that man and woman, husband and wife, are of one kind, equal in every respect, although different forms, different manifestations, of the very same nature.

Eve is Adam's perfect complement, female. She is his perfection and he hers. Together they are humankind whole and complete. Adam and Eve are complementary, but not in the sense that one apart from the other is not fully human. Each, even apart from the other, is fully human. But together, in and through their sexual love, man and woman commence the fulfillment of their human potential as beings in communion, as image of the triune God.

16. I should say here that I regard the "Adam" of Genesis 2 before the creation of Eve to stand for humankind—which the biblical writer is distinguishing from all the other animal kinds that God has created—not yet identified, however, in its wholeness as male and female together. Both creation accounts of Genesis, whatever their differences, ultimately agree that the fullness of our humanity is constituted of male and female. Thus, I intend this discussion of Adam's loneliness and incompleteness, or solitude as John Paul II has put it, mainly as a hermeneutical exercise to help clarify the truth that humankind rightly considered is two-sexed, not to claim that before the creation of Eve humankind existed as solely male, or, for that matter, that Adam might have been androgynous.

The Sacramentality of Marriage

The world itself is sacramental. It is epiphanic, revealing of God its creator. The appointed sacraments of the church are not exceptional realities or super-realities; they are not magic. Rather, they are specifications of the symbolical ontology of creation, and they witness to the fact that humankind is created in the image of God. Each of the sacraments names and uses "natural" elements that are particular to that sacrament. In and through this sacramental action, the epiphanic character of those elements is revealed, pointing to the kingdom of God. Bread and wine are natural symbols of flesh and blood. Christ reveals them as symbols of his body and blood, in and through which he is verily present, and by consuming these translated elements, we enter into the most intimate communion with him as one ecclesial body.

Likewise, male and female are the exclusive elements and symbols of transformation in the sacrament of marriage. These elements must themselves be returned to their proper relationship; they must be translated from their present fallen state of alienation from each other back to their original unity and integrity. Basil exhorts in his *Hexaemeron* (On the Six Days of Creation), "May the bond of nature, may the yoke imposed by the blessings make as one those who were divided."[17] Marriage is a healing of the rift and broken communion between male and female that the fall has brought about. Marriage "in the Lord" (1 Cor. 7:39) unites male and female as God originally intended: as spouses and companions to each other, husband and wife, one Christic and ecclesial being (Eph. 5:30–32).

This sacramental union of bride and groom is no mere cipher or allegory of human relationality, as some proponents of same-sex marriage insist. Bride and groom are not nominal titles that may be bestowed on any two persons, irrespective of their sex or gender, who enter into a "loving relationship." There is nothing incidental, accidental, or volitional about heterosexual humanity, the fact that the male is groom and the female is bride, or that the marital union of a man and a woman is an icon of the eschatological union of Christ and the church.

A Nuptial Humanity

Christ is the groom and the church is his bride of the new creation. The referent of groom is the first man, Adam, and the referent of bride is the first

17. Basil, *On the Hexaemeron*, in *Saint Basil: Exegetic Homilies*, trans. Sr. Agnes Clare Way, C.D.P., The Fathers of the Church 46 (Washington, DC: Catholic University Press of America, 1963), 114. This saying of Basil is also included as a prayer in the Byzantine Rite of Marriage.

woman, Eve. The nuptial Adam-Eve humanity of the book of Genesis, the first book of the Bible, is the analogue of the heavenly nuptials of the marriage of the Lamb in the book of Revelation (19:7), the last book of the Bible. The creation of nuptial humanity is an epiphany of the eternal humanity of God precedent to its complete revelation in the incarnation. The creation of nuptial humanity is a prophecy of the church, which itself, through its nuptial union with Christ, fulfills the goal and purpose of creation. Human willing and choosing cannot change marriage's essence or the symbolism that God has ordained for it.

Thus in the Orthodox faith there could never be such a thing as same-sex marriage. There is not a same-sex equivalent to bride and groom. To insist that there are such equivalencies and to act on this error not only represents marriage as something it is not but also envisions salvation as something it is not. And because same-sex marriage contradicts the church's understanding of salvation, specifically of marriage as restoration of the divine image in nuptial humanity, it is a grave heresy.

Three Key Actions

The essence of marriage as a conjugal love union is symbolized in all Orthodox rites of marriage by three key actions: the joining of the hands of bride and groom, the crowning of the couple, and the sharing of the common cup. At the start of the rite, the celebrant joins the right hands of the bride and groom by which the primordial bond of union proclaimed by Adam is affirmed: "This is now bone of my bones / And flesh of my flesh; / . . . and they shall become one flesh" (Gen. 2:23–24). The Orthodox service recapitulates God's primal act by which Adam and Eve were brought face to face to know each other as "self of self," united in love, the image of God, the perfect communion of the Father, the Son, and the Holy Spirit.

This is followed by the crowning of the couple in which, often to the bemusement of Western Christian or nonreligious guests, the bride and the groom literally receive regal crowns on their heads. This indicates that, like every sacrament, marriage brings the kingdom of God into our midst. As John Chrysostom explains, every marriage is a little church in which the virtues of the kingdom are learned and rehearsed. The bride and groom are king and queen of this new heavenly kingdom of their marriage. And God calls on them to exercise, within the domestic household, that same form of dominion over the world that he instructed the first couple to practice. The crowns are also a reminder that the kingdom of God is won only through self-giving and self-sacrificial love, even as Christ went willingly to the cross.

Last, the sharing of the common cup recalls Christ's blessing of the wedding in Cana of Galilee (John 2:1–12). The water changed to wine is the sign that marriage "in the Lord" (1 Cor. 7:39), as Paul puts it, is a sacrament of the kingdom of God. "Natural" marriage is revealed as the matter or material of the sacrament. Sharing the wine is emblematic of the one-flesh union and the life of mutual love to which husband and wife must aspire. These practices of the shared cup and the remembered events at Cana of Galilee are cast in the marital rites as typologically related to the sacraments of baptism and Eucharist. By marrying "in the Lord," persons may deepen their membership in the body of Christ and as sharers and participants in the divine life (2 Pet. 1:4).

Marriage and Eucharist

As I intimated above, the early church initially saw no need to perform a special ritual for marriage. Rather, the church simply recognized the validity of the marriages that the civil authorities authorized and performed, giving them its blessing. But it also then invited the couple to share the Eucharist together as an emblem of their union in Christ and their belonging to his body. It was not until the ninth and tenth centuries that distinct rites of matrimony emerged. At this time, marriage was gradually removed from the Eucharist altogether, and just the sharing of the common cup remained—although in some locations the common cup and the Eucharist may have continued to exist alongside each other.

Today, under the new regime of *Obergefell v. Hodges*, there are compelling reasons for all the churches to demonstratively rejoin marriage and the Eucharist—that is, to bring them into greater liturgical proximity. In some churches, such as Roman Catholic and Anglican churches, a nuptial mass is optional. Roughly the same is true in Orthodox churches, though the practice is infrequent, as most of the laity is unaware of that possibility. It is a common practice in the Armenian Church for couples to take communion together on a Sunday preceding their wedding. Speaking as an Armenian Orthodox theologian to his own and to other Orthodox churches, I would like the option of a nuptial Eucharist to be formalized and actively encouraged. I will explain why in a moment.

My immediate point is that as the Eucharist is the "home" of Christians, so also is it the home of Christian marriage. The early Christian apologists, who fully acknowledged the legal validity of civil marriage, insisted on this mystical connection between Christian marriage and the Eucharist. The late second-century writer Tertullian in a letter to his wife beautifully expresses this sentiment: "What words can describe the happiness of that marriage which the church unites, the offering strengthens, the blessing seals, the angels proclaim, and the Father declares valid? What a bond is this: two believers who share one hope, one desire, one discipline, the same service!"[18]

In the early ninth century, St. Theodore the Studite mentions two elements that belonged to eucharistic marriage perhaps as early as the fourth century. He informs us that a crowning ceremony existed, followed by a brief prayer, a prayer that is virtually replicated in Orthodox rites of marriage today:

> Thyself, O Master, send down Thy hand from Thy holy dwelling place
> and unite these Thy servant and Thy handmaid.
> And give to those whom Thou unitest harmony of minds;
> Crown them into one flesh;
> Make their marriage honorable;
> Keep their bed undefiled;
> Deign to make their common life blameless.[19]

This simple blessing encapsulates the whole meaning of Orthodox Christian marriage. God marries man and woman, and only man and woman. God is present at every Christian marriage. The Orthodox Church (and other churches) must make it clear to the courts that Christian marriage is a sacrament and, therefore, that as an act of worship it is the under protection of the Constitution from the state's fiat. This is why the churches should endeavor to place marriage in the closest performative proximity to the Eucharist.

Mounting a Defense of Marriage in Our Present Circumstances

Rejoining marriage and the Eucharist is therefore not just a matter of sentiment or correct theology. It is also practical, even strategic. Sometimes the children of God need to be as wise as serpents. Should the day come that the federal government mandates or otherwise pressures churches through threat of punitive sanctions to marry same-sex couples, the free exercise clause of the Constitution—the First Amendment—may become crucial for a defense

18. Tertullian, "To His Wife," in *Marriage in the Early Church*, ed. David G. Hunter (Minneapolis: Fortress, 1992), 38.
19. Cited in John Meyendorff, *Marriage: An Orthodox Perspective* (Crestwood, NY: St. Vladimir's Seminary Press, 1984), 25.

of traditional marital practices. If that time comes, churches must be in the best position to mount an argument that marriage is integral to Christian worship—that it is a mystery of the church linked to baptism and the Eucharist.

Even this defense may not be as easy as it once was. In *Obergefell v. Hodges*, the court appears to have fixed on a conception of marriage that is far removed from sacrament and worship. This is the notion that marriage is an expressive association. Expressive association is closely related to expressive individualism and the idea of autonomy variously expressed. Such a view is likely to be blind to the freedom of an ecclesial body or its communal exercise of prayer and worship. It is telling that in his majority opinion Justice Kennedy makes no mention of the free exercise clause as a protection from overreach by the state. Rather, he speaks in patronizing terms of the protection that the First Amendment gives to "religious organizations and persons" that they may "*seek to teach the principles* that are so fulfilling and so central to their lives and faiths."[20] Teaching is not exactly the exercise of faith that includes worship, blessing, and prayer. If I may say so, Kennedy's words are a chilling reminder of how faint the court's appreciation is of the relation of marriage to the exercise of religion, specifically the church as a praying and worshiping body of believers and marriage as belonging thereto.

This puts churches in America that are opposed to same-sex unions in a precarious and even menacing position. It threatens the sacrament of marriage and, specifically, the Orthodox Church's own understanding of itself as sacramental reality, for so much of the Orthodox Church's liturgical speech is imbued with the symbolism of marriage. But perhaps from this crisis can be seized the opportunity for the formation of a new catechesis that is a joint endeavor of bishops, priests, and laity, of married and single persons alike, to secure the foundations of the church with a renewed understanding and affirmation of the sacral and ecclesial meanings of marriage.

20. Obergefell v. Hodges, 576 U.S. 27 (2015), https://www.supremecourt.gov/opinions/14 pdf/14-556_3204.pdf (emphasis mine).

10

Parenthood

In our day, hyper-individualism and exaggerated notions of personal autonomy flourish and, as I have said in the prior chapter, influence the law. This individualism assumes that the individual is primary and community is derivative and artificial and that, therefore, the individual's claims take precedence over the community.[1]

This individualism is conspicuously reflected in current attitudes and opinions about marriage and divorce, abortion, and physician-assisted suicide, to name a few. Many view marriage as a contract between two autonomous selves who have strong feelings for one another, which may be revoked when those feelings no longer exist. A woman's decision to have an abortion, whether she is single or married, is judged as solely her prerogative. A quarter century ago, Dr. Jack Kevorkian conducted his crusade for the legalization of physician-assisted suicide and euthanasia with the cunning calculation that the logic of the principle of autonomy, deeply imbedded in modern people's minds, would ultimately prevail over traditional moral objections to the practice.[2]

An earlier version of this chapter originally appeared as "The Ecclesial Family: John Chrysostom on Parenthood and Children," in *The Child in Christian Thought*, ed. Marcia J. Bunge, 61–77 (Grand Rapids: Eerdmans, 2001). Used by permission.

1. Robert Bellah, Richard Madsen, William M. Sullivan, Ann Swidler, and Steven M. Tipton, *Habits of the Heart: Individualism and Commitment in American Life* (Berkeley: University of California Press, 1985), 334.

2. See Vigen Guroian, *Life's Living Toward Dying* (Grand Rapids: Eerdmans, 1996), xiii–xxvii.

To the extent that these notions of individualism and autonomy influence contemporary thought on childhood, there is a tendency to define childhood isolated from any serious reflection on the meaning of parenthood. Yet a moment's pause should lead to the recognition that there is scarcely a deeper characteristic of human life than the parent-child nexus.

The Christian faith would have us look more closely at this nexus. Yet in the churches, too little discussion is given to the vocation of parenthood and the child's duties and obligations to parents. Rather, the churches parrot the culture's obsessive interest in individual psychology and personal autonomy. In Christian education, these habits are reflected in division of instruction by age group and the dominance of developmental models of child psychology that overemphasize autonomy and cognitive capabilities. The latter has led to a neglect of effective socialization of children into the community of believers using the church's own resources of sacred narrative and sacramental theology.[3]

In this chapter, I propose to discuss John Chrysostom's seminal Christian reflections on parenthood and the parent-child nexus. Chrysostom (ca. 347–407) is one of the great figures of the early church and of Eastern Christianity in particular. His thoughts on marriage have already been touched on in the prior two chapters. Chrysostom's fame as a bishop, pastor, and preacher is second to none among the Greek fathers—testified by his name, which means "golden-mouthed." Chrysostom spoke of the solidarity of human community, the need for early socialization of the young into the church, and the powerful unitive and communicative love that the parent-child relationship infuses into human society.

He often addressed parents of his day on these matters. As a priest in his homilies at Antioch and later as bishop of Constantinople, the highest episcopal see in the Christian East, he returned time and again to the theme of parenthood. His views are grounded in the trinitarian and christological teachings of the church and integrate both the communal and personalist aspects of the Christian faith. He argues that the Christian family is itself an ecclesial (or churchly) entity wherein adults and children rehearse for membership in the kingdom of heaven. He advances a strong moral teaching about the virtues and responsibilities of parenthood and invests that role with a pressing soteriological significance.

In his day, Chrysostom was concerned with the fact that the religious and moral standards of parenting and childhood that the church prescribed were

3. John L. Boojamra strikes chords that resonate with Chrysostom's own pastoral insights and is critical of prevailing models and methods of Christian education in *Foundations for Christian Education* (Crestwood, NY: St. Vladimir's Seminary Press, 1989).

losing ground to loose and degrading values of popular culture, not so very different from the concerns of people in many churches today. Were he living in our time, Chrysostom would likely remind us that when and where there is a crisis of childhood, there is also bound to be a crisis of parenthood. And he would encourage us, in our present circumstances, to examine closely the parental side of the parent-child relationship. Thus while not neglecting to consider the meaning and moral characteristics of Christian childhood that Chrysostom proposes, in this chapter I want to focus on Chrysostom's virtually unique contribution to a Christian understanding of parenthood, setting aside for the final chapter a discussion focused on childhood.

The Context of John Chrysostom's Ministry

John Chrysostom lived during a time of intense monastic activity, but as he became involved with priestly and episcopal responsibilities within the great urban centers of ancient Antioch and Constantinople, he turned his attention to the family and the domestic life of his parishioners. He applied what he had learned of the monastic discipline to the secular realm and insisted that even the highest Christian virtues embodied in the beatitudes of the Sermon on the Mount (Matt. 5–7) are binding on all Christians and not reserved solely for monks.[4]

The society in which John Chrysostom lived and preached was diverse and in flux, again, not so unlike our own. The pagan culture of antiquity was in distress and decline. Moral standards were deteriorating, and the old pagan religion was losing force, especially in the cities. In the midst of this change, the Christian church had begun to exert a formative influence on state and society. As mentioned in chapter 2, in 313 Emperor Constantine issued the Edict of Milan, which granted the Christian church legal toleration and

---

4. Addressing married persons who were making excuses for themselves, Chrysostom responded, "And if these beatitudes were spoken to solitaries only, and the secular person cannot fulfill them, yet He [Christ] permitted marriage, then He has destroyed all men. . . . And if persons have been hindered by their marriage state, let them know that marriage is not the hindrance, but their purpose which made an ill use of marriage." See John Chrysostom, "Homilies on the Hebrews," in *St. John Chrysostom: Homilies on the Gospel of John and the Epistle to the Hebrews*, in *A Select Library of the Nicene and Post-Nicene Fathers of the Christian Church*, ed. Philip Schaff (New York: Christian Literature Co. 1890), 14: 402. The Eastern Church has never formally declared a hierarchy of Christian life in which celibacy is designated a higher state of Christian living than marriage. Chrysostom's views are echoed by other Eastern Christian writers such as Clement of Alexandria in his *Stromateis*. For further discussion and references, see chap. 4 of my book *Incarnate Love: Essays in Orthodox Ethics* (Notre Dame, IN: University of Notre Dame Press, 1987).

freedom of worship within the empire. And during Chrysostom's own lifetime, Theodosius I, Roman emperor from 379 to 395, established Christianity as the official religion of the state.

However, this success of the church also presented temptations to compromise Christian moral standards. Chrysostom was persuaded that the purity of the faith was in jeopardy as Christians began to assume responsibilities in the secular world. Increasingly, being baptized and belonging to the church were considered advantageous for worldly success. Chrysostom abhorred a cake-frosting variety of Christianity. Constantly, he inveighed against the moral laxity of self-professed Christians and their excessive preoccupation with material possessions, popular entertainments, social status, and political influence. He was especially troubled, even outraged, by the eagerness of some Christian parents to propel their children into the secular professions while neglecting their spiritual and moral formation. This moved him to address the role and responsibilities of parents.

Communal Christianity and the Ecclesial Family

As I have stated, John Chrysostom's understanding of parenthood is biblically inspired and profoundly grounded in the church's trinitarian and christological teaching. Parenthood and childhood must mirror the life of the divine persons of the Trinity. The life of the Trinity is a life of perfectly reciprocal, mutual love. This is exemplified for our sakes in the fatherhood of God and the obedient and sacrificial sonship of the divine Word revealed in the Gospels. God, in Christ and through the Holy Spirit, calls on the family to emulate his love. If it does so, then the Holy Spirit comes to bless and sanctify the love of the spouses for one another and the love that parents and children have for one another. As parents and children assume this trinitarian resemblance in their relations with one another, they become active participants in the divine life.

The godly family is also an image of the church, in so much as its members rehearse together the redeemed and sanctified life, worthy of Christ and the sacrifice he offered on their behalf. In an often-cited passage that belongs to his homily on Ephesians 5:22–23, Chrysostom explicitly compares the Christian household to the church: "If we regulate our households [properly] . . . we will also be fit to oversee the Church, for indeed the household is a little church. Therefore, it is possible for us to surpass all others in virtue by becoming good husbands and wives."[5]

5. John Chrysostom, *On Marriage and Family Life*, trans. Catherine P. Roth and David Anderson (Crestwood, NY: St. Vladimir's Seminary Press, 1986), 57.

The Role That Hospitality Plays

Sometimes Chrysostom draws up his ecclesial analogy through a typological reading of the Old Testament. In his homilies on the book of Acts, Chrysostom maintains that the Abrahamic household, which kept and practiced the virtues of the kingdom of God in an exemplary fashion, was a type and prophecy of the church. Analogously, all members of a Christian household, adults and children alike, must prepare their home and themselves to receive divine visitors and Christ himself, as did Abraham and Sarah. They must at all times demonstrate love and hospitality, even toward strangers.

> Abraham received the strangers in the place where he abode himself; his wife [Sarah] stood in the place of a servant, the guests in the place of masters. He knew not that he was receiving Christ; knew not that he was receiving Angels; so that had he known, he would have lavished his whole substance. But we, who know that we receive Christ, show not even so much zeal. . . . Let our house be Christ's general receptacle.[6]

Elsewhere Chrysostom declares that "everything good" that happened to the Abrahamic household "came because of hospitality."[7] The home that practices this hospitality is a place worthy of the holy one. It is, indeed, a "little church." Chrysostom exhorts, "[Let] the house be a Church, consisting of men and women, 'For where two,' He saith, 'are gathered together in My Name, there am I in the midst'" (Matt. 18:20).[8]

The Image of God, Original Sin, and the Divine Model of Parenthood

Early in his adult life, Chrysostom emphasized these communal and salvific principles in his defense of monasticism. But later, as a pastor and bishop, he argued with equal vigor that the health and mission of the church crucially depend on the seriousness with which parents attended to the moral and religious upbringing of their children.

One of Chrysostom's richest theological statements on parenthood and raising children belongs to his homily on Ephesians 6:1–4 where he implores:

6. John Chrysostom, "Homilies on the Acts," in *St. John Chrysostom: Homilies on the Acts of the Apostles and the Epistle to the Romans,* in *A Select Library of the Nicene and Post-Nicene Fathers of the Christian Church,* 11:277.

7. Chrysostom, *On Marriage and Family Life,* 103–4.

8. Chrysostom, *Homilies on the Acts of the Apostles,* 127.

Let us bring them [our children] up in the discipline and instruction of the
Lord. Great will be the reward in store for us, for if artists who make statues
and paint portraits of kings are held in high esteem, will not God bless ten
thousand times more those who reveal and beautify His royal image (for man
is the image of God)? When we teach our children to be good, to be gentle, to
be forgiving (all these are attributes of God), to be generous, to love their fellow
men, to regard this present age as nothing, we instill virtue in their souls, and
reveal the image of God within them. This, then, is our task: to educate both
our children and ourselves in godliness; otherwise what answer will we have
before Christ's judgment seat? If a man with unruly children is unworthy to be
bishop [Titus 1:6], how can he be worthy of the kingdom of heaven? What do
you think? If we have an undisciplined wife, or unruly children, shall we not
have to render an account for them? Yes, we shall, if we cannot offer to God
what we owe Him, because we can't be saved through individual righteousness.[9]

Here Chrysostom compares parents to artists and children to portraits and
statues. He returns to these metaphors in his other writings to explain the
nature of Christian parenthood.[10] In this passage, Chrysostom is also arguing that parents must uncover and reveal the image of God in their children,
which has been obscured by sin in the world. God expects parents to refine
this image in their children. The office of parent is imitative of Christ's divine
pedagogy. Parents are not the saviors of their children, but they are their natural
teachers. Individual righteousness alone is not sufficient for salvation. When
parents conscientiously assume their parental office and apply themselves to
its pedagogical duties, they also, like their children, grow in godliness and in
conformity to the *imago Dei*.

The Imago Dei *and the Christian Family*

Not surprisingly, the doctrine of the *imago Dei* lies at the center of Chrysostom's anthropology: every human being is created in the image and likeness
of God. This image is social (or communal), inclusive of male and female,
who, as I have written in chapter 9, become by their union as husband and
wife one conjugal entity. In his homily on Ephesians 5:22–23, Chrysostom
states: "[God] did not, on the one hand, fashion woman independently from
man, otherwise man would think of her as essentially different from himself."[11]

9. Chrysostom, *On Marriage and Family Life*, 71.
10. See, for example, "An Address on Vainglory and the Right Way for Parents to Bring Up
Their Children," in *Christianity and Pagan Culture in the Later Roman Empire*, ed. M. L. W.
Laistner (Ithaca, NY: Cornell University Press, 1967), 96. The "address" is appended to the
back of Laistner's volume.
11. Chrysostom, *On Marriage and Family Life*, 44.

Rather, male and female are equally created in the image and likeness of God (Gen. 1:26–27). By their physical union and spiritual communion, man and woman, father and mother, pass on the image of God to their offspring.

Chrysostom's understanding of the sexes and how they conceive the child is not scientific in our modern sense. Nevertheless, the theological, even soteriological, meaning that he attributes to marriage, procreation, and child rearing is, as I have stated repeatedly, deeply trinitarian and christological. He uses the church's language of consubstantiality and *perichoresis* (co-inherence), first employed in dogmatic formulas for the incarnation and the Trinity, when he speaks of the marital union and the community of being that it brings into existence. In his homily on Colossians 4:18, he asks rhetorically,

> How do they become one flesh?. As if she were gold receiving purest gold, the woman receives the man's seed with rich pleasure, and within her it is nourished, cherished, and refined. It is mingled with her own substance and she then returns it as a child! The child is a bridge connecting mother to father, so the three become one flesh. . . . And here the bridge is formed from the substance of each! Just as the head and the rest of the body are one, so it is with the child. That is why Scripture does not say, "They shall be one flesh." But they shall be joined together "into one flesh," namely the child. But suppose there is no child; do they then remain two and not one? No; their intercourse effects the joining of their bodies, and they are made one, just as when perfume is mixed with ointment.[12]

In his homily on Ephesians 5:22–33, Chrysostom explains: "The child is born from the union of their seed, so the three are one flesh. Our relationship to Christ is the same; we become one flesh with Him through communion."[13] Thus the parent-child nexus is the natural extension into the world of the conjugal union of husband and wife. Parenthood is sown into the very fabric of what and who we are as human beings created in the image of a triune God. Furthermore, God has instilled in human beings a natural bond of affection and love between parents and their offspring that assists children to grow in a likeness to God rather than diminish further from it in a sinful world. For although Chrysostom insists that all human beings are made in the image of God, he also agrees with the patristic consensus that sin diminishes the divine image in human beings, brings death into the world, and weakens the capacity for human beings to grow in virtue and love one another.

12. Chrysostom, *On Marriage and Family Life*, 76.
13. Chrysostom, *On Marriage and Family Life*, 51.

Consequences of the Fall

Chrysostom is also a major voice within a consensus of Greek patristic writers who interpret the fall "as an inheritance essentially of mortality rather than sinfulness, sinfulness being merely a consequence of mortality."[14] This Greek patristic understanding of original sin stems from their translation of Romans 5:12, where Paul, speaking of the Genesis story, writes: "As sin came into the world through one man, and through sin, death, so death spread to all men because all men have sinned [*eph' hō pantes hēmarton*]."[15] John Meyendorff points out that there is a major issue in the way this passage was translated into Latin and in how this carries over into English translations. He explains, "The last four Greek words were translated in Latin as *in quo omnes peccaverunt* (in whom [i.e., in Adam] all men have sinned), and this translation was used in the West to justify the doctrine of original guilt inherited from Adam and spread to his descendants."[16]

The original Greek text, however, does not have this meaning. The crux of the matter has to do with the way the Greek *eph' hō*, which means "because," was translated into Latin as *in quo*, which means "in whom." As a result, Latin theology, as it was formulated in a classical way by Augustine, argues that the sin of Adam, as well as his guilt, is passed on to all human beings; whereas Greek theology maintains that death is the consequence of, or punishment for, the sin of Adam and that it is this mortality—not Adam's sin or guilt—that is passed on to the rest of humankind. "How did death come in and prevail?" Chrysostom asks in his homily on Paul's Epistle to the Romans 5:12. "But what means 'for that all have sinned'? Thus; he [Adam] having once fallen, even they [Adam's descendants] that had not eaten of the tree did from him, all of them, become mortal."[17] This condition of mortality, this corruption and destabilization of human existence, gives rise to an irresistible propensity to sin. Stated another way, Adam's mortal illness corrupts human nature and afflicts the entire race with a deeply ingrained propensity for and habit of sinning.

This perspective on sin and death is crucial for Chrysostom's assessment of the office of parent, especially the positive role he believes parents can perform not just in the moral and spiritual formation of their children but

14. John Meyendorff, *Byzantine Theology: Historical Trends and Doctrinal Themes* (New York: Fordham University Press, 1976), 144.

15. See Meyendorff, *Byzantine Theology*, 144.

16. Meyendorff, *Byzantine Theology*, 144.

17. John Chrysostom, *Homilies on the Book of Acts and the Epistle to the Romans*, in *A Select Library of Nicene and Post-Nicene Fathers of the Christian Church* (Grand Rapids: Eerdmans, 1989), 10:401 (homily 10).

also in their children's salvation. In contrast to Western notions of the need for imputed righteousness in order that we be saved, Chrysostom argues that *solidarity with the life of Jesus Christ*, the second Adam (1 Cor. 15:47), is what is necessary for human beings to overcome sin and mortality. Christ in his own body restored the *imago Dei* to its pristine state for all humankind; he healed human nature and brought it to a state of perfect holiness and made the same available to all human beings.

Renovating and Perfecting the Divine Image in Children

These ideas about the renovation of the image of God in humanity not only are the source of Chrysostom's anthropology but also give reason to his exhortation that parents are duty bound to work with God to restore and refine the *imago Dei* in their children. When parents educate their children in virtue, they assume a role comparable to Christ's action for all of humanity. For in word and deed, Christ revealed himself to be the very image of God (Col. 1:15), the prototype of the image of God that was given to Adam and Eve at their creation from which the race declined because of sin. Parents are not the saviors of their children, but they are, according to God's will and design, their natural teachers, as Christ is the divine teacher for all humankind. "This, then, is our task," Chrysostom urges parents, "to educate both ourselves and our children in godliness."[18]

His tract "An Address on Vainglory and the Right Way for Parents to Bring Up Their Children" is a landmark in Christian pastoral theology devoted to the religious education and formation of children. In it, Chrysostom expands on his favorite metaphor of the sculptor and his statue that we already have encountered. He tells parents, "Just as we see artists fashioning their paintings and statues with great precision, so we must care for these wondrous statues of ours. Painters when they have set the canvas on the easel paint on it day by day to accomplish their purpose. Sculptors, too, working in marble, proceed in a similar manner; they remove what is superfluous and add what is lacking. Even so must you proceed. Like the creators of statues so you give all your leisure to fashioning these wondrous statues for God."[19]

Thus, Chrysostom assigns to parents a sacred responsibility for the religious and moral formation of their offspring. He attributes to children a full human status (the *imago Dei*), but he also insists that parents must see to the perfection (increase in likeness to God) of these "wondrous statues"

18. Chrysostom, *On Marriage and Family Life*, 71.
19. Chrysostom, "Address on Vainglory," 96. The "address" is appended to the back of Laistner's volume.

of theirs, their children. Children are God's greatest work, made in his very own image and intended by God to participate in the divine life. Parenthood is right in the thick of a web of human relations, obligations, and synergy of human and divine wills by which salvation comes about. Thus, parents hold not only an ecclesial office but also a soteriological one, a salvific one. God has placed parents in care of their children's bodies and souls, and whether a child inherits the kingdom of heaven critically depends on the care he or she receives from his or her parents.[20]

Baptism

Chrysostom's ideas about sin and the image of God are reflected in his understanding of baptism. This understanding, which is consistent with much that is said in the Christian East, differs in important respects from the familiar Augustinian and Reformed interpretations of the rite. As I have said, Chrysostom understands original sin not in terms of inherited or personal guilt but in terms of an inherited mortality that causes human beings to sin. Augustine believes that even newly born infants participate in Adam's sin. He attributes their relative innocence, or the absence of personal sin, solely to their physical weakness—that is, "being unable to harm anyone else."[21] Nevertheless, he commends infant baptism because infants are born into the grasp of Satan. The baptism of children, then, has first to do with the repossession of the child for Christ.[22]

By contrast, Chrysostom maintains that newborn infants are innocents, wholly without sin. Infants may belong to a corporate human nature mortally wounded by sin with the will weakened and prone to personal sin, but infants are still innocents. In the fourth of his catechetical lectures on baptism, he states, "We do baptize infants. Although they are not guilty of any sins."[23] But if it is true that infants are sinless, then one might ask Chrysostom why the church baptizes them. Like Augustine, Chrysostom attributes a remedial power to baptism. But for him this is just one aspect of the sacrament and by no means exhausts its meaning. Baptism, above all else, is a welcoming

20. Chrysostom nowhere suggests that God cannot find other means to save his children. Children of bad parents are still related to a gracious and merciful God.

21. Martha Ellen Stortz, "'Where or When Was Your Servant Innocent?' Augustine on Childhood," in *The Child in Christian Thought*, ed. Marcia J. Bunge (Grand Rapids: Eerdmans, 2001), 82.

22. Stortz, "'Where or When Was Your Servant Innocent?,'" 96–97.

23. In *The Later Christian Fathers*, ed. and trans. Henry Bettenson (Oxford, UK: Oxford University Press, 1977), 165.

and acceptance by the church of the baptized person into the redeemed and sanctified body of Christ. Baptism is the beginning of a life spent in spiritual combat with evil and instruction in holiness. Baptism launches persons on a deepening journey into the kingdom of heaven. Infants and children are especially needful of being incorporated and socialized into the church just because they benefit most from the care and discipline of adults who are experienced in spiritual warfare.

Salvation, Parenting, and Children

Related to Chrysostom's ideas about the image of God and the role parents play in renovating this image in their children is his belief in the corporate nature of salvation. "We can't be saved through individual righteousness," Chrysostom insists in his homily on Ephesians 6:1–4. And he continues, "If the man who buried his one talent gained nothing, but was punished instead, it is obvious that one's own virtue is not enough for salvation, but the virtue of those for whom we are responsible is also required."[24] The implications for parenthood are striking. Though a parent may lead an otherwise virtuous life, if he or she neglects the needs of the child and fails to instruct the child in godliness, then that virtue does not count for much in the eyes of God. "Not only does God punish children who behave badly toward their parents, not only does he receive favorably those who are good," Chrysostom writes, "but he also does the same thing to the parents, severely punishing those who neglect their children, but honoring and praising those who care for them."[25]

If God is not a monad but rather a triune community of being whose ecstatic communion brings into existence creatures to love, and if humankind is created in God's very own image and likeness, then genuine virtue is an unselfish service of love toward others. And what is more natural and imitative of God's love than the love of parents for their children? Chrysostom's view of love, however, is free of sentimentalism and romanticism. It is a teaching about what we today call "tough love."

In Chrysostom's view the love of God is correlative to the fear of God, the respect, honor, and obedience due to God because God is holy. Something analogous, he says, must obtain in the parent-child relationship. Filial love necessarily includes obedience to Christ, who is perfectly obedient to the Father. Thus Paul exhorts, "Children, obey your parents in the Lord, for

---

24. Chrysostom, *On Marriage and Family Life*, 72.
25. John Chrysostom, *A Comparison between a King and a Monk/Against the Opponents of the Monastic Life*, trans. David G. Hunter (Lewiston, NY: Edwin Mellen, 1988), 132.

this is right. 'Honor your father and mother' (this is the first commandment with a promise) 'that it may be well with you and that you may live long on the earth'" (Eph. 6:1–3 RSV).[26] As for parents, Paul instructs fathers, "Do not provoke your children to anger, but bring them up in the discipline and instruction of the Lord" (Eph. 6:4 RSV). Chrysostom adds, "[Paul] does not say, 'love them.' He would regard such a commandment as superfluous; trusting that nature will draw even the unwilling parent to the love of their children. What does he say? 'Do not provoke your children to anger.'"[27] It follows that parents must not treat their children as slaves or instruments for their own pleasure.

The kind of love to which God calls parents is above natural love and transcends every corruption of it. It is the deepest sort of respect for the child as a divine "statue," an icon of God. This respect obligates parents to bring up their children "in the discipline and instruction of the Lord." Chrysostom proposes a very high and demanding doctrine of the parent-child relationship, which is rooted in fear and love of God.

Chrysostom believes also that the relative weakness and dependency of children establishes certain conditions for their salvation and that of their parents. Parents and children together suffer when the former do not assume responsibility for the latter. In his early tract titled "Against the Opponents of the Monastic Life," likely written just before or about the time of his ordination to the priesthood in 386, Chrysostom teaches this hard truth by commenting on the life of the priest Eli, whose story is told in 1 Samuel. Eli's valuable service to God and Israel is beyond dispute, but he fails to discipline adequately and to correct the behavior of his two adult sons. Their crimes are fornication and gluttony (1 Sam. 2:12–36). For this failure, God does not spare Eli from a violent death. Chrysostom judges Eli and his sons severely. He makes not even the least allowance that a parent might not be responsible for the behavior of his or her children. The hard edge of his monastic training had not yet been softened by his later experience in the pastorate.

> What, then, did God say to Samuel? *He knew that his sons cursed God, and he did not correct them* [1 Sam. 3:13]. However, this is not exactly true because

---

26. Filial obedience is not an absolute. In his homily on Eph. 6:1–4, Chrysostom raises the question, "What if my parents command me to do things that are wrong?" He answers the would-be inquirer as follows: "Paul has left us a provision in this case, by saying, '*Obey your parents in the Lord,*' that is, whenever they tell you to do what is pleasing to God. So, if your father is an unbeliever, or a heretic, and demands that you follow him, you ought not to obey, because what he commands is not in the Lord." Chrysostom, *On Marriage and Family Life*, 66.

27. Chrysostom, *On Marriage and Family Life*, 66–67.

Eli certainly did correct his sons, but God says that his was not true correction. God condemned his warning because it was not sufficiently forceful. Therefore, even if we show concern for our children, if we fail to do what is necessary, it will not be true concern, just as Eli's correction was not a true one. After God had stated the charge against Eli, he added the punishment with great wrath: *For I have sworn, he said, to the house of Eli that the iniquity of Eli's house shall not be expiated by sacrifice or offering for ever* [1 Sam. 3:14]. Do you see God's intense anger and merciless punishment? Eli must perish utterly, he says, not only him and his children, but also his entire household with him, and there will be no remedy to heal his wound. Except for the man's negligence in regard to his children, however, God had no other charge to make against the elder at that time; in all other respects Eli was a marvelous man.[28]

Since the value of children is so great in God's estimate, and their weakness equally evident, parental neglect ranks among the gravest evils and injustices. Speaking of parents who put their own needs before their children's needs and neglect the good of their children's souls, Chrysostom states, "I would say that these parents (and I am not speaking out of anger) are even worse than those who kill their children. . . . God will not easily tolerate those who neglect the ones so dear to him. He cannot labor on behalf of their salvation, while others disdain to show concern for them. . . . When parents are concerned only with their own affairs and do not wish to give priority to their children's, they necessarily neglect their children, as well as their own souls."[29]

We might question Chrysostom's judgment about what constitutes parental neglect of children. On this matter, there was no consensus in his day any more than there is in ours. It is clear, however, that the very high standard to which he holds parents responsible for their children derives from several religious and moral principles that he finds in the Christian gospel and in Jesus's teaching in particular. The most important of these is love of neighbor. Neighbor love entails much more than goodwill; it requires an active interest in the neighbor's salvation. "The Judge demands of us with the same strictness both our own and our neighbor's salvation. That is why Paul everywhere urges everyone to seek not merely their own interest, but also the interest of the neighbor."[30]

My salvation and the salvation of my neighbor are inextricably tied together, Chrysostom argues. And our children are our most proximate

28. Chrysostom, *Comparison/Against the Opponents*, 128–29.
29. Chrysostom, *Comparison/Against the Opponents*, 132–33.
30. Chrysostom, *Comparison/Against the Opponents*, 133.

neighbors. Furthermore, children are among the weakest and most vulnerable members of society. Therefore, the obligation of neighbor love is that much stronger in the parent-child relationship. "Writing to the Romans, Paul ordered them to exercise great care in this matter, urging the strong to be like parents to the weak and persuading the former to be anxious for the salvation of the latter." Paul does not say such things "on his own authority, but on instruction from the Teacher." Chrysostom continues, "For the Only-begotten of God, wishing to teach that this is a necessary duty and that great misfortunes await those who do not wish to fulfill it, said: *Whoever should scandalize one of these little ones, it would be better for him to have a great millstone fastened around his neck and to be drowned in the depths of the sea* [Matt. 18:6]."[31]

On the basis of Gospel passages such as this and on Pauline counsel, Chrysostom concludes that God has seen fit to ground parental obligation for the care and nurture of their own offspring in nature as well as in divine statute. First, God "has endowed nature with a powerful desire which by a kind of inescapable necessity leads parents to care for their children." Second, he has left commandments that fortify this natural bond and make care for one's children every bit as much a duty as caring for oneself.[32]

Parental Responsibility for the Christian Formation of Children

In summary, Chrysostom did not believe that the image of God is destroyed or that it has been so radically distorted by sin that we are forbidden to think about how it might be humanly repaired or refurbished. It is just this optimism about reform and perfectibility (*theosis* or divinization) that moved Chrysostom to exhort parents unremittingly to take up their responsibility to influence and shape the lives of their children by example and through common worship, discipline, and religious education. God, he believed, instills in human beings a natural bond between parents and their offspring that assists in the "perfection" of the young. Parents are in the best position of all to exercise a divine pedagogy that restores in children the original luster of the *imago Dei*. Parenting is not principally about preparing children to be autonomous selves who are successful in a trade or profession but rather about bringing children into the communion of saints.

Chrysostom harshly chastises Christian parents who are more concerned with secular standards of success and goals for living than with the church's

31. Chrysostom, *Comparison/Against the Opponents*, 124–25, 125, 125–26.
32. Chrysostom, *Comparison/Against the Opponents*, 131–32.

standards of right living. Over and against the commercialism and hedonism of his own day, he affirms a Christian asceticism that he would have reach into every corner of the secular world.

> If a child learns a trade, or is highly educated for a lucrative profession, all is nothing compared to the art of detachment from riches; if you want to make your child rich, teach him this. He is truly rich who does not desire great possessions, or surrounds himself with wealth, but who requires nothing. . . . Don't worry about giving him an influential reputation, for worldly wisdom, but ponder deeply how you can teach him to think lightly of this life's passing glories, thus he will become truly renowned and glorious. . . . Don't strive to make him a clever orator, but teach him to love true wisdom. He will suffer if he lacks clever words, but if he lacks wisdom, all the rhetoric in the world can't help him. *A pattern of life is what is needed, not empty speeches; character, not cleverness; deeds, not words.* These things will secure the Kingdom and bestow God's blessings.[33]

Throughout his preaching on the subject of Christian character, Chrysostom keeps in mind this "pattern of life." By what means are children to learn this pattern? Chrysostom gives us a long list that includes worship, the habit of prayer, and instruction in the commandments. Storytelling ranks high on his list. He, of course, prefers stories from Scripture, but he does not exclude pagan stories, which can be used to prepare the child's appetite and imagination for instruction in the Bible. "The child . . . learns the story of raising from the dead. If in pagan legend such marvels are told, one says: 'he made the soul the soul of a hero.' And the child believes and, while he does not know what a hero is, he knows that it is something greater than a man. And as soon as he hears, he marvels. Much more will he do so when he hears of raising from the dead and that the younger brother's [Abel's] soul went up to heaven."[34]

Chrysostom is confident also that the biblical stories are capable of communicating profound moral truths to children. He spends much time in "An Address on Vainglory" explaining to parents how they can accomplish this moral education in their own homes. For example, he suggests juxtaposing the story of Cain and Abel with that of Jacob and Esau. Parents should first draw out the distinct lessons of each story and then compare them so as to identify the common themes of sibling rivalry, envy, and fratricide, and the importance of obedience to God and parents. He urges parents to tell these

---

33. Chrysostom, *On Marriage and Family Life*, 68–69 (emphasis mine).
34. Chrysostom, "Address on Vainglory," 104.

stories to their child not once but often and repeatedly. Then they should say
to the child,

> "Tell me the story of those two brothers." And if he begins to relate the story
> of Cain and Abel, stop him and say: "It is not that one that I want, but the
> one of the other two brothers [Jacob and Esau] in which the father gave his
> blessing." Give him hints but do not as yet tell him their names. When he has
> told you all, spin the sequel of the yarn, and say: "Hear what occurred after-
> wards. Once again, the elder brother, like in the former story, was minded to
> slay his brother."[35]

Chrysostom is even attentive to what we today speak of as "age appropri-
ateness." Thus, he advises parents that when a child is older, they may tell
him more fearful tales—but not too soon, "for thou shouldst not impose so
great a burden on his understanding while he is still tender, lest thou dismay
him." When a child is "ten or eight or even younger let him hear of the
flood, the destruction of Sodom, the descent into Egypt, . . . stories full of
divine punishment. When he is older let him hear also the deeds of the New
Testament—deeds of grace and deeds of hell." He explicitly advises that a
child should not hear of hell until "he is fifteen years old or older."[36]

In this same work, Chrysostom also discusses at length biblical models
of the parent-child relationship and sibling relations. To parents, as we have
seen already, he commends the examples of Abraham and Sarah for their
great virtues of hospitality and obedience to God. He also holds up Hannah
especially, the mother of Samuel, as an exemplar of unselfish parenthood
whose first concern was to see that her only son was fit for the kingdom of
heaven and available to the Lord. Hannah fulfilled the community's office
of parenthood by unselfishly giving her only son to the temple to become
a priest. Godly parents raise their child for God, to be God's servant.
Hannah "gave Samuel to God, and with God she left him, and thus her
marriage was blessed more than ever, because her first concern was for
spiritual things."[37]

Furthermore, Chrysostom encourages parents to name their children after
the righteous and to teach them their lives. Every child should be taught the
great lives, whether of believers or unbelievers. "Let us guide the conversation to the kingdom of heaven and to those men of old, pagan or Christian,

---

35. Chrysostom, "Address on Vainglory," 106. See also "Family and Christian Virtue," chap. 6
in my book *Ethics after Christendom: Toward an Ecclesial Christian Ethic* (Grand Rapids:
Eerdmans, 1994).
36. Chrysostom, "Address on Vainglory," 109.
37. Chrysostom, *On Marriage and Family Life*, 68.

who were illustrious for their self-restraint. Let us constantly flood his ears with talk of them,"[38] he exhorts. Last but not least, he insists on a discipline of prayer and worship. Parents must teach their children "to pray with great fervor and contrition," and he adds with the voice of the strong pastor to a human lot with which we all are too familiar, "and do not tell me that a lad never will conform to these practices."[39]

Conclusion

In my analysis here, we see that John Chrysostom sets forth in his sermons and other writings an impressive theology of parenthood and a recipe for what we of late call the education of character. It is, indeed, striking how so many of the metaphors he employs to exhort parents to seize responsibility for the religious and moral education of their children have to do with leaving an "impression" on the soul or person of a child. "If good precepts are *impressed* on the soul while it is yet tender, no man will be able to destroy them when they have set firm, even as does a waxen *seal*,"[40] he urges. The means by which an impression of good character may be set firm in a child are various, and Chrysostom visits and revisits these in his sermons and tracts.

Various as these means are, however, the end is clear. Chrysostom raises parenthood to cardinal importance as a moral and ecclesial calling, and he justifies doing so on solidly trinitarian and christological grounds. Another way of putting this—not Chrysostom's but my own—is that parents are fellow workers (*synergoi*) with Christ (1 Cor. 3:9) in the garden of childhood. The Son of God calls them to raise their sons and daughters to the full stature of maturity in Christ (Eph. 4:13; Col. 1:28), as members of his body, the one, holy, catholic, and apostolic church.

It is possible that Chrysostom is a far more contemporary figure than he first appears to be. For example, when he chastises parents for their obsession with educating their children in skills for worldly success—"vainglory," as he calls it—is he not also speaking to us? Or when he advises that parents pay serious attention to the moral education of their children by judiciously selecting the images and examples of life that reach their children's eyes and ears, is he not striking a contemporary theme brought sadly and tragically to mind by the plague of bullying and violence that children commit against children on the streets and in our schools? In "An Address on Vainglory,"

38. Chrysostom, "Address on Vainglory," 118.
39. Chrysostom, "Address on Vainglory," 119.
40. Chrysostom, "Address on Vainglory," 95 (emphasis mine).

Chrysostom addresses the education of boys, but we can certainly apply his advice to our daughters also: "First train his soul and then take thought for his reputation,"[41] he insists—not bad advice for any age and perhaps especially our own.

41. Chrysostom, "Address on Vainglory," 119. When he is not talking about children in general and is more specific, Chrysostom's regular practice is to speak of sons and boys, not girls or daughters. Similarly, he more often than not addresses himself to fathers, but he does have things to say about the mother's role in raising children. For example, he freely speaks of mothers reading and telling stories to their children. This is not only a presumed practice but something he encourages.

11

CHILDHOOD

This chapter originally belonged to a volume of commissioned essays on the subject of the vocation of the child. While I value the sacred meaning that Christian writers and communities have invested in vocation, I chose in this instance to discuss the "*office* of child." I did not write "*office* of *the* child" because I wanted to emphasize the objective character of an office as contrasted with vocation, which often carries a subjective connotation. Vocation is used to refer to God's calling of *particular* persons or communities into his service, whereas an office is a *station* into which a person is "placed" or "called," or "steps into." For example, the office of child does not belong to any particular child; rather, all children may hold that office by virtue of being children.

Our English word *office* comes from the Latin *officium*. The meaning of *office* has a lineage reaching back to Aristotle, Cicero, Plutarch, and others, passing through patristic and medieval Christian thought to us. This tradition continues to make a claim on us—for example, when we make the distinction between the office of president and the person in that office. The Latin roots of *office* connote duty, work, and task. *Officium* denotes performance of a task. It, in turn, is the compound of *opus*, meaning "work," and *ficiere*, meaning "to make" or "to do."

An earlier version of this chapter originally appeared as "The Office of Child in the Christian Faith: A Theology of Childhood," in *The Vocation of the Child*, ed. Patrick M. Brennan, 104–24 (Grand Rapids: Eerdmans, 2008). Used by permission.

Historically speaking, within both religious and secular spheres, *office* also signifies a relationship with and responsibility toward others within a community. Because the child assumes his or her office by embracing the role of son or daughter, the office of child is presumptively related to the office of parent within the matrix of marriage and family. The fundamental quality of the office of child is responsibility toward one's parents, family, and the larger community. In other words, the office of child and the office of parent are reciprocally related, inextricably linked to one another. I have said something about this already in the previous chapter.

The offices of parent and child each have their own peculiar set of virtues. Trust, humility, and obedience belong especially to the office of child, whereas the virtues of the office of parent are presence, authority, and loving care.[1] Within the Christian religion, the life of Jesus Christ in his relationship to God the Father is the supreme model of the faithful performance of the office of child as son or daughter. Having set out the etymology of *office*, we will turn to exploring how it functions within a Christian theology of childhood. But let me be clear: though child and childhood overlap in meaning, they are not the same thing. We do not outgrow the office of child even when we mature into adulthood; but we do outgrow childhood. Jesus's relation to God the Father is the model. If one thinks about it, almost everything we know of Jesus is about his adult relationship to God the Father, yet what we find is exemplary of what it means to occupy the office of child. Nonetheless, my primary interest in this chapter is to explore the meaning of that time in our lives when we are children and not yet adults. For it is when we are the youngest of human beings that we first "learn" the office of being a child, an office that we ought to honor even after our parents have passed on.

In our day, when churches lament the weakening of marriage and the family, ironically, they not only have very little of substance to say about childhood, but they also demonstrate scant memory of the meaning of office as it pertains to childhood. Very often, theologians, pastors, and religious educators simply adopt and adapt models of the child and childhood from the disciplines of psychology and sociology. But these models are insufficient, and they may mislead. They do not penetrate the profound theological and even salvific significance that the Christian tradition has credited to childhood (and being

1. The virtues of the office of child are out of favor in our day. For instance, some thinkers, like the philosopher Nietzsche, reject them as signs of weakness. They equate trust, humility, and obedience with servility or self-hatred. For this reason it is important for Christian theology to reclaim the office of child. While it is not the burden of this chapter to prove these critics wrong, I hope that the positive value of these virtues of the office of child will be evident.

a child). The presence of children in the church does not just entail the responsibility to pass the faith on to them; children also are emblematic of what kind of a person the adult Christian needs to become so that he or she might inherit the kingdom of heaven. We can say that childhood is a harbinger of our eternal destiny, even a *prophecy* of it.

Having put down these preliminary observations, the remainder of this chapter divides into three sections. The first is a short discussion of the theological meanings of childhood and the office of child. This is followed by a review and critique of two contemporary views of childhood, the developmental (or stage) theory of childhood and the (postmodernist) social constructionist proposal. A serious contemporary Christian theology of childhood must, in my view, wrestle with these two competing models. In the final section of this chapter, I begin to develop a Christian theology of childhood. As I did in my previous discussion of John Chrysostom's views on the child and parenthood, I turn to a discussion of the sacrament of baptism as a touchstone for this theology.

On the Meaning of Child

The meaning of child is not limited to the small or immature human individual, much as the tenure of the office of child does not terminate at puberty or when a young man or woman leaves home and parents to marry or live independently. At the age of seventy, I still am the child, the son, of my father, Armen Guroian, and my mother, Grace Guroian. And even as they now are deceased, I strive to exercise a responsible sonship in my relationship to them, and that does not end with death.

It goes without saying that we discover the essence of childhood in young children. Likewise, it is fair to say that the office of child is the first office that a human being holds in the community. Ancient strains of Christian spirituality make much of the fact that God in Christ stooped to become a child. Ambrose of Milan counsels that the divine Word, the only begotten son of the father, "was a baby and a child, so that you may be a perfect human."[2] John Saward attempts to retrieve this theology of the birth and childhood of Jesus in his book *The Way of the Lamb: The Spirit of Childhood and the End of the Age*. In the womb of his mother, Mary, "the Son took the way of childhood into the world, and thus united Himself to every child." He need not have done so, however. "He could have created for Himself, as He

2. Ambrose of Milan, *Luke*, ed. Arthur A. Just Jr., Ancient Christian Commentary on Scripture (Downers Grove, IL: IVP, 2003), 3:38.

did for Adam, a human nature in adult form."[3] John Chrysostom explains that it was "to prevent you from thinking that his coming to earth was merely an accommodation, and to give you solid grounds for truly believing that his [Christ's] was real flesh, [and that] he was conceived, born and nurtured."[4]

Insomuch as the Second Person of the Holy Trinity assumed our humanity completely and grew as we grow from embryo to adult, God in Christ has revealed something special about the economy of salvation. Ironically, in order that we "grow" into godlikeness, we must grow into what Paul speaks of as "a perfect man," according to "the measure of the stature of the fullness of Christ" (Eph. 4:13).

The virtues that are typically associated with the child are humility, simplicity, unaffected love, trust, and obedience. Christ exercised these virtues through the whole of his life. Unfortunately, as a consequence of the fall and sin, we are prone with age to shed these gifts of childhood. Yet humanity is not bereft of hope: through the sacrament of baptism God offers every human being the opportunity for a second birth into innocence and the grace to grow young again in his own image, Christ's image (Col. 1:15). Augustine says, "They went [into the baptismal font] as old men [and] they came out as infants."[5] Nerses Shnorhali, the great twelfth-century Armenian bishop and saint, articulates the paradox and the mystery of divine youth in his long poem *Jesus, the Son*:

> Thou [Jesus] didst enter the temple to be presented;
> And thou, the Ancient of Days [Dan. 7:13], the aged man [Simeon]
> took thee up as a child in his saintly arms.
> I who was born in sin from vice,
> Thou didst create me anew at the font.[6]

Developmental Child Psychology and the Postmodernist Critique

In our day, two theories of the child contend for attention and acceptance. The first is the developmental or stage theory of the child. The second is the

---

3. John Saward, *The Way of the Lamb: The Spirit of Childhood and the End of the Age* (San Francisco: Ignatius, 1999), 68–69.

4. John Chrysostom, *Luke*, ed. Arthur A. Just Jr., Ancient Christian Commentary on Scripture (Downers Grove, IL: IVP, 2003), 3:39.

5. Saward, *Way of the Lamb*, 62.

6. Nerses Shnorhali, *Jesus, the Son*, trans. Mischa Kudian (London: Mashtots Press, 1986), 36–37.

postmodernist social constructionist theory of the child. The former issues principally from the field of psychology and the latter from sociology. A Christian theology of childhood that entirely embraces either theory will negate itself and no longer be Christian; but it is possible to incorporate something of each into a theology of childhood.

The writings of Jean Piaget and Lawrence Kohlberg and their followers are representative of the developmental model of the child. The chief premise of developmental theory is that there are natural stages of moral development through which normal, healthy human individuals pass from infancy through adulthood.

Kohlberg argues that individuals necessarily progress through the stages of development one at a time and that they cannot "jump" or "skip" stages, although they can regress. In this sense, the model is "deterministic." The *telos* or goal of the progression is the formation of an autonomous or independent moral conscience. Progress through the various stages of moral development (six for Kohlberg) is not inevitable, however. Human beings must have social interaction to develop as moral beings. They require experience that is educative in the broadest sense, experience that challenges them to move ahead from one stage to the next. Children need to be challenged with dilemmas that prompt them to move on to the higher stages of moral development toward moral autonomy.

Pitted against the developmental and stage model of childhood is a theory of childhood as social construct that postmodernist sociology advances. This theory accuses developmental psychology of two baneful errors: a nature-based determinism (i.e., fixed stages of growth toward moral autonomy) and a philosophical essentialism that falsely defines the child as a universal phenomenon. As we have seen in Kohlberg's case, developmental theory defines childhood as a natural and determinate stage (or series of stages) on the way to "becoming" a complete human being.

Chris Jenks, a representative of the postmodernist school, argues that we should not think of childhood as a set of predetermined natural (biological or psychological) stages of growth and maturation. Childhood is not something fixed on a continuum from irrational, pre-moral immaturity to adulthood, reason, and moral autonomy. "Physical [or mental] morphology," he maintains, "may constitute a form of difference between people in certain circumstances but it is not an adequately intelligible basis for the relationship between the adult and the child."[7] Whereas they ought to be treated as genuine human agents, stage theory, with its essentialist and

---

7. Chris Jenks, *Childhood* (London: Routledge, 2005), 6.

determinist bias, denigrates young people by classifying them as incomplete human beings.[8]

Postmodernists, like Jenks, argue that childhood plays a certain role in the structure of society and as such, it is a construct of such societies rather than a *universal* feature."[9] Thus childhood is a diverse phenomenon. "There is no essential child [but many childhoods] . . . built up through constitutive practices."[10] Childhood is a linguistic-cultural invention that reflects the interests of the adult world and varies according to cultural setting, and developmental child psychology is merely one of these linguistic-cultural inventions.[11] It follows then that no universally valid criteria exist for judging the moral status of the child. There is no "essential" child.

The Christian Alternative to Developmental Theory

Christian theology is obliged to reject the social construct thesis of the postmodernist school. But it can agree with the postmodernists that developmental psychology devalues childhood. That is to say, when one views childhood principally as a stage (or stages) in a determinate course of human maturation, the child may, indeed, be reduced to an epiphenomenon on the path to becoming a morally autonomous adult.

Stanley Hauerwas criticizes moral development theory in just this way. Moral development ultimately concerns itself with "how to reach the last stage of morality," wherein people stop growing morally and have reached a sort of moral autonomy. By this view, childhood, once having been left behind, is of little lasting significance. It is merely "a pre- or non-moral stage of [human] development."[12] Much like the tadpole that metamorphoses into a frog, the importance of childhood is reduced solely to a function of the superior end toward which it invariably moves.

Growth Is Not Perfection

Instead of the tadpole and frog analogy, a better analogy for the child is the oak sapling that grows into a mature tree and leaves lasting rings in the

8. Jenks, *Childhood*, 8–9.

9. Jenks, *Childhood*, 50.

10. Allison James, Chris Jenks, and Alan Prout, *Theorizing Childhood* (Hoboken, NJ: Wiley-Blackwell, 1998), 212.

11. Jenks, *Childhood*, 6.

12. Stanley Hauerwas, *A Community of Character* (Notre Dame, IN: University of Notre Dame Press, 1981), 133.

trunk. Jesus exhorts his listeners to emulate "childlikeness" and make the "childlike" virtues of trust, humility, and obedience their own—not to leave them behind, though he in no way suggests that every child possesses these virtues in exemplary fashion.

The great nineteenth-century English divine John Henry Newman drew from this scriptural record to elaborate on the eternal value of childhood. Newman holds up for special attention the simplicity, innocence, artless love, and openness to mystery and spiritual reality that is found in children. But he adds that children nevertheless lack "formed principles in [their hearts], . . . habits of obedience, . . . [and] true discrimination between the visible and the unseen."[13] In other words, in children these virtues are not yet the perfections of the kingdom of God. A child "is but a type of what is at length to be fulfilled in him . . . , of what God will make of us, if we surrender our hearts to the guidance of His Holy Spirit,"[14] says Newman.

Despite children's lack of discipline and self-control, their status and station have an inherent value. According to Newman, we may forgive children their lack of consistency in virtuous behavior precisely because they are young and inexperienced, while we remain open to what they can teach us about what we need to become in order to inherit the kingdom of God.

As with all figures of speech, even the oak sapling metaphor is limited. It does not suffice for a complete and accurate understanding of childhood. The oak sapling must *necessarily* become an oak tree with a *particular* shape and type of foliage and fruit. Personal life, however, is indeterminate and pluripotent, transcending mere biological growth. Stage and developmental theory maintains that a determinate process of growth from infancy to youth and adulthood arrives at freedom and autonomy when the individual reaches the age of reason. This theory does not, nor is it capable of, resolving this *prima facie* contradiction. How can a determinate process lead to freedom? Developmental psychology does not fully comprehend the self-transcendent (spiritual) nature of personal existence that even children possess.

Once again, we are reminded of the limitations of the analogy of the oak tree. The metaphors of growth that we take from nature simply cannot bring to light the Christian doctrines of radical freedom, sin, and conversion. Sin is

13. John Henry Newman, "The Mind of Little Children," in *Parochial Sermons and Plain Sermons* (San Francisco: Ignatius, 1997), 267.

14. Newman, "Mind of Little Children," 268. I am at this writing a grandfather to five grandchildren, six years of age and under. And I confess that Newman's description of these young people as "a blessed intimation . . . a foretaste of what will be fulfilled in heaven" is apropos of my feelings when they are in my presence. It is an astonishing feeling, one that, in spite of all my reading and writing on the subjects of parenthood and childhood, is a great and wonderful surprise!

not merely a failure in a system, such as when a disease shortens the height or distorts the shape of a tree. A sin is a creation that the self wills into being, although it contradicts the good of the agent and the will of God. "Conversion denotes the necessity of a turning that is so fundamental that the self is placed on a path of growth for which there is no end,"[15] Hauerwas points out, for this "growth" transcends necessity. Perfection is its end; the "growth" is self-directed. It is freedom enacted away from sin and toward God.

Freedom, so understood, explodes the determinacy of developmental theory. It certainly does not originate from a determinate process. That is why, says Hauerwas, the translation of the Christian language of perfection into the language of development is a great misfortune. It robs perfection of its religious and transcendent significance.[16] Christian perfection is sanctification (*theosis* or deification for Orthodox): a self-directed, self-enacted movement toward divine similitude. Holiness, not just rationality or moral conscience, is the earmark of human maturity and perfection. What is more, there is no point along the path to perfection that is inferior to that which comes after it. There is no stage along the way that is mere necessity either.

The Lesson of Child Saints

Christian faith draws important lessons from those it names saints or holy persons—for our purposes, especially, child saints and martyrs—as exemplars of the radical indeterminacy of human existence. The saints leap across psychological boundaries and growth-stage markers. Take for example Saint Peter Chrysologus's fifth-century sermon on Matthew's account of Herod's slaughter of the children of Bethlehem (Matt. 2:16). Chrysologus writes, "He [Christ] gave to them [the children who were slaughtered] the gift of the crown even before their bodies had grown. It was Christ's will that they pass over vice for virtue, attain heaven before earth and share in the divine life immediately."[17]

The Christian church reckons these holy innocents as the first martyrs for Christ. Much theology and spirituality has been developed around this belief. We cannot review that here. But we can take a quick look at three main elements of the theology of the child saint that Chrysologus employs. First, the slaughtered children gained the crowns of holiness even before "their bodies had grown." Spirit transcends nature. Holiness does not follow nature; it is a

15. Hauerwas, *Community of Character*, 131.
16. Hauerwas, *Community of Character*, 130.
17. Peter Chrysologus, *Matthew 1–13*, ed. Manlio Simonetti, Ancient Christian Commentary on Scripture (Downers Grove, IL: IVP, 2001), 1a:34.

"gift" of God. Second, "it was Christ's will that they pass over vice for virtue." Virtue, too, is a gift and not merely an achievement of human conscience or the fruit of biological maturation. Third, they "attain[ed] heaven before earth." The end or telos of human existence is not natural; it is spiritual. Spiritual "maturity" is something quite different from biological or psychological maturity. We may experience heaven on earth. Perfection and beatitude are not the result of living a full natural life, as the purple of the grape is the result of ripening a full season. Rather, human freedom is at play. Who we are and what we may become do not depend solely on natural processes. Even human freedom does not entirely explain human perfection—for divine will and grace surpass and may even bypass nature and history.

The Shortcomings of Postmodernist Social Constructionism

Developmental psychology swings the pendulum too far toward the pole of naturalism and determinism. Postmodernism points this out. The theory of social construction, however, swings the pendulum to the opposite pole of a radical historicism and cultural relativism. It claims to affirm human freedom, but this is not a transcendental freedom. This is not freedom oriented to a spiritual end, such as the *imago Dei*.

Furthermore, social constructionism rejects the epistemological and ontological realism of the Christian tradition.[18] As I have said already, it rejects the notion of the "essential" child. This would not be so troublesome if all that was meant by this denial was that, as an exercise in *thought*, we ought not to abstract the child from time and context. But social constructionism insists on more than that. Just as there is no essential child, so too there is no universal human nature.

At this juncture, social constructionism and Christianity part company completely. The Christian faith affirms the existence of universal human nature, although it certainly does not embrace this as a naked metaphysical proposition, as postmodernists often accuse. Rather, Christianity grounds its doctrine of a universal human nature in the central Christian dogma of the incarnation, which itself is no mere idea but rather an action of God. God in Jesus Christ assumed our "flesh," our whole humanity. The divine Word became a human child, and his childhood is, if for no other reason than this, universally significant for humankind. The childhood of the incarnate Word predicates a universal human nature as well as a spiritual end for human

18. James, Jenks, and Prout, *Theorizing Childhood*, 17–19.

existence. Following the logic of the postmodernist position, however, even if one were to grant for argument's sake that God actually did become a human child in ancient Palestine, it is not possible that that event could have an ontological, let alone a salvific, bearing in all times and places. This is how radical the postmodernist's historicism actually is. Without denying our human historicity, we must judge that this historicism is a belief and not the provable fact that it often claims for itself. Having set down these criticisms of the developmental and social constructionist models, we may discuss the distinguishing features of a Christian theology of childhood.

A Christian Theology of Childhood

Childhood and Parenthood: What Has Sex Got to Do with It?

Sexuality does not belong to the divine life, but it most certainly belongs to human existence. The Son is begotten of the Father in perfect freedom, whereas human procreation, parenthood, and childhood derive from both natural determinacy and sexual love. There is no such thing as pure instinct in the human being. Human eros is not merely a sexual urge. Eros includes spirit, freedom, and choice. We cannot explain or account for human parental and filial love solely on the basis of animal sexual drive or a motherly or fatherly instinct to care for the child. We may say that human fathers sire their young and that mothers give birth to them. But being sired and being born do not alone make a child or a son or a daughter. Siring and giving birth alone do not make a father or mother either.

The extraordinary Victorian writer George MacDonald asks in his *Unspoken Sermons*: "Was Jesus ever less divine than God?" His answer is, "Never!"[19] But if this is so, then childhood must always have belonged to divine being. The Word became flesh at a particular moment in time; he grew from an infant into a man over a span of years. Nevertheless, the Word is eternally begotten of the Father; the Word is eternally the Father's child. Even before his conception and birth by a woman, even before Christ assumed the office of human son, his divine hypostasis is related to the Father as Son and he occupies the office of divine sonship. Childhood and sonship and daughterhood have a divine origin.

The seer of the book of Revelation states a related mystery. Jesus Christ is "the Lamb slain from the foundation of the world" (13:8). Our humanity

19. George MacDonald, "The Child in the Midst," in *Unspoken Sermons* (Whitehorn, CA: Johannesen, 1997), 13.

is preexistent within the life of God, through the Son, from all eternity. Childhood is itself an eternal attribute of God. Newman writes, "What shall we say of the Eternal God but that He, *because* He is eternal, is ever young, without a beginning, and therefore without change, and, in the fulness and perfection of His incomprehensible attributes, now just what He was a million years ago? He is truly called in Scripture the 'Ancient of Days,' and is therefore infinitely venerable, yet he needs not old age to make Him venerable."[20] God has created humankind in his own image, and that image includes childhood.

Mary Ann Hinsdale has demonstrated that the twentieth-century Roman Catholic theologian Karl Rahner was similarly persuaded. Rahner believed that childhood is not restricted to "the first phase of our biological lives but is 'a basic condition' always appropriate to human existence lived rightly."[21] He believed that "human childhood is not transferred by some dubious process of metaphorical or poetic transference to a quite different reality which we called the childhood of God, but rather has its ultimate basis [in God's existence]. . . . Childhood is only truly understood, only realises the ultimate depths of its own nature, when it is seen as based upon the foundation of the childhood of God."[22]

"Whoever Receives One of These Little Children"

The ninth chapter of the Gospel of Mark presents us with the scene wherein the disciples are arguing among themselves over which of them will hold the highest office in the kingdom. Jesus lifts up a child and says to his disciples: "Whoever receives one of these little children in My name receives Me; and whoever receives Me, receives not Me but Him who sent Me" (Mark 9:37). MacDonald believes that these verses "record a lesson our Lord gave his disciples against ambition, against emulation."[23] Jesus teaches the disciples a lesson concerning the true divine and redemptive nature of childhood.[24] MacDonald adds that "the recognition of the *childhood as divine* . . . will show the disciples how vain the strife after relative place or honour in the great kingdom. . . . When he tells them to receive such a little child in his name, it must surely imply something in common between them all—something in

20. Quoted by Saward, *Way of the Lamb*, 66–67n26.
21. Mary Ann Hinsdale, "'Infinite Openness to the Infinite': Karl Rahner's Contribution to Modern Catholic Thought on the Child," in *The Child in Christian Thought*, ed. Marcia J. Bunge (Grand Rapids: Eerdmans, 2001), 427.
22. Hinsdale, "'Infinite Openness,'" 427–28.
23. MacDonald, "Child in the Midst," 2.
24. MacDonald, "Child in the Midst," 7.

which the child and Jesus meet—something in which the child and the disciples meet. What else can that be than the spiritual childhood?"[25]

This is to say that when Jesus states, "Whoever receives these little children in My name receives Me," he means more than that he desires that the disciples receive the little child as himself. He also reveals two fundamental realities about God and the kingdom of heaven. First, the relation of children to their parents is an image of Jesus's own relationship to God the Father. Second, every baptized human being enters into a new relationship as adoptive son or daughter of God the Father and brother or sister of Jesus.

Caryll Houselander writes in her modern classic of spirituality *The Passion of the Infant Christ*: "In our tenderness for those whom we love, above all our love for children, we know God in His image and likeness in ourselves. We come to know God as Father and Mother and Lover. . . . We learn the simplicity, the humility and trust of children, but only if we dare to love one another."[26] MacDonald adds: "To receive a child in the name of Jesus is to receive Jesus; to receive Jesus is to receive God; therefore to receive the child is to receive God himself."[27] God is not just father of the divine Word, but stepfather to all who are baptized. God is not just a friend in Christ, but the stepbrother of all who are baptized. Through the Spirit and in Christ, persons, children and adults alike, increase in God's own image, an image that illumines the full meaning and purpose of the offices of child and parent.

Bios and *Zoe*

Neither psychology nor sociology comprehends these transcendent, spiritual origins of childhood. Nor, by the very rules of inquiry that each follows, can either account for the offices of son and daughter and father and mother. Not mere nature, instinct, or even freedom enables child or parent to fulfill his or her respective office. We must take into account the spiritual dimension of human existence and the role that love plays.

Nevertheless, freedom and choice are powerful predicates of human parenthood and childhood, as they also are evidences of spirit in nature. The Gospel narratives of the conception and birth of Jesus emphasize this, as do the Christian feasts of the annunciation and nativity that explore the meaning of these narratives. Mary became a mother despite the fact that her

25. MacDonald, "Child in the Midst," 7 (emphasis mine).
26. Caryll Houselander, *The Passion of the Infant Christ* (New York: Sheed and Ward, 1949), 79–80.
27. MacDonald, "Child in the Midst," 9.

motherhood did not issue from her sexual nature or from conjugal union. Mary freely accepted the call of God to assume the office of mother to God the Son. Joseph was not Jesus's biological father, yet Joseph, of his own free willing, consented to be the stepfather of the incarnate Son of God, as God is stepfather to every baptized person. The Word eternally chose Mary and Joseph to be his earthly parents and accepted the office of human son through a supreme act of kenotic love so that all humankind might inherit eternal life as God's children and as his own brothers and sisters.

Thus the Gospels attest that the parent-child nexus, though rooted in nature and human biology and reaching diverse forms in history, is transcendentally grounded in God's eternal triune being. Human parenthood and childhood may be grounded in *bios* (biological) existence, yet both originate and have their fulfillment in what C. S. Lewis calls *zoe* (spiritual) existence.[28] *Bios* is the realm of necessity and *zoe* the realm of transcendental freedom. Natural law defines and gives shape to *bios*. The virtues constitute *zoe*; for in the strictest and deepest sense all virtues are spiritual, since virtue is an attribute of personhood, and personhood is the divine image in humankind.

"God caused us to be loved by our parents for this reason, that we might have mentors in virtue," writes Chrysostom. "You see," he adds, "God does not make fathers only for having children . . . nor . . . mothers [only] to give birth to children. . . . It is not nature but virtue that makes parents."[29] Likewise Cyril of Jerusalem observes, "For like as Mary was called mother of John [the apostle], because of her parental affection, not from having given him birth, so Joseph also was called father of Christ, not for having begotten Him (*for he knew her not*, as the Gospel says, *until she had brought forth her first-born Son*), but because of the care bestowed on His nurture."[30]

From this theological perspective, we can see that the holy family is not the exception to the rule, as some mistakenly characterize it but rather the fullest human expression of the offices of parent and child and the relationship they strengthen and perfect. For in the end, to be a human parent or human son or daughter is an act of freedom, a willingness to be so when love is present. Even the fact that Jesus is eternally begotten of the Father does not stand in the way of our emulating the holy family. This is because God the Father is the author of the office of sonship or daughterhood much as he is also the author of the office of fatherhood and motherhood. The Father reveals himself

---

28. C. S. Lewis, *Mere Christianity* (San Francisco: HarperCollins, 2001), bk. 4, chap. 10.

29. Chrysostom, *Old Testament Homilies*, vol. 1, *Homilies on Hannah, David and Saul*, trans. Robert Charles Hill (Brookline, MA: Holy Cross Orthodox Press, 2003), 71.

30. Cyril of Jerusalem, "Catechetical Lectures," in *A Select Library of Nicene and Post-Nicene Fathers of the Christian Church*, second series (Grand Rapids: Eerdmans, 1978), 7:46.

as the Father at Jesus's baptism in the waters of the Jordan and again also on Mount Tabor, where Jesus is transfigured before the eyes of Peter, James, and John. At Jesus's baptism, the Father announces: "You are My beloved Son, in whom I am well pleased" (Mark 1:11), and on Mount Tabor, "This is My beloved Son. Hear Him!" (9:7).

Cyril comments, "We came into holy sonship not of necessity but by choice."[31] Every human child is a potential son or daughter of God. We cannot say the same about the lion cub or the canine puppy. Jesus is not only the pioneer of our salvation but also our model of human sonship and daughterhood and of the divine sonship and daughterhood that baptism confers on us. Cyril says of Christ, and as a reminder to all who are baptized, that "He [Christ] obeys the Father, yielding, not a forced obedience, but a self-chosen accordance; for He is not a servant, that He should be subjected by force, but a Son, that He should comply of His free choice and natural love."[32] God the father affords the same relationship and status to those who believe in Christ his son. Thus, we come by this station not according to virtue alone or merely by reason of our human nature but by our freely given obedience to the Father, who loves each one of us as his own son or daughter.

Christian Anthropology and the Divine Character of Childhood

The primary speech of Christian anthropology is transformational: it is not the language of growth naturalistically conceived. To repeat what I have been saying, the Christian faith is perfectionist, not developmental or, for that matter, social constructionist. Hauerwas rightly maintains that the Christian idea of maturity (or perfection) suggests a much "more radical transformation and continued growth"[33] than child development theory imagines. In summary, from the standpoint of Christian belief, human "growth" transcends mere biological maturation. It is "growth" toward a spiritual perfection that transcends the natural course of life from conception to death. Because of sin and a corrupted will, however, human "maturation" into spiritual life also requires penance and conversion, enabled by God's freely offered grace through the power of the Holy Spirit.

Contrary to postmodernism's radical doctrine of historicity, the human person does not just enact his or her own history but may partake of and participate in a transcendent spiritual dimension of divine life, which God

---

31. Cyril, "Catechetical Lectures," 47.
32. Cyril, "Catechetical Lectures," 113.
33. Hauerwas, *Community of Character*, 131.

graciously offers to the creature that he has created in his very own image. On the one hand, the spiritual dimension of human existence is indeterminate: it entails freedom. On the other hand, this freedom is not open ended; it has an end (or *telos*) that is transnatural and transhistorical. God, not nature or history, gives human existence meaning, purpose, and direction. God accomplishes this through creative actions, by making humankind free and self-transcendent. Our humanity is grounded in the eternal Spirit of God and God's perfect freedom. Paul writes: "The Lord is the Spirit, and where the Spirit of the Lord is, there is freedom" (2 Cor. 3:17 RSV).

Therefore, according to Christian anthropology, childhood has a footing both in nature and nature's determinism and in the historicity that is the outcome of immanent freedom. God also has planted in all human beings a sort of force that impels and propels them into a spiritual dimension. The image of God is neither static nor merely a character trait or combination of human capacities. It is an inclination or movement toward a personal relationship in communion with God, toward a perfection of divine similitude, a participation in the love and life of God, the Father, the Son, and the Holy Spirit. Like the tree whose branches reach to the sky, humankind, though made of dust, reaches toward spirit.

This capacity of transcendent participation in the life of the Spirit is no less present in children than in adults. If it were absent in children, the church could not justify infant and child baptism. Indeed, this inclination toward godmanhood and god-womanhood may be more pronounced, or at least more pristine, in children than in adults because in children the original corruption of sin has not progressed as far as in adults; the habit of sin is still young.

Childhood and Original Sin

As I have shown in the preceding chapter, in contrast to Western theologies—influenced by Augustine—that attribute an "inherited" or "original guilt" to all human beings, no matter their age, the Orthodox tradition believes that although all human beings are born into a sinful world, all at the start are also free from actual sin and do not carry the guilt of Adam. Infants, therefore, are innocents. Chrysostom writes, "We do baptize infants, although they are not guilty of any sins."[34] All human beings develop the habit of sin and may accumulate personal guilt as they experience life. Young children, however, are in a real sense more like what all Christians must become than are adults. Christians must become spiritual children.

---

34. John Chrysostom, *The Later Christian Fathers*, ed. and trans. Henry Bettenson (Oxford, UK: Oxford University Press, 1977), 169.

Legal scholar Joseph Vining comments in his book *From Newton's Sleep* that the spiritual dimension of human existence is entirely different from both "the biological (determinacy), which is a given," and "the malleable constrictions, called socially constructed," which connote what is "wholly changeable and with no necessity whatever to it."[35] This spiritual dimension of human life has, however, its own peculiar "determinacy." God destines us to be his adoptive sons and daughters—though paradoxically what God destines is also what we freely choose. When Paul speaks of the Christian coming into the stature of the fullness of Christ, he is identifying this spiritual dimension of human existence (Eph. 4:13). He is pointing to a mystical (i.e., hidden) synergy of human will and divine energy, a movement of the human person toward holiness, wholeness, and perfection set in motion by God's creation of human beings in his own image and their perfection in Christ.

This perfection is not an end state, a mere stasis, however. Rather it is an everlasting participation in the divine life (2 Pet. 1:3–4), a transtemporal communion of the saints (1 Thess. 3:11–13) that is perpetually transformation but not change, destiny but not necessity. The offices of child and parent in their relation to one another are trajectories on this path to holiness, wholeness, and perfection. The primary way that God reveals these trajectories and makes them available to us is through the Christian sacrament of baptism.

On Baptism and the Meaning of Childhood

> Know you what it is to be a child? It is to have a spirit yet streaming from the waters of Baptism.
>
>   Francis Thompson, from "Shelley"[36]

By baptism we become children of God, and by being made a child of God, adds Clement of Alexandria, we are also "being made perfect . . . [and] immortal."[37] In other words, our biological, chronological childhood is both preparation for and symbol of the office of child of God, a spiritual, transtemporal childhood. Clement also argues that when Jesus speaks of children and childhood, he has in mind that "we are the children."[38] And

---

35. Joseph Vining, *From Newton's Sleep* (Princeton: Princeton University Press, 1995), 12–13.

36. Thompson's essay "Shelley" originally appeared in the *Dublin Review* in July 1908.

37. Clement of Alexandria, "The Instructor," in *Ante-Nicene Fathers* (Peabody, MA: Hendrickson, 2004), 2:215.

38. Clement, "Instructor," 212.

when God places children in our presence, God is instructing us in the virtues we need to fulfill the office of child of God that God bestows on us by our baptisms. Clement continues, "On the question . . . 'which of them should be the greater,' Jesus placed a little child in the midst, saying, 'Whosoever shall humble himself as this little child, the same shall be the greater in the kingdom of heaven' (Matt. 18:4). He does not then use the appellation of children on account of their very limited amount of understanding from their age, as some have thought."[39]

"Unless you are converted," Jesus says, "and become as little children, you will by no means enter the kingdom of heaven" (Matt. 18:3). In Clement's analysis, our Lord commends to us the virtues of trust, humility, and obedience that belong to children.[40] In this sense, children are our best guides to filling the office of sons and daughters of God. Clement's comments are neither naive nor romantic. If we presume that the Christian doctrine of original sin (or our ancestral sin, as Orthodox theology prefers to call it) applies to children, then young children, let us say as young as one or two years old, are most certainly not pure innocents. The resistance of even the young child to these virtues bears a peculiar kind of witness, however, to the fact that they do belong quintessentially to childhood, since this behavior is in utter contradiction to our intuitive sense of how children ought to be.

These virtues of trust, humility, and obedience are essential not only for "natural" childhood and the "natural" relationship of children with their parents but also for Christian men and women in their relationship to God as his adopted sons and daughters. Real human maturity is not the same thing as chronological adulthood; the end of which is senility and death. Real human maturity is the rebirth of innocence (or, perhaps, in Paul Ricoeur's famous turn of phrase, a "second naïveté").

We arrive at a central paradox of the Christian life that John Henry Newman identifies. As we have seen, Newman argues that childhood is "a type of the perfect Christian state." Christ said that we must become as little children to enter his kingdom for "in them we are bound to see Christian perfection." But God does not ask us to perform what is impossible and return by our powers alone to our original innocence in the garden of Eden or to become literal children once again. "We are not, we cannot [literally] be children [again]; grown men have faculties, passions, aims, principles, views, duties, which children have not."[41]

39. Clement, "Instructor," 213.
40. Newman, "Mind of Little Children," 1024.
41. Newman, "Mind of Little Children," 1024.

We rightly desire that our children mature into responsible adults. Yet ironically in wishing this we forget that the kingdom of heaven more nearly resembles our state of childhood with its innocence than does spoiled adulthood. Children share in the original or ancestral sin of Adam, and the "old Adam" in them is already corrupting their innocence. Yet they do not "know" sin intimately, or at least they do not experience its consequences as their common base of knowledge. In some real and substantial sense, they have not yet eaten from the tree of knowledge. Only a child or a simpleton will wonder how there might be evil people in the world.

Jesus understood these matters. That is why, according to Newman, Jesus did the unexpected and took a child in his arms as a specimen and example of what a disciple of his must become. "In aiming to be children again, we are aiming to be Adam on his creation," in the special sense that "children are saved, not by their purposes and habits of obedience, not by faith and works, but by the influence of baptismal grace [alone]; [as] into Adam God 'breathed the breath of life, and man became a living soul' (Gen. 2:7)."[42] We, in our fallen and sin-smudged condition, in our adulterated adulthood, have but small traces of Eden left within us or that show on our faces, except for the few who are holy. We may be baptized as biological children or as adults, but in either case by baptism we become *spiritual* children. In adulthood, far more so than in childhood, we need cleansing, refreshment, and spiritual rehabilitation. Yet even if we were baptized as infants, baptism may be the source of this cleaning and refreshment throughout our lives. God breathes the breath of life into us once again, and over and over again, as our baptisms are perpetually renewed in eucharistic worship.

Conclusion

Synchronically, the office of parent may seem more important than the office of child. Indeed, in our culture the former is almost always assumed to be the superior. Yet this is an inversion of the wisdom of Christ and of the church fathers. Diachronically, and even more especially from the perspective of Christian soteriology and eschatology, the office of child and the virtues associated with it are more significant than the office of parent and its virtues. Paul writes that baptism sets the Christian free on a path of perfection, toward divine likeness "from glory to glory" (2 Cor. 3:18). God assists his adoptive children on that path by the example of his only begotten Son. In the ancient baptismal

42. Newman, "Mind of Little Children," 1027.

hymn that Paul incorporated into his Letter to the Philippians, he predicates Christ's filial relationship to God the father in trust, humility, and obedience. "He [Christ] humbled Himself and became obedient to the point of death, even the death of the cross" (Phil. 2:8). Thus God calls every Christian to this very same office and the virtues that belong to it. Each person whom the church baptizes God adopts as his son or daughter. And God sends each of them "the Spirit of His Son" so that they might cry out, "Abba, Father!" (Gal. 4:6).

The transformation and translation into *zoe* life that baptism inaugurates does not efface or negate nature. Baptismal grace builds on human nature. The temporal human offices of child and parent have their own integrity (the integrity of creation), even as God also employs these offices in his redemptive work. I have said that the virtues of office of child are more significant in the scheme of redemption and sanctification than are the virtues of the office of parent. And I have hinted that the evidence for this is the incarnation itself, that Jesus through his life, death, and resurrection fulfilled all the requirements of the office of child and, thereby, showed us what perfection truly is.

This is a strong reason why Christian theology resists and rejects conceptions of childhood that conceive of it as either an ephemeral stage of human existence or that deny its universal status. When we become adults and parents, we do not simply leave behind the office of child like the crab that sheds its first shell for a second and a third. Through the whole of our lives, we naturally continue to relate to our parents as their children. We also find it needful to "remember" and, in some real sense, recapitulate our childhood, so that we will be good and successful parents. Similarly, in our relationship with God, we never wholly cease to be children nor do we completely "outgrow" the virtues of childhood, although they take on a different meaning and character. Newman writes, "As habits of holiness are matured, principle, reason, and self-discipline are unnecessary; a moral instinct takes their place in the breast, or rather, to speak more reverently, the Spirit is sovereign there. . . . We act from love."[43]

When we come to the end of our earthly lives, we also leave behind the office of parent, even adulthood itself. We render up the office of parent to God alone. As spiritual children, we lovingly and trustingly give ourselves over completely to God's parental care. Ironically, we complete our course of natural existence by accepting the office of child as the way to eternal life. This, indeed, is "the measure of the stature of the fullness of Christ" (Eph. 4:13). In this way, we fulfill perfectly the office of son or daughter no longer in relation to human parents but wholly in relation to God and, by this path, receive God's eternal blessing.

43. Newman, "Mind of Little Children," 1028.

Conclusion

In the introduction, I furnished readers with a look into the background of my theological existence and especially the experiences and the convictions that contributed to this book. I closed the introduction with a glance forward to the conclusion and promised that rather than providing a summation of the book, the conclusion extends an invitation to readers to broaden and deepen their knowledge and understanding of the Orthodox Church and its theology.

During my teaching years at the University of Virginia from 2008 to 2015, I was free to develop courses in Orthodox Christianity on both introductory and advanced levels. In these concluding pages, I discuss the reading lists of two syllabi from these courses. It is not possible in such a short space to account for or describe everything in these reading lists or to deeply discuss the thought that went into making my selections. I have, however, added bibliographic information so you, the reader, may easily find the books, chapters, and articles that are listed.

Both lists reflect many years of reading and study. I suspect that most college and university teachers would agree that much time and work go into constructing a good syllabus—much more than most who use and benefit from it ever imagine. Nonetheless, this labor is intrinsically rewarding. It can be a highly creative and satisfying activity, an almost unique occasion to review and organize one's own learning.

The first reading list is for the course "Themes in Eastern Orthodoxy: An Introduction." This course was designed for upper-level undergraduate students. The readings commence with a study of the Byzantine formation of the Orthodox faith and its distinctive dogmatic, liturgical, and ecclesiastical characteristics. The balance of the readings introduces the sacramental and iconographic tradition of the Orthodox Church and also Orthodoxy's engagement with the modern world. The second reading list is from the course "Prospects in Eastern Orthodox Theology." This course was for graduate and upper-level undergraduate students. All the selections are from modern and contemporary Orthodox theology and are heavily weighted toward dogmatic themes, although by no means limited to these. I endeavored to include as many modern and contemporary Orthodox voices as possible without committing the error of filling the plate so full that it becomes a muddle of different flavors. I am confident that the assembled texts open up a comprehensive view of the shape, scope, and tenor of contemporary Orthodox theology.

A General Introduction to the Orthodox Church

For readers who are looking for an introductory text on Orthodox Christianity, I recommend two books in particular. First published in 1963, Bishop Kallistos Ware's *The Orthodox Church* (new ed., Penguin Books, 1993) is now a classic in the field. In the first half of the book, Ware offers a historical account of the beginnings of Christianity, the formation of the Orthodox Church, and Orthodoxy's global reach. In the second half, he introduces his readers to the beliefs, sacraments, practices, and ecumenical activities of the Orthodox Church.

John McGuckin's *The Orthodox Church: An Introduction to Its History, Doctrine, and Spiritual Culture* (Wiley-Blackwell, 2008) is also a classic. Much like Ware, McGuckin begins with the history of the Orthodox Church. However, the greater portion of his book is given over to discussions of the important characteristics and aspects of Orthodox Christian belief and practice. This includes lengthy, detailed chapters on doctrine, tradition, liturgy, and the sacraments.

Themes in Eastern Orthodoxy: An Introduction

"Themes in Eastern Orthodoxy" was a course in Christian theology, not a history of the Orthodox Church. Nonetheless, John Meyendorff's *Byzantine Theology: Historical Trends and Doctrinal Themes* does attend to history. The book recounts the historical development of Orthodox Christianity's thematic core. Meyendorff covers the millennium during which the basic character of Orthodox Christianity took shape. The book, as the subtitle indicates, is in two parts: "Historical Trends" and "Doctrinal Themes."

These two components of the book complement one another. "Historical Trends" narrates the rise and development of the christological issue in the fifth century through the iconoclast crisis and the great schism of the eleventh century and closes with the final three centuries of Byzantium during which the liturgical worship of the church was regularized. Meyendorff also introduces the reader to the great architects of Byzantine theology who refined its doctrine of God, cosmology, soteriology, monastic theology, and sacramentology. Among the most important of these figures are Maximus the Confessor (580–662), the patriarch Photius (810–895), Symeon the New Theologian (949–1022), Gregory Palamas (1296–1359), and Nicholas Cabasilas (1322). All are neglected in most standard courses on Christianity and Christian theology.

The second half of the book recapitulates and reintroduces the history of doctrine and ecclesiological development. This time around, however, the doctrinal and ecclesiastical developments are thematically organized and discussed for their theology. Meyendorff demonstrates how thought and ideas had consequences and lent to Byzantium a cohesive vision of the world. *Byzantine Theology* is challenging. It is not the typical introductory text. I found that it was necessary to give strong lectures to accompany the reading. We would spend a full six weeks of the semester on the book and its subject matter. The effect was a total immersion into the language and thought patterns of Byzantine Christianity. I assigned John McGuckin's *The Westminster Handbook of Patristic Theology* as a sort of "pony" for the course. The hundreds of entries in the *Handbook* range over the first seven hundred years of Christianity and make it an invaluable aid to students for whom the theological language of the patristic and Byzantium era is foreign.

During the study of *Byzantine Theology*, I also included readings from the contemporary efforts of the Eastern Orthodox, Oriental Orthodox, and Roman Catholic churches to reconcile long-standing disagreements over Christology, namely, how to speak in agreement about the duality of Christ's identity as a person who is both fully divine and fully human. While they did not deny that Christ is fully divine and fully human, several of the ancient churches—Armenian, Coptic, Syrian, and Ethiopian Orthodox—ultimately rejected the two natures formula of the fourth ecumenical Council at Chalcedon in 451. In 1989 and then again in 1990, representatives of the non-Chalcedonian, Oriental Orthodox churches met with representatives from Eastern Orthodox churches to examine and discuss the historical sources of their disagreement over Christology. These consultations concluded that, in light of this history and what we have learned about the linguistic and theological reasons that contributed to disagreement and misunderstanding, Christology should no longer be a source of division. In the "Second Agreed Statement" the members of the joint commission agreed that the Christology of the Oriental Orthodox churches is not heretical and called for all anathemas to be lifted. These decisions of the joint commission were not binding on any of the churches, Byzantine or Oriental Orthodox.

In the interim since these meetings, the various churches have weighed in on the commission's findings with different assessments. Meanwhile, the Roman Catholic Church and Oriental Orthodox churches have also worked on a common language through which this ancient source of division between them might be overcome.

I put my students through this exercise in contemporary ecumenism not just to sharpen their understanding of the historical christological controversy but also to enable them to see that even so ancient a dispute can have an impact on and important consequences for how the Christian churches relate to one another today.

Liturgy and Sacraments

Alexander Schmemann's *For the Life of the World* is, undoubtedly, the book by an Orthodox writer that is most widely read in North America. In this book, Schmemann does not define the sacraments so much as he *envisions* them. For this reason, there is nothing scholastic about the book. Schmemann does not introduce the reader to arcane or esoteric terms and define them, but rather conducts the reader on a sojourn through the sacraments. The two essays that in later editions are included at the back of the book as appendixes are some of his most refined and provocative writing on the contrast between sacramental and secular visions of life.

Faith and Spirituality

Kallistos Ware's *The Orthodox Way* is a special way of entry into Orthodoxy as a lived theology. Rather than introduce students to a text that is specifically on Orthodox dogmatic theology, I chose a book that is less formal and more engaging existentially. Ware achieves this effect through his fluid and graceful literary style and manner of presentation. The titles of the six chapters and the epilogue all begin with "God"—for example, "God as Mystery," "God as Man," and "God as Prayer." But these chapters are not just about God. Each chapter also demonstrates how thinking about God as one of these "things" or "activities"—man, prayer, and so on—is at the same moment also a meditation on the many ways in which God meets and addresses the human being.

The prologue and epilogue are very effective front and back "covers" to the book. The former is titled "Signposts on the Way" and the latter, "God as Eternity." In the prologue, Ware informs his readers that they are about to enter "on a journey through the inward space of the heart, a journey not measured by the hours of our watch or the days of the calendar, for it is a journey out of time into eternity."[1] The "way" to God is through participation in the divine life. The journey into God's eternity is marked by signposts to which saints and great Christian men and women have testified. Ware includes pithy excerpts from these writings to close each chapter.

The Icon and Its Theology

The icon and its theology is an immense subject with a vast array of images that modern technology makes available to us. During my years at the University of Virginia, I introduced a seminar on iconographic art and its theology and taught it three times. Orthodox Christianity cannot be understood apart from attention to this art and material culture.

Some will undoubtedly object, but for my purposes I do not restrict the meaning of iconography to sacred art painted on wood but include also the arts of illuminated Bible manuscripts and carvings in stone, as in the Armenian tradition, as well as mosaic and mural art. The first text in this section is of seventh- and eighth-century John of Damascus's *Three Treatises on the Divine Images*. The St. Vladimir's Seminary Press edition of these treatises is especially useful. It includes Orthodox historian and translator Andrew Louth's lucid introduction to this important patristic text.

Meyendorff's *Byzantine Theology* discusses the iconoclast controversy and the theology that emerged from it. Louth succinctly reviews that controversy once again but focuses his attention on John of Damascus's treatises in the defense of icons. He clarifies what John's principal arguments are and the terminology he employs. The first treatise sufficed for our purposes.

Many books are available that introduce the icon and its role in Orthodox worship and belief. Three that I have found to be useful in the classroom are Leonid Ouspensky's and Vladimir Lossky's *The Meaning of Icons*; John Baggley's *Doors of Perception: Icons and Their Spiritual Significance*; and Michael Quenot's *The Resurrection and the Icon*. The difficulty, style, and approach of these books differ, but each successfully introduces the icon and its theology to the reader.

For my syllabus, however, I selected Gabriel Bunge's *The Rublev Trinity*. This book is not just about one particular icon; it is also a beautifully written treatise on the theology of the icon and iconography. Andrei Rublev's life

---

1. Kallistos Ware, *The Orthodox Way* (Crestwood, NY: St. Vladimir's Seminary Press, 1995), 7.

bridges the fourteenth and fifteenth centuries. His icon of the Trinity, with its sources in the ancient Christian art of Abraham's hospitality toward his three angelic visitors, may be the most well-known of all Russian icons.

Bunge discusses the history behind Rublev's icon and interprets the religious art and iconography that belongs to it. He closes the book by discussing an issue that has been debated ever since Rublev composed his icon. Is it possible to identify in the images of the three figures which is the Father, and the Son, and the Holy Spirit? Although they do not directly engage Bunge's thesis, Paul Evdokimov and Clementa Antonova propose contrasting interpretations of the icon. This juxtaposition of interpretations invites students to try their own hand at "reading" an icon.

In chapter 1, I emphasized the strong relationship between religion, art, and culture. Religion that hasn't a culture and doesn't create culture has never existed so far as I know. Orthodox Christianity has produced a variety of forms of material culture. Iconographic art is one. Iconography is not mere religious art suited for display in a museum. It's home is liturgy; it is incarnational, it occasions prayer and memorializes the communion of saints.

It would be absurd to study Orthodox Christianity without experiencing the worship of the church and its material culture. To bring the icon into the classroom is useful, but it is not revealing of how it functions liturgically and shapes Orthodox piety. Thus my students visited St. Maximos the Confessor Skete (of the Bulgarian Orthodox Diocese), in Palmyra, Virginia, not far from the University of Virginia.

At St. Maximos Skete my students met Fr. Mefodii, an iconographer, and Fr. Kyrill, a translator of liturgical texts. Their combined talents experienced within such a religious compound gave "body" to much of our book learning. The visits began with a worship service, followed by a lecture and visit to Fr. Mefodii's art studio where he demonstrated the art of "writing" icons.

Catholicity, Ecumenism, and the Unity of the Church

Questions about the ecclesiology of the Orthodox Church almost inevitably arise in any attempt at introducing its formation, beliefs, and practices. How does the Orthodox Church differ from Protestantism, since it also does not recognize papal supremacy with its claims to jurisdiction or headship over all Christians? Again, how is the Orthodox Church different from the Roman Catholic Church, since it shares with Roman Catholicism a belief in the seven sacraments and is structurally hierarchical, similar to the Roman Catholic Church?

I decided to limit the inquiry to the question of authority in the church, specifically, how Orthodoxy and Roman Catholicism differ on the authority of the bishop of Rome. All readings for this section reflect contemporary discussions of papal primacy and the efforts of Orthodox and Roman Catholics to resolve their disagreements. The selections are weighted toward Orthodox writings since the course is on Orthodoxy. But I thought it was important to include several pronouncements of contemporary popes. Thus, we hear from Popes John Paul II, Benedict XVI, and Francis. My selection of Orthodox writers is also limited. I included representatives of three traditions: Greek, Russian, and Armenian.

Church and World

Alexander Schmemann's *Church, World, Mission* was published in 1979. It is a collection of essays. Four trenchantly argued essays start it off. In these essays, Schmemann assesses Orthodox Christianity's struggle to maintain its identity and mission in its Western diaspora. These first four chapters of the book comprise half of its over two hundred pages. Titles such as "The 'Orthodox World,' Past and Present" and "The World in Orthodox Thought and Experience" are revealing of Schmemann's concerns.

In chapter 3, I mentioned Schmemann's visit to Loyola College in 1983, where I taught at the time. One afternoon we strolled together around the campus. I mentioned to Fr. Alexander how much I appreciated and learned from *Church, World, Mission*, especially its opening chapters. With a broad grin and mischievous chuckle, he responded: "If the bishops read it, I would be excommunicated." An overstatement for sure but proof, as well, of how seriously Schmemann regarded these writings.

Prospects in Eastern Orthodox Theology

I taught "Prospects in Eastern Orthodox Theology" for fall semester of 2014. This followed two earlier attempts to field a course for graduate students and advanced undergraduates on modern and contemporary Orthodox theology. Initially I had envisioned the course as an introduction to a half dozen or so of the most eminent figures in modern Orthodox theology, such as Georges Florovsky, Vladimir Lossky, Sergius Bulgakov, Paul Evdokimov, Alexander Schmemann, and John Zizioulas. On my third attempt, I decided to construct a syllabus with the flavor of a course in Orthodox Christian dogmatics. "Prospects" is divided into fourteen distinct sections with titles that reflect this subject matter, such as "God and Creation," "The Fall and

Sin," "Redemption in Christ," "Mary and Holiness," and "Eschatology." For each section I selected representative writings that are in the mainstream of Orthodox theology. There are differences in manner of presentation and stress on this or that aspect of a doctrine or theological topic, but rarely are there sharp disagreements.

It was not my intention while settling on this method of selection to give the impression that among contemporary Orthodox theologians there are not arguments over how the faith should be presented. Differences do exist, and, in fact, some of these show up in the selections. For instance, there is an ongoing debate about how much modern Orthodox theology should depend on the great deposit of patristic writings. And, for example, to what extent ought the patristic writings be mediated through philosophical lenses other than the neo-Platonic and Aristotelian frameworks within which the fathers worked? Some insist that Orthodox theology must hew closely to the fathers, their language, and their method. Others are open to the ad hoc appropriation and use of philosophical language different from that of the fathers and the great councils in order to interpret them. Still others argue that Orthodox theology needs to break free from the worldview of the fathers entirely and adopt new philosophical frameworks in order to communicate the faith effectively to modern people.

An early sounding in this debate opens the course reading list. In 1959 at a World Council of Churches Orthodox Faith and Order Consultation, Georges Florovsky presented an important paper titled "The Ethos of the Orthodox Church." In it Florovsky called for an Orthodox theology that is in "historic continuity" with the fathers, a "neo-patristic synthesis" free of Western theological influences that deviate from the great "Tradition of the Undivided Church."[2]

I could have constructed the course to reflect this and other debates. That would have been to venture into what is sometimes called metatheology. I judged, however, that to get into the thick of this sort of inquiry or to highlight a debate such as this would miss the mark for the needs of advanced undergraduates and graduate students who possessed little or no background in Orthodox theology. So I decided on a simpler and more straightforward approach to introduce a healthy sample of modern and contemporary Orthodox writers on important topics and let the theologians speak for themselves.

In the second section, "God and Creation," the articles by Vladimir Lossky, Georges Florovsky, Dumitru Staniloae, and John Zizioulas demonstrate, each

2. Georges Florovsky, "The Ethos of the Orthodox Church," *The Ecumenical Review* 12, no. 2 (1960): 17.

in their own way, how the Eastern and Western doctrines of God differ. It is often said that the late Latin inclusion of the *filioque* clause in the Nicene Creed—that the Holy Spirit proceeds from the Father and *the Son*—is emblematic of this difference. However, the differing approaches to a doctrine of God, East and West, are not wholly accounted for by this particular piece of history. There is not room here to describe or discuss the characteristics of Western approaches to a doctrine of God, Roman Catholic and Protestant. But these Orthodox writings all emphasize something distinctive about Orthodox theology: the priority of the divine persons when addressing God's identity and activity of creating and redeeming the world. Florovsky obliquely approaches this matter in his discussion of Athanasius's distinction between "being" and "will." This distinction, of course, carries on into the trinitarian theology of the Cappadocians and then into that of Maximus the Confessor and Gregory Palamas.

Zizioulas further develops this distinctive "personalism" of Orthodox theology in his essay "The Father as Cause: Personhood Generating Otherness." God the Father, acting out of his absolute freedom, is the eternal source of both divine and human personhood. The unity of the Godhead is not so much a substance but a relationship of three persons characterized by the common love that unites them. The Father is the "cause" of both this freedom and this love. Zizioulas concludes, "The one God is the Father of Jesus Christ and the Spirator of the Holy Spirit: the Trinity *depends ontologically on the Father* and is not in itself, that is, *qua* Trinity, the one God. If the Trinity is God, it is only because the Father makes it Trinity by granting it *hypostases*."[3] This description of the Godhead is a far remove from a notion prevalent in Western theology that the Holy Spirit is the love that binds together the Trinity or at least communicates the love of the Father and Son to one another.

As regards Mariology, the selections in section 13, "Mary and Holiness," present several perspectives on her person and her importance to the life of the church that might not be anticipated by Protestant or Roman Catholic readers. Respecting Mary, it is common for both Orthodox and Roman Catholic commentators to turn to the doctrine of immaculate conception to explain the difference between Roman Catholic and Orthodox Mariology.

This, however, is not entirely helpful. There is no question that one reason the Orthodox Church has not designated as doctrine the concept of the immaculate conception is that it veers dangerously near to isolating Mary from the rest of humankind by its claim that she was exempt from the otherwise

3. John Zizioulas, "The Father as Cause: Personhood Generating Otherness," in *Communion and Otherness* (London: T&T Clark, 2006), 154.

universally shared condition of original sin. A reason why the Orthodox Church retains the title "Theotokos" (lit. God-bearer) for Mary is that it adheres to the ancient conviction of the fathers of the Council of Ephesus (431) that the honor we give to Mary presumes her special relationship as mother of the Son of God.

As may be seen in the selection from Vladimir Lossky and the chapter from my book *The Melody of Faith*, Mary *is* venerated for her holiness. Mary *is* the *Panagia*, the "All Holy, Mother of God." This belongs also to Roman Catholic belief and piety. I submit, however, that Orthodoxy emphasizes more strongly than Roman Catholicism that Mary's holiness issues from her *doing*, her *free willing* to be the Theotokos. Thus, in Orthodoxy, there is not the compelling reason, as in Roman Catholicism, for Mary's exemption from original sin, her immaculate conception.

As I have stated, some sections of the syllabus clearly venture beyond strictly dogmatic subject matter. In these instances, my selection for readings was governed by one of two criteria. In the first instance, I was interested in simply offering several important theological topics under a general heading, such as in section 10, "God and Mystery," and section 12, "The Orthodox Christian Vision." The titles of the sections speak for themselves.

In other instances, such as section 9, "The Church and Political Order," and section 14, "Women and the Priesthood," my purpose was not just to introduce a salient issue but to include statements by several theologians who differ in their approach to the issue or who disagree about where the Orthodox Church ought to stand on it. Section 9, "The Church and Political Order," brings together three contrasting approaches to how Orthodoxy ought to comport itself within the democratic societies in which it is located, especially the United States. Aristotle Papanikolaou and I certainly can claim some common ground. We both approve of open and free societies. Nonetheless, we have very different evaluations of liberal democracy and its consistency with the Orthodox faith. Papanikolaou, Stanley Harakas, and I each have different and, in certain respects, conflicting interpretations of how Orthodoxy, with its history of the doctrine of *symphonia* (the notion that the church and state should complement each other, with neither dominant over the other), must or even can adjust to the American doctrine of a separation of church and state.

Something similar holds for the readings under section 14, "Women and the Priesthood." In this section I have included representative essays by three Orthodox theologians: Fr. Thomas Hopko, Sr. Nonna Verna Harrison, and Elisabeth Behr-Sigel. In his essay "Presbyter/Bishop: A Masculine Ministry," the late Thomas Hopko strongly opposes the ordination of women to the priesthood. He argues that it is *incorrect*, however, to say that women are excluded from the priesthood "simply because they are women." Rather, women and men have different callings in Christ, different spiritual gifts with which God respectively endows the sexes. The essential dignity of persons is in no manner compromised by this, God's design. Sacramental blessing is not limited to one sacrament. Nonna Verna Harrison, who is still active and writing, is also strongly opposed to women in the priesthood. She grounds her argument in the patristic tradition and its theological anthropology as well as in the symbolic imagery of the Orthodox liturgy.

Elisabeth Behr-Sigel, who passed away in 2005 at ninety-eight years of age, was a pioneer for women in the Orthodox Church. Behr-Sigel is respectful of the tradition's judgment that women cannot belong to the priesthood, but she reminds us that tradition is not a dead record and is, rather, a living thing that in Vladimir Lossky's words is also "the critical spirit of the Church."[4] In this "spirit" Behr-Sigel criticizes the marginalization of women in the church through false theological anthropologies that regard them as, in effect, inferior to men. She pleads for an openness to discussion of the issue and calls for the reinvigoration of the ancient office of deaconess. As an aside, in contrast to the Byzantine Orthodox churches, the office of deaconess has endured in the Armenian Church through the twentieth and twenty-first centuries within monastic communities in the Middle East and Armenia.[5]

Let me add that were there a substantial article or book by an important theologian in the Orthodox Church that argues for women to be priests, I would have included it or some portion of it. Meanwhile, it is revealing of the procedure of Orthodox theology that to support their positions, Hopko, Harrison, and Behr-Sigel all argue from three sources of authority in the church: Scripture, tradition, and liturgy. This is an earmark of Orthodox theology in general.

Concluding Remarks

I hope that this rather "unorthodox" conclusion is a help to the reader who desires to learn more about Orthodox Christianity, a spur and encouragement, if you will, to read even beyond the contents of this book and the chapters within it. I recognize that this book and the two appended reading lists demand a fairly high level of theological literacy. Nevertheless, I know

4. Vladimir Lossky, *In the Image and Likeness of God* (Crestwood, NY: St. Vladimir's Seminary Press, 1974), 156.

5. See Abel Oghlukian, *The Deaconess in the Armenian Church: A Brief Survey* (New Rochelle, NY: St. Nersess Armenian Seminary, 1994).

that in addition to teachers of religion, there are others outside the walls of the academy who would welcome a reliable guide to the Orthodox faith and its theology. I created these syllabi with the immediate goal of including Orthodox Christianity in a religious studies curriculum from which it was otherwise absent. And it may well be that the main value of this book belongs to religious pedagogy and academic study. Still, it is greatly satisfying also to make these reading lists available to other audiences who seek direction for investigating the Orthodox faith.

Course Syllabi

FURTHER READING IN ORTHODOX THEOLOGY

Themes in Eastern Orthodoxy: An Introduction

I. Historical Background

"Common Declaration of John Paul II and Catholicos Karekin I," December 13, 1996. http://www.vatican.va/roman_curia/pontifical_councils/chrstuni/anc-orient-ch -docs/rc_pc_christuni_doc_19961213_jp-ii-karekin-i_en.html.

Fenwick, John. "Orthodox Churches." In *Encyclopedia of Christianity*, edited by John Bowden, 854–64. New York: Oxford University Press, 2005.

Guroian, Vigen. "Fully God and Fully Man—Rome and Armenian Orthodox Settle a War of Words." *National Catholic Register*, July 6, 1997.

"Joint Commission on the Theological Dialogue between the Orthodox Church and the Oriental Orthodox Churches: First Agreed Statement," June 20–24, 1989. In *Restoring the Unity in Faith: The Orthodox-Oriental Orthodox Dialogue; An Introduction with Texts*. Edited by Thomas FitzGerald and Emmanuel Gratsias, 58–62. Brookline, MA: Holy Cross Orthodox Press, 2007.

"Joint Commission on the Theological Dialogue between the Orthodox Church and the Oriental Orthodox Churches: Second Agreed Statement," September 23, 1990. In *Restoring the Unity in Faith*, 63–68.

McGuckin, John Anthony. *The Westminster Handbook to Patristic Theology*. Louisville: Westminster John Knox, 2004. (For use as reference throughout.)

Meyendorff, John. *Byzantine Theology: Historical Trends and Doctrinal Themes*. New York: Fordham University Press, 1976.

Nersoyan, Tiran. "Problems of Consensus in Christology." In *Armenian Church Historical Studies: Matters of Doctrine and Administration*, 155–74. New York: St. Vartan Press, 1996.

II. Liturgy and Sacrament

Schmemann, Alexander. *For the Life of the World*. 2nd ed. Crestwood, NY: St. Vladimir's Seminary Press, 1973.

III. Faith and Spirituality

Ware, Kallistos. *The Orthodox Way*. Crestwood, NY: St. Vladimir's Seminary Press, 1995.

IV. A Study in the Icon and Its Theology

Antonova, Clemena. "Sample Analysis: An Analysis of Rublev's Trinity Icon." In *Space, Time, and Presence in the Icon: Seeing the World with the Eyes of God*, 157–66. Burlington, VT: Ashgate, 2010.

Bunge, Gabriel. *The Rublev Trinity*. Crestwood, NY: St. Vladimir's Seminary Press, 2007.

Evdokimov, Paul. "Andrei Rublev's Icon of the Holy Trinity." In *The Art of the Icon: A Theology of Beauty*, 243–57. Renando, CA: Oakwood Publications, 1990.

John of Damascus. *Three Treatises on the Divine Images*. Translated by Andrew Louth. Crestwood, NY: St. Vladimir's Seminary Press, 2003.

V. Catholicity, Ecumenism, and the Unity of the Church

Benedict XVI. "Address of His Holiness Benedict XVI," September 24, 2011. Meeting with Representatives of Orthodox and Oriental Orthodox Churches. https://w2.vatican.va/content/benedict-xvi/en/speeches/2011/september/documents/hf_ben-xvi_spe_20110924_orthodox-freiburg.html.

"Common Declaration of Pope Francis and Ecumenical Patriarch Bartholomew I." Salt and Light Media, May 25, 2014. http://saltandlighttv.org/blogfeed/getpost.php?id=56302.

Guroian, Vigen. "The Problem of Papal Primacy." In *The Orthodox Reality*, chapter 7. Grand Rapids: Baker Academic, 2018.

John Paul II. *Ut Unum Sint* (excerpts), May 25, 1995. https://w2.vatican.va/content/john-paul-ii/en/encyclicals/documents/hf_jp-ii_enc_25051995_ut-unum-sint.html.

"Joint Declaration of Pope Francis and Patriarch Kirill." Vatican Radio, February 12, 2016. http://en.radiovaticana.va/news/2016/02/12/joint_declaration_of_pope_fran cis_and_patriarch_kirill/1208117.

Meyendorff, John. "The Meaning of Tradition." In *Living Tradition*, 13–26. Crestwood, NY: St. Vladimir's Seminary Press, 1978.

———. "Rome and Orthodoxy: Is Authority Still the Issue?" In *Living Tradition*, 63–79.

Zizioulas, John. "Primacy in the Church: An Orthodox Approach." In *The One and the Many: Studies on God, Man, the Church, and the World Today*, 262–73. Alhambra, CA: Sebastian Press, 2010.

VI. Church and World

Guroian, Vigen. "Orthodoxy and American Religion." In *The Orthodox Reality*, chapter 5. Grand Rapids: Baker Academic, 2018.

Schmemann, Alexander. *Church, World, Mission: Reflections on Orthodoxy in the West.* Chaps. 1–4, pp. 7–117. Crestwood, NY: St. Vladimir's Seminary Press, 1979.

Prospects in Eastern Orthodox Theology

I. Orthodoxy and Theology

Bulgakov, Sergius. "Dogma and Dogmatic Theology." In *Tradition Alive: On the Church and the Christian Life in Our Time; Readings from the Eastern Church*, edited by Michael Plekon, 67–80. Lanham, MD: Rowman & Littlefield, 2003.

Florovsky, Georges. "The Ethos of the Orthodox Church." *The Ecumenical Review* 12, no. 2 (1960): 183–98.

Lossky, Vladimir. "Prologue: Faith and Theology." In *Orthodox Theology: An Introduction*, 13–25. Crestwood, NY: St. Vladimir's Seminary Press, 1978.

Schmemann, Alexander. "Liturgy and Theology." In *Liturgy and Tradition: Theological Reflections of Alexander Schmemann*, edited by Thomas Fisch, 49–68. Crestwood, NY: St. Vladimir's Seminary Press, 1990.

II. God and Creation

Florovsky, Georges. "St. Athanasius' Concept of Creation." In *Aspects of Church History*, 39–62. Vol. 4 of *The Collected Works of Georges Florovsky*. Belmont, MA: Nordland, 1975.

Lossky, Vladimir. "The Creation." In *Orthodox Theology: An Introduction*, 51–78. Crestwood, NY: St. Vladimir's Seminary Press, 2001.

———. "The Two Monotheisms." In *Orthodox Theology*, 27–49.

Staniloae, Dumitru. "The Holy Trinity: Structure of Supreme Love." In *Revelation and Knowledge of the Triune God*, 245–80. Vol. 1. of *Orthodox Dogmatic Theology: The Experience of God*. Brookline, MA: Holy Cross Orthodox Press, 1998.

Zizioulas, John. "The Father as Cause: Personhood Generating Otherness." In *Communion and Otherness*, 113–54. London: T&T Clark, 2006.

III. The Fall and Sin

Lossky, Vladimir. "Original Sin." In *Orthodox Theology*, 79–94.

Staniloae, Dumitru. "The Fall." In *The World: Creation and Deification*, 163–89. Vol. 2 of *Orthodox Dogmatic Theology: The Experience of God*. Brookline, MA: Holy Cross Orthodox Press, 2000.

Zizioulas, John. "Creation and Salvation." In *Lectures in Christian Dogmatics*, edited by Douglas H. Knight, 83–100. London: T&T Clark, 2008.

IV. Redemption in Christ

Bulgakov, Sergius. "The Work of Christ: Section B; Redemption." In *The Lamb of God*, 342–72. Grand Rapids: Eerdmans, 2008.

Guroian, Vigen. "Divine Therapy." In *The Melody of Faith: Theology in an Orthodox Key*, 43–64. Grand Rapids: Eerdmans, 2010.

Lossky, Vladimir. "Christological Dogma." In *Orthodox Theology*, 95–118.

———. "Postscript: Image and Likeness." In *Orthodox Theology*, 119–37.

Zizioulas, John. "'Created' and 'Uncreated': The Existential Significance of Chalcedonian Christology." In *Communion and Otherness*, 250–85.

V. Theological Anthropology

Clément, Olivier. "Persons in Communion." In *On Human Being*, 43–54. London: New City Press, 2000.

Evdokimov, Paul. *Orthodoxy*. Pt. 1, chaps. 1 and 2, pp. 55–92. Hyde Park, NY: New City Press, 1979.

Lossky, Vladimir. "Catholic Consciousness: Anthropological Implications of the Dogma of the Church." In *In the Image and Likeness of God*, 183–94. Crestwood, NY: St. Vladimir's Seminary Press, 1974.

Zizioulas, John. "On Being a Person." In *Communion and Otherness*, 99–112.

VI. Eschatology

Evdokimov, Paul. "Part Five: The Eschaton or the Last Things." In *Orthodoxy*, 309–40.

Guroian, Vigen. "The Luminous Moment of the Apocalypse." In *Melody of Faith*, 25–42.

Lossky, Vladimir. "Dominion and Kingship: An Eschatological Study." In *In the Image and Likeness of God*, 211–27.

Schmemann, Alexander. "Liturgy and Eschatology." In *Liturgy and Tradition*, 89–100.

VII. Eucharist and Liturgy

Schmemann, Alexander. *The Eucharist*. Crestwood, NY: St. Vladimir's Seminary Press, 1988.

VIII. Liturgy and Ethics

Guroian, Vigen. *Incarnate Love*. 2nd ed. Chaps. 3–6. Notre Dame, IN: University of Notre Dame Press, 2002.

> These four chapters constitute the contents of part 2 of *Incarnate Love*, "Liturgical Ethics." They are "Liturgy and the Lost Eschatological Vision of Christian Ethics," "The Gift of the Holy Spirit," "Seeing Worship as Ethics," and "An Ethic of Marriage and Family."

Yannaras, Christos. *The Freedom of Morality*. Chaps. 3–7, 9. Crestwood, NY: St. Vladimir's Seminary Press, 1984.

> These short chapters are too numerous to list. They cover such subjects as Gospel ethics and the ascetical and liturgical sources of Orthodox ethics.

IX. The Church and Political Order

Guroian, Vigen. "Godless Theosis: A Review of the Mystical as Political." *First Things*, April 2014. https://www.firstthings.com/article/2014/04/godless-theosis.

———. "Orthodoxy and the American Order." In *Incarnate Love*, 163–88.

———. "The Problem of a Social Ethic." In *Incarnate Love*, 141–62.

———. "The Struggle for the Soul of the Church: American Reflections." In *Ethics after Christendom: Toward an Ecclesial Christian Ethic*, 83–101. Grand Rapids: Eerdmans, 1994.

Harakas, Stanley. "Orthodox State-Church Theory and American Democracy." *Greek Orthodox Theological Review* 21 (1975): 285–307.

Papanikolaou, Aristotle. "Divine-Human Communion and the Common Good." In *The Mystical as Political: Democracy and Non-Radical Orthodoxy*, 131–62. Notre Dame, IN: University of Notre Dame Press, 2012.

———. "Eucharist or Democracy?" In *The Mystical as Political*, 55–86.

X. God and Mystery

Hart, David Bentley. "'God' Is Not a Proper Name." In *The Experience of God: Being, Consciousness, Bliss*, 13–45. New Haven: Yale University Press, 2013.

Sherrard, Philip. "The Presence of Evil." In *Christianity: Lineaments of a Sacred Tradition*, 159–79. Brookline, MA: Holy Cross Orthodox Press, 1998.

Ware, Kallistos. "Dare We Hope for the Salvation of All?" In *The Inner Kingdom*, 193–216. Crestwood, NY: St. Vladimir's Seminary Press, 2000.

XI. Beauty: Theological Aesthetics

Clément, Olivier. "The Third Beauty." In *On Human Being*, 126–44.

Evdokimov, Paul. *The Art of the Icon: A Theology of Beauty*. Renando, CA: Oakwood Publications, 1990. Chapters 1, 2, and 5.

Hart, David Bentley. "Introduction: III. Beauty." In *The Beauty of the Infinite: The Aesthetics of Christian Truth*, 15–28. Grand Rapids: Eerdmans, 2003.

XII. The Orthodox Christian Vision

Chryssavgis, John. "The World of the Icon." In *Beyond the Shattered Image: Insights into and Orthodox Christian*, 121–40. Minneapolis, MN: Light and Life, 2007.

Schmemann, Alexander. "Appendix 1: 'Worship in a Secular Age.'" In *The Life of the World*, 117–34. Crestwood, NY: St. Vladimir's Seminary Press, 1973.

———. "Appendix 2: 'Sacrament and Symbol.'" In *The Life of the World*, 135–50.

Sherrard, Philip. "Christianity and the Desecration of the Cosmos." In *Christianity: Lineaments of a Sacred Tradition*, 200–231.

XIII. Mary and Holiness

Bulgakov, Sergius. "The Glorification of the Mother of God." In *The Burning Bush: On the Orthodox Veneration of the Mother of God*, 65–116. Grand Rapids: Eerdmans, 2009.

Evdokimov, Paul. "Theotokos: Archetype of the Feminine." In *Woman and the Salvation of the World*, 211–25. Crestwood, NY: St. Vladimir's Seminary Press, 1994.

Guroian, Vigen. "Mother of God, Mother of Holiness." In *Melody of Faith*, 65–92.

Lossky, Vladimir. "Panagia." In *In the Image and Likeness of God*, 195–210.

XIV. Women and the Priesthood

Behr-Sigel, Elisabeth. "The Ordination of Women: Also a Question for the Ortho-dox Churches." In *The Ordination of Women in the Orthodox Church*, edited by Elisabeth Behr-Sigel and Kallistos Ware, 11–48. Geneva: WCC, 2000.

Harrison, Nonna Verna. "Orthodox Arguments Against the Ordination of Women as Priests." In *Women and the Priesthood*, edited by Thomas Hopko, 165–87. Crestwood, NY: St. Vladimir's Seminary Press, 1999.

Hopko, Thomas. "Presbyter/Bishop: A Masculine Ministry." In *Women and the Priest-hood*, 139–64.

Index